Ena

This is simply an outstanding book! With so many false christs lurking in the world and in our churches today, Pastor Richard deftly gets to the heart of such idolatry. Written with superb narrative wit and great pastoral care, he provides a brilliant tool for the diagnosis, prescription, and curative treatment of such pervasive idolatries. Capturing the plight of multiple misbeliefs with clear and accessible language, Pastor Richard faithfully presents the real Jesus Christ, bloodied and crucified for you, and regularly given to you through His Word and Sacrament. This is a gem for our time!

Rev. Dr. Lucas V. Woodford
Senior Pastor, Zion Lutheran Church and School, Mayer, Minnesota

Matt Richard has given us a wonderful read, filled with real-life situations that are clear and understandable. His kind and pastoral writing style gives the reader sound biblical theology in a very user-friendly format. He helps us see the many false "christs" around us, pointing out the spiritual dangers of each. Then, he gently shares the real Jesus and therefore the real Gospel in each chapter. I highly recommend this book!

Rev. Dr. Mark J. Buchhop
Immanuel Lutheran Church, Warren, Minnesota
Retired Campus Pastor, University of North Dakota

Have you ever wondered why Christians seem to believe such different things about Jesus? It's clear that Matt Richard has, using every tool in his considerable arsenal to bring good order to the chaos. His writing style is highly conversational and relational, applying theological precision to everyday scenarios so that the reader can learn to recognize how each "false christ" impacts a person's practices and views. His patient "learning by listening" approach to dialogue is a great model for us all.

Heather Choate Davis
Author, Speaker, Theologian

Timely, engaging, and accessibly written, Richard helps ground and orient his readers in a climate that treats Jesus more as an idea, something for us to imagine and shape, than a real, historical person and the Savior. This is a worthwhile read for pastors hoping to better reach their flock. Moreover, it is an extremely helpful book for laypeople who want to better know the true Jesus and recognize the false christs Jesus Himself warned would sprout up and be proclaimed after His Ascension.

Wade Johnston, PhD
Assistant Professor of Theology
Wisconsin Lutheran College, Milwaukee, Wisconsin

....

It's hard to sell people a dead man on a cross. It's not easy to worship a God you don't get to choose. But it does little good to find a Jesus who doesn't really exist. With real-life narratives and passionate focus, Pastor Richard shares how easy it is to craft a "better" Jesus, one made after our own image, an idol to which we plaster the name "Jesus." More important, he reminds us why it's better to be a doorkeeper in the house of the true God than to reign in the halls of gods that can't help us. The real Jesus has stood up. He is risen, and Pastor Richard will leave you feeling confident that the real Jesus has done this great thing precisely for you.

Rev. Jonathan Fisk
Host and Producer at KFUO Radio, Creative Director of
Worldview Everlasting, podcaster at RevFisk Raw, and author of the book
BROKEN: Seven Christian Rules that Every Christian Ought to Break

....

Rev. Dr. Matthew Richard provides a series of highly relatable examples of the false christs that American culture has enticed ordinary Christians with. Specifically, these christs offer salvation either through an antinomian rejection of the Law or a legalist rejection of the Gospel. Such false christs are ultimately a byproduct of fallen humanity's compulsion to reject God's objective Word in favor of the individual's inner thoughts and feelings (enthusiasm). In a most excellent manner, Richard gives the reader tools for identifying these false christs and helpful responses to those who devote themselves to such idols.

Jack D. Kilcrease, PhD
Professor of Historical and Systematic Theology
Institute of Lutheran Theology, Brookings, South Dakota

....

Jesus is an object of fascination for believers and unbelievers alike. But the question remains: "which Jesus?" Is He the Jesus of whom the Scriptures testify and the creeds confess, or is it a plastic Jesus molded by human impulses and imagination? Pastor Matthew Richard has provided a crisp and conversational apologetic for critiquing faulty images of Jesus while inviting both Christians and non-Christians to engage the One whom the Scriptures present as Lord. An added bonus is the discussion questions, making *Will the Real Jesus Please Stand Up?* an excellent book to use with an adult study group.

Rev. John T. Pless
Assistant Professor of Pastoral Ministry and Missions
Concordia Theological Seminary, Fort Wayne, Indiana

....

It should be easy to help people understand Jesus—simply read the New Testament! But with so many views of "Jesus" floating around in the media, the news, and classrooms, and so many interpretations of the Bible, it can be a challenge to help people see Jesus, revealed in His Word, and crucified, risen, and ascended for all. Pastor Richard will not only help you talk about Jesus with people you meet every day, but also help steer you through all the noise so that you can listen to—and find hope in—the real Jesus.

Jeffrey Kloha, STM, PhD
Provost Professor of Exegetical Theology, Concordia Seminary, St. Louis, Missouri

....

This is a very timely and well-organized book, perfectly written for the lay person to not only identify the false christs that we, sinners, often inadvertently create for ourselves, but to better understand why people do so. Pastor Richards brilliantly provides his readers with a detailed education in contemporary Christology. More important, he presents us with the true Jesus and constant instruction and encouragement to respond with the true Gospel in genuine empathy and love to those caught up by false christs.

Sandra Ostapowich
Higher Things Conferences Executive, Plano, Texas

....

Matthew Richard writes with a pastoral heart. With each counterfeit christ he encounters, he responds with compassion, clarity, and most of all, faithfulness to God's Word. In this book, Dr. Richard identifies philosophical concepts, cultural landmines, and deep theological truths, and yet he writes in a simple conversational tone that connects with every reader. This book is a "must-have" for our conversations with those holding onto their false christs and when we ourselves slip into these same errors. Above all else, this book is all about Jesus—the real One!

Rev. Dr. James A. Baneck
Executive Director of Pastoral Education, LCMS

....

Jesus asked His disciples, "Who do men say that I am?" Pastor Richard surveys the answers of our time, identifying twelve false christs, all fashioned to suit our sinful desires. With theological tact and pastoral skill, he dismantles these idols, all while tending to the main thing: confessing the true Christ, the Savior of the world. This book will challenge, equip, and most especially comfort you. God be praised for this book!

Pastor Bryan Wolfmueller
Hope Lutheran Church, Aurora, Colorado
Host of Table Talk Radio; author of Has American Christianity Failed?

....

"That is not the Jesus I know!" How many times have we heard this? Pastor Richard takes us on an enlightening and structured journey of identifying twelve common false christs encountered in Christianity. He does this by providing the reader with easy-to-understand and theologically rich discernment tools. From start to finish, the reader will walk away with a better understanding of who the "real Jesus" is and how He alone stands for poor wretched sinners. Pastor Richard writes with depth, insight, and experience. A definite must for any Christian seeking to faithfully follow Jesus.

Rev. Eric Ekong
Trinity Lutheran Ministries
Trinity Lutheran Church, Jackson, Michigan

....

With one eye on the truth of Scripture and the other on our changing culture, Dr. Richard separates the real biblical Jesus from our culture's many attempts to remake Him in its own image. He identifies the tendency of fallen humans, inflamed by relativistic views of truth, to recreate the person of Jesus into a soothing salve that can be spread over false ideologies. Drawing upon a holistic reading of Scripture, Dr. Richard presents us with the real biblical Jesus, who came not to justify sin, but to justify sinners through His substitutionary death and life-giving resurrection.

Rev. Brad J. Soenksen
Grace Lutheran Church
Erhard, Minnesota

....

An everyday guide to Christology. Pastor Richard both unmasks the identity of many "false christs" and shows how the devil, the world, and our own sinfulness lead us to worship these idols. Extremely accessible, and yet also full of solid theology, this little book teaches how to evangelically engage the people we meet in our everyday life, recognize when a "false christ" is being proclaimed, and offers Christians a useful guide for engaging our erring neighbor with humility, all the while looking for the opportunity to confess the real Jesus, in whom alone we have real salvation.

Pastor David Warner
LCMS Church Planter in Spain

....

Everyone seems a bit too eager to answer Jesus' old question, "Who do *you* say that I am?" This book will help take some of the subtlety out of the devil's craft. With compassion and detail, Pastor Matt Richard exposes twelve deadly twists that *flesh and blood* have put on Jesus (and therefore the Gospel) so that you can confess Him truthfully as the *Father in heaven has revealed* Him.

Rev. Sean Daenzer
Trinity Lutheran, Great Bend, North Dakota
Peace Lutheran, Barney, North Dakota

....

Rev. Richard shows us who the genuine Jesus is by exposing a dozen popular false christs that compete with Him in today's religious marketplace. Good theology well written is always a pleasure to read, especially when the topic is the person and work of our Savior, Jesus Christ. This is an excellent book, written in a conversational and easy-to-read style. Rev. Richard refutes false conceptions about who Jesus is, what He has done for us, and what He says to us. He does so clearly and pastorally.

Pastor Rolf D. Preus
Trinity Lutheran Church, Sidney, Montana;
St. John Lutheran Church, Fairview, Montana

....

The landscape of life in the twenty-first century is filled with a confusing number of "customized christs." Matthew Richard handily summarizes how to recognize these manufactured messiahs who might sway some of us, but cannot save any of us, so that we might stand up for the real Jesus.

The Rev. John Arthur Nunes, PhD
President, Concordia College—New York

....

False idols and fake christs are everywhere. This book is a bold and engaging critique of the many false christs in the twenty-first century. It depicts twelve false christs and reveals how they are nothing more than shams, counterfeits, and falsifications of Jesus. Pastor Richard has written a winsome book that points out not only the failures of false christs but also the firm truth of the real Christ Jesus.

Rev. A. Trevor Sutton
Associate Pastor, St. Luke Lutheran Church, Lansing, Michigan
Author of Being Lutheran

....

In C. S. Lewis's *The Great Divorce*, an angel offered to kill the red lizard perched on a man's shoulder and so set him free from a comfortably cherished substitute savior along with its lies and false comfort. Reluctantly he allowed the angel to kill his whispering lizard and so was delivered from its tyranny and destruction. With the insight of that angel and the skill of a surgeon, Dr. Richard wields the sword of God's Word to diagnose and remove the red lizards in false christ's clothing that people have embraced rather than the real Jesus revealed in Holy Scripture. Will the real Jesus stand up? Indeed, not only does the real Jesus stand up throughout the pages of Dr. Richard's book, but the real Jesus also slays the lizards and dragons who try to take His place and lead His people astray.

Rev. Joshua D. Reimche, Pastor
Our Savior Lutheran, Bottineau, North Dakota
Immanuel Lutheran, Willow Creek, North Dakota
St. Paul Lutheran, Rugby, North Dakota

....

WILL THE
Real Jesus
please stand up?

· · · · · · · · · · ·

12 FALSE CHRISTS

Matthew Richard

CONCORDIA PUBLISHING HOUSE · SAINT LOUIS

Published by Concordia Publishing House
3558 S. Jefferson Ave., St. Louis, MO 63118–3968
1-800-325-3040 • cph.org

Manufactured in the United States of America

Library of Congress Cataloging-in-Publication Data

Names: Richard, Matthew Rev. Dr., author.
Title: Will the real Jesus please stand up? : 12 false Christs / Matthew Richard.
Description: Saint Louis : Concordia Publishing House, 2017. | Includes bibliographical references and index.
Identifiers: LCCN 2017025004 (print) | LCCN 2017038507 (ebook) | ISBN 9780758657206 | ISBN 9780758657190 (alk. paper)
Subjects: LCSH: Jesus Christ—Person and offices.. | Christianity—North America.
Classification: LCC BT203 (ebook) | LCC BT203 .R53 2017 (print) | DDC 232—dc23
LC record available at https://lccn.loc.gov/2017025004

4   5   6   7   8   9   10   26   25   24   23   22   21   20   19

Contents

Acknowledgments

Writing a book obviously requires a great amount of time and help from many individuals. Therefore, I say "thank you" to the following people not casually but with a profound sense of gratitude.

First of all, I want to thank my family. Serenity, you have been an incredible support to me in this endeavor. You have listened, read, interacted, and helped me immensely in this book. You are not only my wife and best friend but a theologian whom I truly respect. Matthias, Anya, and Alaythia, thank you for giving of your time and being gracious to Daddy when playtime had to wait just ten more minutes.

Second, I want to thank several of you who offered feedback during my writing process: Serenity, Carol, Leon, Rebeka, Lauri, Chris, Tana, Sandra, Sean, Ellie, Brad, David, and Joshua. Your insights were excellent and most helpful.

Finally, I want to thank Laura and Barbara, my editors. Your professionalism and editorial understanding have been most beneficial to this project, as well as to me personally as a writer.

Sub Cruce.

Introduction
Free Will, Idolatry, and Postmodern Relativism

I have met a lot of Jesus Christs in my life. I have met them on the Delta 5849 flight to St. Louis. I have met them at coffee shops, at college, on social media, and on the streets. I have even met them in the church, on mission trips, at assisted-living apartments, at church picnics, at small-group home Bible studies, at weddings, and at my office. Indeed, in my short life, I have met a lot of Jesuses. All of them different; all of them unique.

But wait a minute, how can there be more than one Jesus? Does not the Bible and history clearly show us that there is only one Jesus of Nazareth, the son of Mary and Joseph? Yes, the Bible teaches there is only one Jesus Christ. There is only one authentic and real Jesus Christ. As we confess in the Apostles' Creed, there is one Jesus Christ "who was conceived by the Holy Spirit, born of the virgin Mary, suffered under Pontius Pilate, was crucified, died and was buried. He descended into hell. The third day He rose again from the dead." However, despite there being only one Jesus, we find an overabundance of forgeries in North America.

There is no shortage of false christs in the twenty-first century.

These false christs are portrayed, talked about, and beloved within our large North American culture. Like all the Santa Clauses scattered across our malls during the Christmas season, there are dozens upon dozens of look-alike false christs scattered across America's churches and in homes. Like all the Elvises roaming the streets of Vegas, these look-alike christs roam in and out of our spiritual conversations and lives and beliefs. These christs may look like Jesus and sound like Jesus, but they are nothing more than counterfeits. They are pseudo christs. They are false christs. Like the mall Santa Clauses and the

Vegas Elvises, they are not real, even though they are embraced, loved, promoted, revered, and sometimes even taught by well-meaning, yet misinformed Christians.

Who exactly are these false christs? Do you know them? Do you worship them? You might be surprised at the answers. In the upcoming chapters of this book, we will meet twelve of them. The chances are good you have already met some of these false christs, most likely in different places and within different circumstances. But before we meet these twelve false christs, we must pause and ask ourselves a question. How did these false christs come to be in the first place? I have several theories about why this is.

For starters, we live in a culture that offers an abundance of choices and exalts everyone's personal free will—we are encouraged to do what we want, whenever we want. We are told that we are masters and commanders of our lives. This leads us to try and individualize everything to suit our fancy. For example, we personalize our social circles by friending people on Facebook and unfriending others. We personalize our feeds on Twitter to see only what we want to see, allowing us to ignore that which we find irrelevant. We also personalize our cable channel listings, our radio channels on music apps, our sub sandwiches, our fantasy football teams, and our smartphones—just to name a few of the many things which we personalize to suit our preferences. If we can personalize our music, movies, and food, why can't we customize Jesus the way we want?

If we can personalize our music, movies, and food, why can't we customize Jesus the way we want?

There is a second reason why I believe there are so many false christs. To explain this second reason, let us consider Peter, one of Jesus' disciples. Peter is best known for his remarkable confession about Jesus: "You are the Christ, the Son of the living God" (see Matthew 16:13–20). After Peter's confession of whom Jesus is, Jesus goes on to explain what it means for Him to be the Son of the Living God. Jesus revealed that He, as the real Christ, must go to Jerusalem to suffer many things from the elders and chief priests and scribes and be killed, and on the third day be raised (16:21). Peter, though, had a hard time accepting this explanation, especially the suffering and dying part. As a result, Peter ultimately chewed Jesus out (well, Bibles use the word "rebuked") because he didn't like what he was hearing. Peter took Jesus aside and began to scold Him, saying, "Far be it from You, Lord! This shall never happen to You" (16:22). On the surface, we might just

THE MYTH OF FREE WILL

Free will exalts mankind's ability to "choose." While it is true that mankind is free to choose things such as what kind of food to eat or what kind of car to drive, it is not true that mankind can choose salvation, choose Jesus, choose whom we will serve, choose to surrender, choose to be obedient, and so on. In a nutshell, free will theology teaches that mankind can choose good over evil. Considering this, we need to ask ourselves: if our wills are free, then why do we continue to sin and choose evil? It seems to me that if our wills are free, it would be simple for us to say "no" to sin and "yes" to righteousness—problem solved. However, as we look at history, we see that this was not the case for millions of people (Christians included) over the last several thousand years.

Furthermore, if our wills are so free, what is stopping us from implementing all the principles and helpful tips in self-help books? Why the lack of success? Let me take this a step further: if our wills are free, why would we even need self-help books or books aiding and encouraging us how to become a better or a more righteously driven person? Doesn't the very presence of improvement books showing us how to become better validate that we are not free? Ultimately, the reason for the importance of this discussion about free will is that the very Gospel is at stake. In other words, the more a person believes in a free will, the less they will believe in their need for a Savior. The more they will see themselves as bound, the more they will cry out for a Savior. The more perceived freedom, the less the need; the greater the realization of bondage, the greater the need.

assume Peter is scared for his friend. What is wrong with that? Well, what went wrong with Peter is what goes wrong with our culture. When individuals—like Peter—do not like who Jesus really is, they reject what Jesus says about Himself. However, they don't stop with rejecting Jesus; rather, they redefine Him. Yes, when the real Jesus does not fit into a person's narrative and when He does not agree with the way a person figures things should be, He is changed so that He can be supportive of that individual's wants, desires, values, and worldview.

This temptation to redefine Jesus is not only prevalent in our culture today, but it certainly was during the Early Church as well. If I were in Peter's shoes, I am pretty sure that I would have recoiled in horror at Jesus' talk of suffering and death. Like Peter, I would have said something like, "Jesus, if You have power over creation, death, and the devil, let all this silly talk of suffering and death stop! It is depressing! You are God. This despairing talk should not concern us." Tragically, we Christians—with the culture—commandeer this great confession and then redefine who Jesus is according to our hopes and our dreams and our desires. We do this because it is this way with our idolatrous hearts.

I have heard it said that idolatry occurs anytime a person thinks about the Lord in ways that are unworthy of Him. Otherwise stated, idolatry is essentially creating a false image of the Lord. That seems simple enough; however, we must take note that there is something rather sneaky with idolatry. Idolatry allows the opportunity to not entirely reject the Lord, but an opportunity to redefine the Lord according to a particular, desired perspective. Idolatry takes the real Jesus captive in the imagination and then chisels away that which is offensive and then glues on extra things that are wanted. Our mind works like a hammer and chisel, forming the real Jesus into a

Our mind works like a hammer and chisel, forming the real Jesus into a creature of our making—carving out that which is uncomfortable and adding enhancements to please our desires.

creature of our making—carving out that which is uncomfortable and adding enhancements to please our desires. (See the story of the Golden Calf in Exodus 32.)

More specifically, this tactic of not completely rejecting the Lord but redefining Him according to our personal agendas is the result of the sinful nature at work. Keep in mind that the sinful nature—that is, mankind's corrupt and evil nature everyone has inherited from Adam's fall into sin—does not believe the Gospel, never has believed the Gospel, and never will believe the Gospel. The sinful nature operates from the context of unbelief.

> *We typically reshape and reform the Lord into the image of ourselves. Life is easier when Jesus is redefined to fit our own agenda and dreams.*

This sinful nature wants independence, not dependence. This sinful nature wants to have everything, including the Lord, underneath its thumb. This freedom and control can be cleverly attained through the means of idolatry. (To learn more about the impact of original sin and

IDOLATRY

When we think about the topic of idolatry, it is easy to imagine primitive people groups worshiping and showing their devotion to false deities carved out of stone or wood. While there may be some truth to this general characterization of idolatry, we need to be on guard from such an oversimplification of the subject. This harmless generalization can actually obstruct us from understanding the heart of idolatry. In the words of Martin Luther in his Large Catechism, "[Idolatry] happens not merely by erecting an image and worshiping it, but rather it happens in the heart" (I 20–21). This means that idolatry is so much bigger than worshiping simple wood carvings. Idolatry can happen when we take the Lord and carve Him out in our imaginations to the way we think He should be (i.e., we create a different god) and then we attach our hearts to the false god that we have created in our imaginations. Anytime our fear, love, and trust of the real Jesus is transferred to an imposter christ, we have broken the First Commandment by idolatry.

the sinful nature, there is a beneficial section in the Apology of the Augsburg Confession, the second article. The Apology of the Augsburg Confession is the Lutheran response to the debates in the sixteenth century about original sin and the sinful nature.) Succinctly stated, the sinful nature is sly in that it will not boldly reject Jesus and the Gospel for fear of being exposed. Rather, the old sinful nature will attempt to redefine Jesus into its image, desires, dreams, hopes, and aspirations. Indeed, idolatry allows a person to redefine and reconstruct the Lord into an image of the one who is committing idolatry. We typically reshape and reform the Lord into the image of ourselves. Life is easier when Jesus is redefined to fit our own agenda and dreams. That is to say, things do not go well when Jesus disagrees with our outlooks on life—for we cannot live with ongoing cognitive dissonance.

COGNITIVE DISSONANCE

If you have ever been to a junior high school band concert, you have experienced dissonance, though maybe not intentionally. Dissonance happens when band members play the wrong notes. Maybe an F-sharp is to be played, but half the band plays a G, which results in a sound that makes you cringe. You might even want to plug your ears and slam your head against the chair in front of you. Cognitive dissonance is much like this, but instead of musical notes colliding, conflicting thoughts, ideas, and beliefs are crashing into one another.

In regard to Christianity, a person cannot embrace the Christian faith without Jesus. However, if the Jesus as proclaimed in the Bible does not agree with a person's desires, dreams, hopes, and aspirations, there will be cognitive dissonance. A person with cognitive dissonance cannot endure such dissonance for a long period of time. The dissonance in the mind must be resolved. It can be resolved in one of two ways: either the person repents of their wrong desires, dreams, hopes, and aspirations, bringing them into harmony with Jesus, or the person attempts to change the person, work, teaching, and words of Jesus. In regard to cognitive dissonance, it can only be neutralized by repentance or by creating an idol.

The third and final reason for all these false christs is that our current culture is suspicious of claims of objective truth (an objective fixed standard). Our current culture is embedded in a mind-set called postmodern relativism. Don't let this long philosophical word scare you! Simply put, postmodern relativism says there are no such things as objective standards

Our current culture is suspicious of claims of objective truth (an objective fixed standard).

of truth—truth is what a person believes it to be. Postmodern relativism also says what is true for one person might not be true for another person—truth is relative because it varies from person to person. Therefore, if there is no such thing as objective truth, then truth is up to the individual person, which means nobody can definitively say who Jesus is. Any attempt to definitively and objectively define who Jesus is, such as through the ancient Holy Scriptures, is often met with harsh criticism. Practically speaking, in postmodern relativism, everyone can have whatever view of Jesus they want; everyone is right, for there are no objective rules. However, if a person points out differences, they are immediately told they are not being very loving and should stop judging. Furthermore, postmodernists may ask: "What gives you the right to religiously control *my* personal spirituality?"

POSTMODERN RELATIVISM

Thousands of years ago, there were people called Sophists. The Sophists basically believed that mankind was the measuring stick of all things—each person could judge for him or herself what was good, bad, and beautiful. Furthermore, Sophists were skeptical of anything that expressed itself as an objective universal truth.

Fast forward to the 1970s, and we see that the ancient ideology of the Sophists has emerged in the North American culture through postmodern relativism. Postmodern relativism basically teaches that there is no such thing as objective and universal truths and that what is true for one person may not be true for another.

Our culture is used to choices—and lots of them. Our culture allows the sinful heart to go the way of idolatry. Therefore, our culture rejects a really important objective truth (that is, a rejection of the Holy Scripture's testimony about Jesus). Our culture also believes that truth varies from person to person. All of this is what allows for such a great diversity of false christs in North America. Choice, idolatry, a rejection of truth: this is the landscape that we find ourselves in, and this is the landscape through which this book attempts to maneuver.

As we journey through the following pages, I introduce you to twelve false christs I have personally encountered over the past twenty years of my life. As previously mentioned, these false christs have been made known to me through individuals I have crossed paths with in various contexts and places. Therefore, these people will be introduced to you as well. As a pastor, I assure you I am not revealing confidential information nor sharing any stories that occurred within the private context of personal confession. I have kept real identities secret by changing names and circumstances. (Think of the people, places, and conversations as works of fiction based upon real life events.) Specifically, you will hear the stories of how these individuals have gone the way of idolatry and in what way various Western cultural ideologies have influenced them.

As you are introduced to the various people in the upcoming chapters of this book, you may find them to be quite familiar. Perhaps the way they talk about life and their view of who Jesus is will remind you of yourself or your own interactions with acquaintances in your life. Or, your friends and family members might hold views similar to those you will meet in this book. If you have not already, then you most likely will in the future. When you do have encounters and conversations, you may wonder how you can respond. Therefore, at the end of each chapter, I will include a brief section titled "How to Respond." Think of this section as a Christian apologetic and evangelism approach—a way of bolstering our defense of the Christian faith and an encouragement to confess the real Jesus in our everyday conversations. This section will give you ideas of how to respond not only to the people in this book but also to those in your life who subscribe to a false christ.

By the end of this book, we are going to desperately want the real Jesus to please stand up in the midst of all the false christs, telling us for Himself who He really is. As we ponder the last chapter of this book and hear about the real Jesus Christ, we will then be able to contrast the real Jesus with all the false christs. We can then clearly answer who Jesus is, for this is the most important answer and confession the Christian can give. Why? Because who we say Jesus is not only reveals the identity of Jesus but also influences how we understand the Church, how we read the Bible, how we live, and how we know the truth. Who Jesus is has lasting ramifications in this life and the next.

So, join me as we encounter:

The Mascot
The Option among Many
The Good Teacher
The Therapist
The Giver of Bling
The National Patriot
The Social Justice Warrior
The Moral Example
The New Moses
The Mystical Friend
The Feminized
The Teddy Bear

Join me in asking, "Will the real Jesus please stand up?"

Let's discuss the **Introduction**

Read Matthew 16:13–28. The following questions are going to force you to consider the topic of Jesus' identity and what happens when people set their minds on the things of man.

1. During the time of Jesus, what were people saying about His identity? Did everybody agree? (See Matthew 16:13–14.) Who do people say Jesus is today?

2. As we look at Matthew 16:15–19, what was Peter's confession about Jesus' identity? According to Jesus, how was this confession revealed to Peter? What does this revelation mean regarding the Church and the gates of hell?

3. In verse 21, how did Jesus further expound on Peter's confession? In verse 22 how did Peter respond to Jesus' further explanation of His identity? Did he accept it or reject it? Why do you think Peter responded the way that he did?

4. What was Jesus' response to Peter in Matthew 16:23? Why did Jesus respond the way that He did? Does Jesus' response surprise you? Why or why not?

5. What happens when we set our mind on things of man and not the things of God when attempting to define Jesus? What happens when our minds are set on the things of God (i.e., the Scriptures) when trying to identify Jesus?

6. Before you read the rest of the book, write down some of the examples of false christs you have experienced in your life. What context did you experience these idols in? After you finish the book, look back at your list and see if you can match any of them to a specific chapter.

Meet Jillian, the Ethical Hedonist

Our plane was cruising at an altitude of thirty-one thousand feet, and the flight attendants were passing out drinks. My neighbor Jillian, a typical Midwestern woman in her late twenties or early thirties, was pouring her small bottle of wine into a small, red, plastic airline cup as we were talking. Since take off, I had learned she is married and a mother of three. After the flight attendant had moved to the next row, she continued our conversation, saying, "Lately, I have had all sorts of issues with Jesus. I don't want to. But I do. And I don't care for that, and I don't like what I feel are contradictions, and I don't believe some of it, and I feel bad about all of those feelings."

Jillian had grown up in a small rural town, attended the local church, participated in youth group, and was homeschooled. In her early twenties, though, she had drifted away from consistent church attendance. The busyness of life, college, marriage, and three kids had brought about her uneven church attendance, and she had never seemed to recover the consistency that she once had.

Although Jillian grew up in a fairly small conservative Midwestern town and in what appeared to be a very stable family, she found great conflict with her family upbringing and some of the teachings of Jesus. Her parents' values and beliefs had not changed—they still attended Jillian's childhood church faithfully each week, where her dad was on the board of trustees and her mom was very active in the altar guild. Needless to say, she was experiencing cognitive dissonance. Jillian was unable to reconcile how she got to the point where she and her family were on different sides of the aisle on so many things—things like sexual ethics, God's Law, and the doctrine of hell. Furthermore, she was unable to understand why she was at odds with Jesus. When Jillian's parents and childhood pastor talked about Jesus, it seemed that Jesus was too stern, too critical, and talked about hell too much for her liking. Not only was Jillian a bit offended by this but she also felt disenchanted and confused. Why had Jillian become so different from her parents and those around her if she was raised with the same values and taught the same things? Why did she struggle with Jesus when she once felt so comfortable with Him?

We obviously have a lot to unpack and understand with Jillian; therefore, why don't we start with the conflict that she was having with her upbringing, family, and Jesus.

To understand the conflict Jillian is experiencing, we must conclude that there are only three plausible reasons for the disunion: Jillian's family and Jesus had changed, Jillian had changed, or all three had changed to some degree. In our conversation, I learned the church she attended still had the same pastor, and I gathered the church was not one that was easily tossed to and fro by the waves of culture and carried about by every wind of man-made doctrine. Therefore, we can conclude with a fair amount of certainty that her childhood congregation and its teachings about Jesus had not changed. Furthermore, it sounded like Jillian's family was and is a hardworking and proud Midwestern family that sticks to their guns. That means the most likely scenario is that Jillian herself had changed.

But had Jillian really changed? According to Jillian, she had not officially left the church, she had not renounced her Baptism, and she still attended church services several times a year with her family around Christmas and Easter.

So, what is going on with Jillian? After talking with her a little more, it became apparent that even though Jillian's circumstances and context had not changed, her worldview had. In other words, the only thing that had drastically altered in Jillian's life from the time of her childhood to the time of her conversation with me was that her perspective on life had shifted. The way that Jillian viewed the world, considered the Christian faith, and understood Jesus, had all changed since childhood, moving away from both her family's and her church's perspective. Indeed, for many years, the way she saw life, reality, and herself, had been changing, even though she was relatively unaware of the slow transformation that had been occurring to her worldview for some time.

Very simply stated, Jillian's presuppositions about life, the world, and Jesus were now different. But what caused her worldview to change? It is important to pause and think through what has happened to Jillian, for her story will be a consistent pattern with many of the other individuals in this book. Let's pull back the layers to investigate what is going on beneath the surface.

As we already know, the younger Jillian viewed things one way; however, as she got older, she began to view the same things differently. This change, which we will learn about in the upcoming paragraphs, is what is causing her confusion and making her uncomfortable. People

WORLDVIEW

The way people view or think about the world and themselves is what we call a worldview. A worldview is a person's perception of reality. It is the lens through which they view his or her life. For example, we have heard it said before that some people view life through rose-colored glasses. This is an idiom that is used to show that some people will always view life from an optimistic perspective. Their lens (i.e., worldview) causes them to see all of life's events—the good, the bad, and the ugly—from a positive perspective. Because of their rose-colored worldview, they do not see the glass as half empty, but will always see it as half full.

are relatively unaware of their own worldview and even more so unaware of changes to their worldview until they come into conflict with other individuals who hold worldviews contrary to their own. For example, Jillian's circumstances and context had remained consistent (she didn't renounce the Christian faith, she did not disconnect her family ties, and she still lived in the community she grew up in); however, as she engaged her family, friends, and her church, it was evident there were differing views over sexuality, God's Law, the doctrine of hell, and the Jesus from her childhood. But what changed her worldview? The change in her worldview was caused by an adjustment in her presuppositions—that is to say, assumptions. In other words, one, two, three, or more fundamental presuppositions in Jillian's life changed, which

PRESUPPOSITIONS

Think about an eye exam. A patient's face is pressed against a mechanism with all sorts of dials, knobs, and lenses attached to it. The doctor makes several adjustments to the mechanism to bring forth a lens for the person to look through. Depending on the settings, the patient will see through a blurry lens or a clear lens. Presuppositions are similar to the dials and knobs the doctor uses to choose various lenses. Presuppositions (i.e., assumptions that might be true or might be false) function to determine the kind of worldview a person looks through. True presuppositions help a person see reality clearly, whereas false presuppositions distort reality.

These presuppositions come from a lot of different places and circumstances such as political allegiance, emotional state, religious experiences, psychological dysfunctions, physical environment, theological heritage, language, social conditioning, gender, intelligence, and culture values—to name a few. For example, if a person presupposes that good and evil are tied solely to pleasure and pain, then a person would view things in life that produce pain as evil and things that produce pleasure as good. In summary, presuppositions shape and determine a person's worldview.

subconsciously were forcing her to see things differently with Jesus and the Christian faith, which then brought about the uncomfortable divisions she was experiencing with her family and her upbringing. So what presuppositions changed?

After a couple more sips of her drink, Jillian looked out the airplane window for a moment and then said, "You know what I've come to really hate lately—and I hate the word *hate*? I hate when people are judged, because it is so sad to be judged. It just hurts me and makes me feel tense, gloomy, and kind of angry. But, I also know when something is right and when people should not be judged. Okay, so here is how I know what is right and what is wrong. When something is good, I just know with every fiber of my being that it is not sinful. Yes, when something is good—truly good—I'm 100 percent passionate about it, and my heart and soul and mind are in a really positive and good place."

It may seem odd to be having a theological conversation over Jesus, sin, and theology while traveling at 31,000 feet on a plane, but for pastors, this seems to be a rather typical occurrence—at least in my experience. Pastors can be safe spaces for people to discuss issues of a spiritual nature when there is no long-term commitment to an ongoing relationship. Furthermore, people often share their theological and spiritual insights with pastors, either as a way to connect with a "man of the cloth" or to spiritually validate themselves before a clergy person—perhaps even to validate themselves before God.

Regardless of Jillian's motives, she paused, took another sip of wine, swallowed, and continued, "But then there is a problem. Some of my Christian family members and longtime friends will talk about Jesus and talk about the Bible and morals and stuff . . . and in my heart and mind of my own ideas, what they are telling me is the farthest thing from Christ I could imagine. We used to agree on everything. Now I don't know what to think about this totally, and I don't want to stop wrestling with this, but I just know that there are certain things I can no longer believe. There are certain things that I know

Jesus would never support. The Jesus I know is not like these other people's Jesus."

At this point, it would be easy for us to aggressively jump on Jillian's authentic admission in believing in a false christ. It would be easy to

We may be able to see ways in which we have followed Jillian's false christ, which will lead us to repentance and asking for forgiveness from the real Jesus.

militantly strip her views apart and prove her wrong. It is always tempting to point out another person's logical inconsistencies and then celebrate in victory our sound logic and rightness. However, we must be prudent, gentle, and compassionate. Our goal in examining Jillian's thoughts, and others in this book, is not to prove her wrong and us readers right so that we can tally up brownie points before God, but rather our goal is to examine where Jillian has been tragically ensnared into believing in a false christ. Indeed, by studying Jillian's reflections and comments, we will not only learn a little about her idolatry, but we may be able to see our own errors as well. We may be able to see ways in which we have followed Jillian's false christ, which will lead us to repentance and asking for forgiveness from the real Jesus.

What can we learn from Jillian's comments? Looking a bit closer at her remarks, we can clearly see an emerging presupposition in Jillian, a presupposition that is at work in her worldview. Jillian is very averse to anything that is negative and very favorable to anything that is positive, which rationally makes sense. However, it is important to

Good and evil have become pleasure and pain.

note that Jillian takes this a step further; she ties her moral judgments of right and wrong to that which gives her pleasure and pain. To rephrase this, that which causes her discomfort and pain is evil, and that which grants her comfort and pleasure is good. And how does she discern pleasure and pain? She understands pleasure and pain by the fiber of her being—she knows pleasure and pain by what she feels. For Jillian, good and evil have become pleasure and pain.

For example, one issue Jillian mentioned was how she was upset with her parents and childhood church for their stance on sex being reserved for marriage only. In other words, when the church taught that sex was a gift reserved "only" for a husband and wife within the blessed estate of marriage (the Sixth Commandment), she deemed this as repressive and wrong because it caused her to feel judged and feel emotional pain for her past premarital sex with her now husband. For Jillian, sex before marriage made her happy, so it can't be that bad. Hearing that her premarital sex was wrong caused her unhappiness and emotional pain; therefore, she believed that this teaching was wrong and evil. This belief is not unique to Jillian; it is prevalent in our culture, a culture that believes the key to happiness is total and unlimited sex, much like how the Austrian neurologist, Sigmund Freud, taught. Therefore, any restraint to the goal of sexual happiness, such as reserving the happy gift of sex for a husband and wife in marriage, is deemed as repressive, judgmental, and mean—it causes unhappiness. And as we already know, this way of thinking equates unhappiness and emotional pain automatically with the categorical term *evil*.

ETHICAL HEDONISM

Hedonism teaches that the ultimate goal of mankind is the pursuit of pleasure. Therefore, that which is pleasurable is good; that which is painful is bad. The ethical component of hedonism is that the pursuit of pleasure is the ultimate goal, only insofar as others are not being hurt.

When ethical hedonism infiltrates Christianity, it sounds something like this, "God wants my life to be about success and happiness. As long as I do not hurt anyone, my choices are my choices." However, when ethical hedonism takes a firm root in a person, it might sound something like this, "Everyone has the right to be happy without feeling guilty. Furthermore, I would far rather be happy than right any day."

Regarding pleasure and pain, Jillian also does something else. She places pleasure, not pain, at the center of her life as the ultimate goal and the ultimate good. Therefore, pleasure as the "ultimate" is the presupposition that permeates her worldview. In other words, Jillian's worldview is not linked to an objective standard but linked to her individualized feelings, with the ultimate goal being the pursuit of pleasure. She is what we would call an ethical hedonist.

Jillian's worldview is not linked to an objective standard but linked to her individualized feelings, with the ultimate goal being the pursuit of pleasure.

Hedonism is nothing new. It is as old as humanity. Consider Adam and Eve. In Genesis, God commanded Adam and Eve not to eat from the tree in the midst of the garden. However, after the devil tempted Adam and Eve, Eve saw that the tree was good for food and that it was a delight to her eyes. Instead of trusting God's Word not to eat from the tree, Eve was tempted by the idea of immediate pleasure and ate the fruit. Eve tragically exchanged God's Word for pleasure, which resulted in havoc being wreaked upon humanity. (See Genesis 3:1–7.)

Jillian's lens has been tainted by ethical hedonism. Not only is her vision for her life tainted by ethical hedonism, but it has also tainted the way she understands Jesus. She has manipulated and changed Jesus into an idol of her choice. (Keep in mind that this false christ is an idol; it does not exist, except in the minds of people like Jillian.) Indeed, since Jillian is subconsciously an ethical hedonist, she has also concluded that Jesus is too, or that He supports the ideology of ethical hedonists, at the least.

He won't boo; he is a loyal fan, who never gets angry or upset with his followers.

Meet our first false christ: the Mascot. This false christ is nothing more than a hedonistic idol with pom-poms. With his pom-poms, this idol stands on the sidelines of life encouraging people in their pursuit of happiness. He always cheers and always supports. Since this false christ goes the way of hedonism, he will never bring

THE MASCOT

about any pain for the individual. He won't boo; he is a loyal fan, who never gets angry or upset with his followers. He will even defend them from criticism. This means that the Mascot will never confront the sinful nature with God's Ten Commandments; he will never call for repentance, and he will never talk about hell and damnation. Indeed, he will never condemn, correct, or criticize, which means that he waters down the Word of God to avoid unnecessary conflicts. He is an all-around nice guy who encourages his followers in their pursuits of pleasure and happiness. If the follower is happy and finding pleasure, this false christ is even happier. If the follower is experiencing pain, this false christ is sad as well and says to his follower, "You deserve to be happy! Do whatever it takes to find happiness."

Looking a bit more specifically at the Mascot, we must take note of three crucial characteristics of this false christ: (1) he accepts ethical hedonism (which we have already covered), (2) he avoids the Law, and (3) he avoids the doctrine of hell. But what are the implications of avoiding these last two subjects?

IS IT WRONG FOR A CHRISTIAN TO PURSUE HAPPINESS?

Joy must be distinguished from our culture's understanding of happiness and pleasure. Cultural happiness and pleasure tend to be seen within an individual's power—something people can attempt to force and manipulate and conjure up. Christian joy, though, is not the same. That is to say, joy does not anchor a person in joy itself, but rather biblical joy is a mental state or emotional gratitude for good things received. That's right, joy points to something else, something outside of us; it points to and longs for something grand that is given. In a word, joy is not fixed to an artificial feeling or an emotion; it does not chase after itself. Joy desires, anticipates, and receives gifts. But what are these gifts and who is the giver of these gifts? The Gift-Giver is none other than the Lord Himself. And the gifts He gives are Himself, His name upon our head and heart in Baptism, and His Word in the Bible and in the Sacraments. All gifts, all for us, so that we might have everlasting joy.

A person like Jillian who follows this false christ, who is all about the Good News of the Gospel but avoids teaching or proclaiming the Law, will be led to something called lawlessness. Note that the word *Law* refers to the Ten Commandments: God's prohibitions (don't do that) and God's will (do this). Since the Mascot does not embrace or teach the Law of God, this false christ is not serious about righteousness, holiness, or sin. Therefore, if the Law is not present, sin will be carelessly minimized, and mankind will end up being unrestricted to the point that the apostle Paul says: "their god is their belly and they glory in their shame, with minds set on earthly things" (Philippians 3:19). In other words, by following the Mascot, a person can eat, drink, and be merry with no limitations, no guilt, and no shame. Pleasure can reign supreme.

By following the Mascot, a person can eat, drink, and be merry with no limitations, no guilt, and no shame. Pleasure can reign supreme.

Examining the Mascot a bit more, we find that this false christ—like the hedonist who follows him—has no interest in God's Law because

LAWLESSNESS

Lawlessness is the rejection of God's Law as clearly expressed in the Ten Commandments. Lawlessness in Christianity is when a person abuses the Gospel and disregards the Law. A lawless person believes that grace gives them a license to sin. They say, "I am under grace; therefore, the Law is no longer applicable. I am going to do whatever makes me happy. I am going to follow the desires of *my* heart because I am free." The life of a person who embraces lawlessness is marked by liberty from binding religious ethics (i.e., Law) and an apparent happy disposition of free, unrestricted living according to whatever gives oneself pleasure. Lawlessness is the polar opposite of Legalism. Whereas Lawlessness rejects the Law and abuses the Gospel, Legalism abuses the Law and rejects the Gospel. Both of these are hellish errors, for they do not embrace God's two words of Law *and* Gospel—Law that reveals sin and Gospel that absolves sin.

God's Law functions like a sharp javelin that breaks through the conscience and wounds. In other words, the Mascot will not exchange his pom-poms for the Law because the Law of God functions like a hammer that shatters mankind's sinful endeavors, exposes our foolish schemes, and topples our naïve utopic dreams. This false christ cannot tolerate or allow God's Word of Law to prick the soul, shut his followers' mouths, reveal sin, and kill the old sinful nature, for this is in direct conflict with his goal to minimize pain. (See Romans 3:19–20 and 2 Corinthians 3:6, where the apostle Paul talks about the work of the Law.) Indeed, the Mascot and the hedonist cannot have God's Law, for it would bring about painful convictions of sin which would destroy the central focus of pleasure.

This brings us back to Jillian and the third characteristic of the Mascot: the avoidance of the doctrine of hell. She had just finished up her wine, and the flight attendant came down to collect the trash. We were in our descent to St. Louis and would land in about twenty-three

SWEET POISON

Sin tastes sweet but it is also a poison to the body and soul. Because of this, nobody sins to cause pain and destruction in their life. In fact, it is quite the opposite. Like sweet poison, sin goes down smoothly at first, but in the end, it kills. Take, for example, pornography. Driven by the hedonistic desire for pleasure, a person will click on a pornographic website and enjoy a five-minute video. However, as the short video grants pleasure, the sinful nature wants to continue the pleasure and increase the pleasure. So, a short five-minute video entices a person to more extreme versions of pornography and these more extreme versions of pornography lead a person into sexual darkness where in the end a marriage is ruined, a job is lost, and a once polished reputation is ruined. James captures this progression in his epistle, "But each person is tempted when he is lured and enticed by his own desire. Then desire, when it has conceived gives birth to sin, and sin when it is fully grown brings forth death" (James 1:13–15).

minutes. She turned to me and said, "I had a friend who was dying. His heart actually stopped beating. He was totally gone for three minutes or something like that. But, somehow, he came back to life. He wasn't ready to go—if you know what I mean. Anyway, after he came back from the dead, he said that he saw a big black dragon coming to eat him, which freaks me out! I asked him about the dragon and told him that maybe he was brought back to life to get right with God. But dang, he said that he could care less about God. He actually flipped God off and stated that he couldn't care less about God. He died four days later in the hospital. . . . So, yeah, do you believe that he is in hell?" She paused for a second, not giving me much time to respond before she continued her thought. "I just . . . I just don't believe he is. I know Jesus talks about hell in the Bible, but maybe Jesus wasn't sure about hell. Or maybe the people writing down the Bible were wrong about hell and didn't accurately record Jesus correctly. Maybe hell isn't that bad; maybe it is exaggerated or misworded or something like that. Could hell maybe be like a lesser heaven; could it be not as good as heaven but still okay?"

Let's look at the Mascot's rejection of the doctrine of hell. Hell does not exist with this false christ—it can't. If this false christ would teach or preach or embrace the doctrine of hell, it would affirm that this world that we live in has moral significance. Otherwise stated, if there is a hell, our lives have moral consequence—we can't do whatever we want

Simply stated, if there is a hell, hedonism does not work, and the false christ can't function.

because we know there will be consequences to our thoughts, words, and deeds. Let us think of it this way: if there is such a thing as a moral consequence, then there is a judgment. If there is a judgment, then what we think, say, and do has consequences. If what we think, say, and do has consequences according to an objective standard of God's Law and not a person's feelings, then some of the things that we embrace according to pleasure might be wrong, and some of the things that bring about pain might be right. Simply stated, if there is a hell, hedonism does not work, and the false christ can't function.

Do we see how hedonism and this first false christ—the Mascot—are essentially opposed to the real Jesus and the real Gospel? Indeed, when the Mascot denies the Law and denies hell, he essentially denies the reality, problem, and consequence of sin in this present life. In other words, if there is no such thing as sin, there is no need for the Gospel, and if we do not need the Gospel, "the truth is not in us" (1 John 1:8).

Responding to Jillian

What is the main thing that drives and controls Jillian's thoughts, logic, and decisions regarding Christianity and her views about Jesus?

A MORALLY CONSEQUENTIAL WORLD?

In the Book of Acts, we read about the apostle Paul talking to the Athenians. In his sermon, Paul says that God "has fixed a day on which he will judge the world in righteousness by a man whom he has appointed" (17:31). More specifically, the apostle Paul is attempting to move the people from what has been referred to before as a morally inconsequential worldview to a morally consequential worldview. He is doing this in order to reveal their problem of sin, so that he might reveal the solution to sin, the real Jesus Christ. In other words, if there is no hell and if there is no Law and if there is no judgment, then there is no problem and no consequence of sin (i.e., inconsequential). If there is no problem or consequence of sin, then a person does not need the real Jesus Christ. Indeed, faith cannot enter a heart that has not been crumpled. A person does not call for a doctor until he realizes he is sick. A lost sheep does not desire the shepherd until he knows he is lost. We cannot understand the Gospel unless we first hear about the problem of our sin. We cannot understand the assurance of Mount Calvary unless we have heard the thunder of Mount Sinai. We cannot appreciate the future blessedness of heaven without understanding the dreadful fiery threats of hell.

Jillian has been taken captive by Hedonism. Therefore, everything she does is controlled by this belief that pleasure is good and pain is evil. Thus, she had created the idol of the Mascot. This presents a great difficulty in having any conversation with her because if we offend her or cause her any discomfort, she will immediately sense pain and then label our actions as being evil and, as a consequence, possibly label us as being evil people as well.

So, when we respond to Jillian—and others like her—it is of utmost importance that we pray that the Lord would give us great compassion and gentleness, lest we get easily lumped into the category of evil, resulting in the conversation coming to a close. Considering all of this, if we are able to visit at length with Jillian, our main goal will be to help her understand how much she bases everything upon her feelings of pleasure (good) and of pain (evil). The best way to help Jillian with this is to ask her questions about herself. For example, "Jillian, you said earlier that when something is good, you feel passionate and positive and good about it. Right? Have there ever been times where you have felt good about something, and then it turned out, in the end, to be bad? And have there been things that you thought were bad and then, in fact, turned out to be good?" By asking these questions, we are attempting to reveal to Jillian that automatically labeling pleasure as "good" and pain as "evil" is not foolproof. These questions are attempting to dislodge her from the irrationality of Hedonism, but to do so gently.

Now, if she proceeds to answer these questions, we must continue with great compassion and integrity. When the errors in a person's worldview and presuppositions are revealed, they will often respond defensively or withdraw in insecurity. A defensive response will attempt to justify the Hedonistic worldview and presuppositions. This is usually done in a firm aggressive tone to convey the message that we shouldn't push the issue. This generally means that the discussion will come to a close, but, Lord willing, the topic might come up again another day. On the other hand, if the response is one of insecurity, we may need to be ready to confess. Yes, confess! Keep in mind that Christians do not argue people into the Christian faith, but rather, we confess the real Jesus. So, if someone like Jillian shows signs of doubt over her Hedonism and asks us how we understand goodness and evil, we can then confess Law and Gospel. We can confess that we know right and wrong by the Ten Commandments and we can confess that

> *The goal is to confess the Word—both Law and Gospel—so that all would be gifted repentance of sin and faith in the real Jesus.*

we know forgiveness by God's Word of promise. Keep in mind that the goal is never to beat people like Jillian in a debate but to confess the real Jesus who came to purchase and win them from sin, death, and the devil. The goal is to confess the Word—both Law and Gospel—so that all would be gifted repentance of sin and faith in the real Jesus.

Will the Real Jesus Please Stand Up?

What the world does not need is the Mascot who encourages us to base reality on our feelings. We do not need a smooth talking and agreeable false christ who exalts pleasure and criticizes pain. This false christ does nothing except feed our sinful nature. A false christ without the Law of God who speaks pleasantries into ears only perpetuates a narcissistic epidemic of self-saturated persons chasing after the lusts of the flesh. Dear friends, we do not need our ears tickled by being pointed to hedonistic feelings, but rather, we need the voice of the Lord even when it causes us pain; we need the voice of the true Jesus that does not waver, does not fluctuate, and does not sway or follow the delusions of our amoral culture or our self-centered feelings. In the words of the apostle Paul, we need the word "in season and out of season . . . for the time is coming when people will not endure sound teaching, but having itching ears they will accumulate for themselves teachers to suit their own passion" (2 Timothy 4:2–3). Yes, we need the voice of the real Jesus to break through the glitter and shallow talk to drive us to repentance (which many times is very painful but needed) and then lavishly pronounce forgiveness to us, not only to free us from sin's slavish ways and the hell that we deserve, but to also create and sustain faith in us (see Mark 1:15). We must not be ensnared in the Mascot but desperately seek the real Jesus, for only in the real Jesus do we receive real happiness, joy, and peace that surpasses all understanding.

Let's discuss *the Mascot*

1. What are the three main characteristics of the Mascot?

The following questions should cause you to contemplate ethical hedonism, lawlessness, and the doctrine of hell. As you discuss these ideologies, contemplate how they are embedded in the Mascot; consider how they are diametrically opposed to Biblical Christianity and the Real Jesus.

2. What does the Bible say about ethical hedonism?

a. Read Ecclesiastes 2:1–11. Solomon said, "And whatever my eyes desired I did not keep from them. I kept my heart from no pleasure" (2:10). In other words, Solomon tested the pleasures of the world and his reaction to them. After this hedonistic experiment of Solomon, what was Solomon's conclusion about pleasure? What can you expect if you were to center your life on the pursuit of pleasure?

b. Read Philippians 3:12–20. The apostle Paul describes certain people who live by the god of their belly. How does Paul describe these people? Who are these people in relation to Jesus? What is their end? On what do they base their mind-set?

3. What does the Bible say about lawlessness?

a. Examine Romans 3:20 and Romans 7:7. What is the primary function of the Law? What happens when we reject the Law?

b. Why can the Christian not keep on sinning that grace may abound? See Romans 6:1–11.

4. Consider what the Bible says about the doctrine of hell, its implications, and the final judgment of mankind. Read Matthew 25:31–46. What does Jesus say about the great judgment? Does Jesus say there is or is not a judgment? Does Jesus say there is or is not hell?

5. In your own words, why does the Mascot avoid the doctrines of hell and the Law so much?

6. Why is the real Jesus not compatible with ethical hedonism, lawlessness, and the denial of hell?

7. With all of these texts in mind and what you read at the end of chapter 1, how can or do you interact with someone who has the Mascot as their idol?

THE OPTION AMONG MANY

2

Meet Tamar, The Religious Pluralist

It had been a rough morning, and traffic was congested on the 210 Freeway as I headed west toward Pasadena, California. I had some time to spare, though, and I had an epiphany. Suddenly the thought of a drink at my favorite coffee shop brightened my morning and motivated me to the next exit. Venti vanilla latte, please!

However, after the barista made my latte and called my name, my day got worse. No open tables! There was only one available seat at the counter where you have to sit uncomfortably close to complete strangers.

As I approached the open spot, I noticed the guy next to it was talking on his cellphone. He looked up at me with his coffee in one hand and a phone in the other and gave me a half-smile, as if to say, "That seat is open."

I sat down on the stool and set my latte on the counter. Then I pulled out my laptop to get a little work done on the upcoming week's sermon while I waited for the traffic to thin out on the 210. I was studying the Gospel of John with the help of new software I had just downloaded.

"Hey man, what kind of computer program is that? What kind of language is on that screen?" a voice said to me from my right.

I looked over at the curious stranger who had put his cell phone down and was now leaning toward my computer screen with what seemed to be an intriguing interest.

"It's Bible software I just downloaded, and the language is Koine Greek," I said.

He scrunched his face, "Koine what? What did you just say?"

"Koine Greek. It's the language that the New Testament was originally written in," I said.

He introduced himself to me as Tamar, and I learned he was in his mid to late twenties. He was a native to the Los Angeles area and had never really traveled beyond the Los Angeles Metro and Inland Valley areas. As the conversation developed, I learned he was soon to be married—his bachelor party was to begin that night—and was an owner of a sandwich franchise located near the coffee shop. His sandwich shop made Lebanese-style pitas filled with lean meats, cheeses, fresh veggies, and creative toppings. He had great enthusiasm sharing how his sandwich shop was an on-the-go healthy meal option for all ages. Besides his business franchise and excitement for pita sandwiches, he shared with me that he identified as a spiritual person, but definitely not religious, even though his parents and grandparents were devout Armenian Orthodox Christians.

As Tamar lifted his coffee to take a drink, he paused and directed our conversation away from the typical small talk saying, "You know, I have this gut feeling that all the religions of the world lead to the same place. I mean, they are all totally different approaches, but they all lead to the same place. Every dude goes to heaven or whatever the end looks like. And you, as a pastor, are showing people one of the many avenues and ways to heaven, or nirvana, or the pearly gates—whatever you want to call it." Tamar took a big sip of his coffee and went on to say, "But you know, I have watched a lot of these different spiritual leaders on television. You know—those history documentary channels. I guess I'm a part of the ongoing conversation about dudes like Muhammad, Buddha, Confucius, Ron Hubbard, and that one guy . . . Joseph Smith."

"What about Jesus Christ?" I asked.

Tamar tilted his head to the side, took another sip of his coffee, and said, "Jesus? He is for sure the real thing, just like all those other spiritual gurus. The way that I see it, all these dudes like Jesus, Muhammad, and Confucius are superspiritual guys who have their own spin on the human experience and the way to the afterlife. Jesus is just one option among many."

Meet our second false christ: the Option among Many. This second false christ is not exclusive—he is not *the* way, *the* truth, and *the* life (John 14:6), but merely *a* way, *a* truth, and *a* life. He promotes unity and tolerance at all costs—he just gushes with love. Because he is nonexclusive, this false christ is loved by the world and can get along with any religion of the day. This false christ is a champion of religious coexistence; he not only understands other world religions but promotes them as valid options as well.

As we learned from Jillian in chapter 1, this false christ is a make-believe idol—constructed by a person's presuppositions about who Jesus is to them personally. To put it another way, Tamar's presuppositions have tainted his worldview (the lens in which he views reality).

RELIGIOUS PLURALISM

Many religions have exclusivity. Exclusivity is admitting or omitting certain teachings, practices, and rituals based upon the religion's core doctrines. For example, the religion of Islam has the shahada that states, "There is no god but Allah and Muhammad is the prophet of Allah." In Christianity, Jesus has famously stated in John 14:6 that He is not *a* way and *a* truth and *a* life, but uses a definitive article to convey that He is *the* way and *the* truth and *the* life. Both Islam and Christianity are exclusive of each other. In other words, at the core of every world religion—except the ideology of religious pluralism—is exclusivity, for that is what distinguishes one religion from the next. Religious pluralism, though, removes the exclusivity and puts all the religions of the world on an equal playing field and says that they are all the same and lead to the same end.

This lens then alters the way in which he understands the real Jesus. Therefore, Tamar constructs a false christ in his mind—one that does not exist, except according to his own personal preferences.

Considering this, we must ask ourselves what presuppositions are present in Tamar and his comments above. What preconceived notions influence his worldview and cause him to see Jesus so incorrectly that he ends up creating a false christ? Examining Tamar's comments more thoroughly, we can see a prominent presupposition embedded in Tamar's comments: all religions and their leaders/founders are equal.

Tamar is a religious pluralist. He believes all religions are equally valid and all function as various paths to God and the eternal end. However, how is Tamar able to pull off the idea that all religions are equally valid and all lead to the same eternal end? How can he make Jesus just one option among many?

The first thing that Tamar has to do is strip all the various religions of their exclusivity. At the core of all the religions of the world are exclusive claims. These claims are what shape and form each religion

DOCTRINE AND PRACTICE

As Christians, our doctrine is derived from the Word of God, the Holy Scriptures. Doctrine describes reality: who we are, who God is, what our problem of sin is, and the Lord's solution to that sin. As a result, our Christian doctrine (the teachings of the Bible) shapes and forms the practices of the Christian and the practices of the Church. Christians are captive to the Word of God and shaped by the teachings (doctrine) of the Word. To lose sight of Christian doctrine is to lose the pillar of our faith and summon troublesome alternatives. Keep in mind that the apostle Paul warned young Timothy and Titus some seven times in the Pastoral Epistles (1 Timothy, 2 Timothy, and Titus) to watch the sound doctrine of the Church, for a church and a Christian who do not possess sound doctrine are like reeds blowing in the ideological winds of the world. The Word of God, Christian doctrine, and practice are inseparable, and interdependent.

in a particular way. Keep in mind that every religion has a collection of doctrines that come from a particular source (for example, Islam has the Qur'an and Muhammad, Christianity has the Bible and Jesus, Mormons have the Book of Mormon and Joseph Smith). These sources are either particular holy books or particular holy people, and they function as sources of the religion's doctrine. With that said, if all these particular holy books or particular holy people were in agreement, then all the world religions would look the same. However, since they are not all in agreement, the various world religions, which are founded upon these books and teachers, then indeed look very different. So, back to Tamar. For Tamar to remove the exclusivity of various religions, he must separate them from their exclusive doctrines and separate their doctrines from their exclusive sources. Then, and only then, can one even attempt to put all the religions on the same playing field. (This is a common characteristic of a religious pluralist such as Tamar. Rarely will they ever reference the core leader or holy book of a particular religion because they must avoid exclusive claims.)

Everything that is exclusive about Jesus must be filtered out for religious pluralists like Tamar. Verses about Jesus saying that He is *the* truth and that no one comes to the Father *except* through Him (John 14:6) must be downplayed and ignored at all costs. In creating this false christ, the Option among Many, religious pluralists temper Jesus' exclusive salvation claims as revealed in the Bible and exchange them for ones that are inclusive. Indeed, the Option among Many is disconnected from the Bible so that this false christ can coexist and cohabitate with all the other religions of the world.

Staring into my almost finished latte, I let Tamar's comments sink in and swirl around in my brain. "Okay, Tamar, I am a bit confused. I understand that what you are saying is that Jesus is one option among many and that you believe all roads lead to the same place; however, Jesus does say that in the Bible that the only way to heaven is through Him and—"

Tamar leaned in and immediately interrupted me, "I am totally passionate and sold about Jesus' acceptance of all. People forget that Jesus is all about tolerance and not hate—after all, that's what He taught. So, yeah, I guess I subscribe to the non-hater Jesus who accepts everyone."

Here we learn from our new friend Tamar that not only is this false christ nonexclusive, but we further learn that the Option among Many is all about generic love and tolerance, and definitely not about hate. Although Tamar may separate Christianity and Jesus from the exclusive claims of the Bible in his own mind, he cannot prevent devout followers from doing so; therefore, he will have to offset any exclusivity by appealing to the generic qualities of love and tolerance of his false christ. The only way to have all of these spiritual leaders hang out together, after all, is for them to avoid playing spiritual king-of-the-hill with one another.

> *However, the word tolerance in our contemporary culture has evolved to mean that a person should not only put up with another person's point of view but must also celebrate, enable, and promote that person's point of view, regardless if one agrees with it or not.*

The word *tolerance* used to mean the ability of a person to put up with another point of view, even though they disagreed with it. However, the word tolerance in our contemporary culture has evolved to mean that a person should not only put up with another person's point of view but must also celebrate, enable, and promote that person's point of view, regardless if one agrees with it or not. Any opposition to this modern view of tolerance is immediately viewed as hateful and not loving. In other words, the modern view of tolerance is equated with love, and exclusivity is equated with hate. Therefore, to embrace any element of exclusivity is seen as intolerance, and this intolerance is seen as not loving, and this lack of love is then equated with hate.

As we are learning from Tamar, the Option among Many is not only a false christ who has been stripped of exclusivity but also one who promotes a modern view of tolerance and love. Although these characteristics of tolerance and love sound genuine and pious, they are used to suppress and attack exclusive truth claims that would reveal differences between Christianity and other world religions. Truth claims such as those made in 1 Timothy 2:5, which states, "There is one God and one mediator between God and men." And who is that mediator? That mediator is not Islam's Muhammad or the Mormon's Joseph Smith or Hinduism's Buddha, but the man Jesus Christ. Upon hearing this, those holding the modern view of tolerance and love immediately flinch and then proceed to attack the exclusive truth claim as being too divisive, too judgmental, and not something spoken in the best interest of religious world peace. Indeed, because Tamar's presuppositions are that all religions and their leaders are equal, and that everybody ends

TOLERANCE VERSUS LOVE

Generally speaking, the Bible frowns upon tolerance. For example, in Revelation 2, the pastor of the Church of Thyatira was condemned for tolerating a false teacher in the church, whereas the pastor of the Church of Ephesus was commended for not tolerating false teaching. Considering this, a better way to think about this subject is not with the idea of tolerance, but love. As we hear from 1 Corinthians 13, love is patient and kind but at the same time it does not rejoice in wrongdoing. Indeed, love covers a multitude of sin (1 Peter 4:8) and the Christian is called to speak the truth in love (Ephesians 4:15). In other words, tolerance is not a Christian virtue but more often than not a pagan virtue. On the other hand, love is a Christian virtue that tolerates no evil while it rejoices in true goodness, as it quietly gives sacrificially.

In Jesus, we do not see tolerance, but we see love. If Jesus would have gone the way of tolerance, He would *not* have gone to the cross but would have left us in our sins. And if we were left in our sins, we would be left with damnation. So much for the way of tolerance! But because of His great love for us and His rich mercy, Jesus could not tolerate our sin. Indeed, the Son of God could not tolerate our sin, so He was compelled to the cross—in love—to do something about it.

up in heaven, he must not only diminish the exclusive truth claims of Christianity but also suppress them by accusing these truth claims as intolerant or unloving.

There is a final component of Tamar's presuppositions that we need to address: his belief of universalism. As previously stated, Tamar's religious pluralism makes Jesus and Christianity into just one of the many roads leading to the ultimate end. However, what also permeates Tamar's worldview is the belief that everyone, in the end, will safely arrive at some sort of immortal and eternal goodness known as heaven

WHAT IS LOVE?

Many people will talk about love; however, many will fail to identify what they mean by the word *love*. Thankfully, the Bible clearly teaches that love is the fulfillment of the Law (i.e., God's Commandments). Therefore, real love will never disagree with God's Commandments, and the real Commandments of God will never obstruct love. What this means is that when there is a conflict between love and a law, it is due to either a man-centered view of love or a man-made law, or both. True love is expressed when we keep the Commandments of God toward our neighbor; God's Law is fulfilled when our neighbor is properly loved. (See Romans 13:10 and John 14:15 where Jesus and Paul talk about love being the fulfilment of the Law.)

Love seeks to honor God and Him alone for our good and joy. Love seeks the proper teaching about the Lord in accurate doctrine. Love seeks to remember the Sabbath and God's Word. Love seeks to respect those in authority like parents and governing officials. Love seeks to preserve life, especially those that are weak and insignificant—those unable to protect themselves in the womb or at the end of life. Love seeks to protect marriage from pornography, divorce, and adultery. Love seeks to defend our neighbor's possessions and it seeks to defend our neighbor's reputation. Love seeks to rest in contentment. Love is sacrificing oneself for the good of another, as seen in the actions of Jesus laying His life down for mankind (1 John 3:16).

THE OPTION AMONG MANY

or nirvana or the next life. For Tamar, the exact term that is used to describe the end is not of great importance, only that everyone ends up at the same place and that same place is good and pleasant.

Since Tamar admitted that he subscribed to the loving and tolerant Jesus, I decided to push back gently with a question, "Yes, I hear what you are saying Tamar. So, if Jesus is just one of the ways to heaven and since Jesus is all about love, what does that mean for people's eternal destiny? Does that put everyone into eternal life?"

"For sure man," Tamar responded. "Everyone will be in the afterlife since there is no such thing as hell. You see, hell doesn't exist; it's made up. Why would a loving God send people to hell? Jesus wouldn't do that because He is love!"

Tamar's comment is a perfect example of how the teaching of universalism works. If all religions and religious leaders lead us to the ultimate end of God, and if God is all about love, then a good and loving God would not condemn people to eternal torment in hell. In the case of some universalists—like Tamar—there is a rejection of hell altogether. These universalists reason that hell is against the character and nature and qualities of a loving God. It seems that both Jillian (the ethical hedonist from chapter 1) and Tamar struggle with the doctrine of hell, for this doctrine not only undercuts their worldview but causes them both cognitive dissonance.

Let us break Tamar's comments down a bit more thoroughly. It is interesting to note that regarding Tamar's religious pluralism and his universalism he is not content with what we call a binary system.

The Bible lays out what are called binary oppositions, kind of like our concept of opposites—up and down or yes and no. The Bible speaks of sin and righteousness, hell and heaven, darkness and light, Satan and Jesus, dead and alive, and so on. These binary oppositions are pairs of opposites. Generally speaking, the Bible will label one of the pair as good/favorable and the other as bad/unfavorable. In other words, righteousness is better than sin, heaven is better than hell, light is better than darkness, Jesus is better than Satan, and life is better than death. What makes these items a part of a binary system is that they are listed together in a pair, and then precedence is given to one over the other. However, what if a person does not like the partiality given? For example, what if someone happens to prefer sin over righteousness and does not like the fact that sin is placed in a negative light? Well, a person can fight to change the partiality from righteousness to sin. Or—and here is the point that we need to grasp—a person can reject the binary system altogether. Instead of trying to flip the opposites and change which one is good, a person actually decides to reject the binary pairs altogether, throwing the whole system out.

BINARY OPPOSITIONS IN THE BIBLE

The Bible is full of binary oppositions. For example, sin and righteousness, hell and heaven, darkness and light, Satan and Jesus, dead and alive, female and male, Law and Gospel, single and married, son and father, slave and free, young and old, wife and husband, and so on.

Although the Bible has binary oppositions, we must be careful to not assume that the Bible always gives primacy to one of the binary opposites and negativity to the other. In other words, while it is true that heaven is good and hell is bad and that Jesus is good and Satan is bad, we need to be careful of applying this to all binary opposites. For example, saying that the Law is bad and that the Gospel is good or that wives are bad and husbands are good is not the testimony of Scripture. While some of the binary oppositions have definite bad and good polarity, there are other times when the binary oppositions serve each other. Indeed, the Law serves the Gospel. Wives submit to their husbands, and husbands give up their lives for their wives. Sons honor their fathers, and fathers provide for and teach their sons. In other words, not all binary oppositions in the Bible are to be categorized in a good versus evil polarity. Sometimes binary opposites in the Bible are either good and evil, or both evil, or both good.

In the case of the Bible's confession, it is very clear that Jesus is truth and all other religious leaders and religions are false. This is the exclusivity that the Bible expresses. This leaves only two options: either Jesus is the truth and deserves partiality over other world religions, or Jesus is false and the Bible is wrong and the other religions deserve partiality. But Tamar has introduced us to a false christ who proclaims that another option can be enacted. That option is to throw out the binary opposition completely. Yes, throw it all out! This false christ makes no exclusive claims, and he is the same as everyone else. With this false christ, there is no such thing as heaven versus hell. There is no such thing as an exclusive Jesus. Everything is love and tolerance, and everybody ends up in the same good and happy eternal place. This false christ seems to be incredibly easy to follow because he does not seem to care about anything except generic and vague inspirational-sounding phrases found on many coffee mugs at favorite coffee shops around our land. With that thought in my mind, Tamar looked at his watch, realized that he was late for a meeting, and thanked me for the conversation. I, too, gathered my belongings and thanked him for the conversation, while giving him my card with my contact information. As we walked together to the exit, I handed my now empty coffee mug with an inspirational quote about faith emblazoned on it to the waitress and went back to the traffic battle on the 210.

Responding to Tamar

What is the main thing that drives and controls Tamar's thoughts, logic, and decisions regarding Christianity and his views about Jesus? As we have learned, Tamar has embraced religious pluralism. Therefore, everything he does is controlled by this mind-set that all religions are equally valid and that all religions function as various paths to God or the eternal end. As we have learned, Tamar does this by keeping all religions from competing and then accentuating love and tolerance to smooth everything over, thus creating the Option among Many.

When we respond to Tamar—and others like him—our first goal is to allow all the religions to speak for themselves. To do this, it's important we have done our homework so we know about various religions and are able to identify the exclusive assertions they make.

Only when the real Jesus is distinguished from everything else, can the clear and unique message of the Gospel ring forth.

In a situation like the one I was in with Tamar, it would be beneficial to simply ask him something like this, "Islam teaches that there is no god but Allah and Muhammad is the prophet of Allah; however, Christianity says that Jesus is the way and the truth and the life, that there is no other way to God except through Jesus. How can they both claim to be exclusive and still both be correct?" This question will no doubt bring forth cognitive dissonance for Tamar, which is our intended goal. Remember, as we learned in the Introduction, many times people create a false christ in their mind to reconcile away the cognitive dissonance they experience. We, however, will attempt to do the exact opposite by bringing that cognitive dissonance back into play. In fact, our goal should be to bring cognitive dissonance to the forefront. The reason why? Only when the real Jesus is distinguished from everything else, can the clear and unique message of the Gospel ring forth. And when the clear and unique message of the Gospel rings forth, it can then be heard as the power of God unto people's salvation.

As in Jillian's situation, we are not trying to bring forth cognitive dissonance to somehow destroy Tamar's worldview in vengeance. Our goal is not to somehow prove that Christianity is superior (even though it is); rather, we advocate to bring about cognitive dissonance so we might have an opportunity for a clear confession of the real Jesus to be heard, for we know that faith in the real Jesus only comes by hearing the Word.

Will the Real Jesus Please Stand Up?

What Tamar and others do not need is yet another Option among Many. Indeed, a false christ who is not the way, the truth, and the life is nothing more than one of the many flavorings on a coffee menu. In fact, a false christ who gushes only generic love and stands for nothing except one-word slogans is no deity worth following or respecting. A false christ who is unable to stand for something will ultimately fall for anything. Dear friends, we do not need a non-exclusive, politically correct false christ—society and politics are already filled with people like this. Instead, we need, as the apostle John's Gospel states, "the way, and the truth, and the life" (14:6). We need the real Jesus. We need the real Jesus who is exclusive to false idols and false religions. We need the real Jesus who Peter speaks of in Acts 4:12, "There is salvation in no one else, for there is no other name under heaven by which we must be saved." We need the only one who "takes away the sin of the world" as John the Baptist says in John 1:29. Humanity needs not just another option—another choice—but the exclusive one who chose to give Himself up as a ransom for all (1 Timothy 2:5–6).

Let's discuss the **Option among Many**

1. What are the three key characteristics of the Option among Many?

Using the provided verses below and the Leader's Guide in the Appendix, contemplate the following ways in which the real Jesus Christ qualifies as the exclusive Lord and Savior, not just the Option among Many:

2. Read Isaiah 7:14, Matthew 1:18, and Luke 1:26–38. How was Jesus exclusive in His conception and birth? How are His conception and birth different from other religious leaders?

3. Read John 1:14. How was Jesus exclusive in His incarnation? How is His incarnation different from other world religions? *Note: For a definition of "incarnation," see chapter 3.*

4. Read Romans 5:19 and Galatians 4:4–5. How was Jesus exclusive in His life? How is His life different from other world religions?

5. Read Isaiah 53:6 and 2 Corinthians 5:21. How was Jesus exclusive in His death? How is His death different from other world religions?

6. Read Romans 6:9 and 1 Corinthians 15:3–7, 17. How was Jesus exclusive in His resurrection? Why is the resurrection of Jesus so incredibly important to the Christian faith and how is it exclusive?

7. As we consider our friends who are "spiritual, not religious," how can we most effectively communicate the truths we just studied—the ones proclaimed in the Apostles' Creed and the Nicene Creed?

Meet Mr. Darby, The Possible Atheist

Things were relatively consistent each week with my undergraduate English class. I would arrive at class, pick my usual seat, pull my binder out of my backpack, and prepare for the lecture. As always, though, about three-quarters of the way through the lecture, our professor, Mr. Darby, would take some subtle, yet intentional, jab at Christianity. It was like he couldn't help it. Or maybe he could. Maybe he spent the evening before thinking of the jab he would take.

I had heard about his antics from other Christian friends. Mr. Darby would say something religiously provocative—even though it had nothing to do with the course he was teaching—and then would hone in to see which Christians in the classroom would squirm. He would then direct his gaze toward the Christian students and prod them a little more, hoping to draw them out into the open, to then pounce on them with his perceived superior intellect.

As for me, I was but a babe in the Christian faith and knew I would be outwitted if I challenged Mr. Darby publicly. So, I remained silent.

"Religion is solely thesis," Mr. Darby said one day in his class. "However, science is the quest to understand through theory and research. Christianity is vastly theoretical; it is not real."

This particular day, one of my Christian classmates had had enough. My classmate forcefully interrupted Mr. Darby, saying, "What about Jesus? Was He not real? Was He a thesis?"

Mr. Darby was taken aback by the forceful interruption. He literally took a small step backward, composed himself, and then responded in a smooth tone, "Ah, yes. Jesus. It is my view that there was probably a guy named Jesus who inspired the Christian religion. Jesus most likely existed, but He was no different than all the other religious leaders of the day. I don't doubt that He was probably a profound teacher; however, that was all He was. He was nothing more than a good teacher who taught people good things."

"What about all the miracles and Jesus rising from the dead?" my classmate challenged.

It was evident Mr. Darby did not appreciate the tone in which he was being addressed. He adjusted his tie and straightened his posture and said, "I am not getting sucked into a 'Christianity is a real' debate!"

My classmate's face scrunched up as if frustration had set in, and with a certain amount of sassiness said, "It was just a question!"

Mr. Darby did not waste any time and countered, "You've seen those wacko television evangelists. Everybody knows that what they tout as miracles are nothing more than a highly-induced state of excitement. These frauds turn the emotional faucet on and amp up their charisma."

"I didn't ask about televangelists. I asked about Jesus. What about all of Jesus' miracles and Jesus rising from the dead?" my classmate asked a second time.

Mr. Darby paused and took two steps forward, "Listen now, God is not real, which means that Jesus was not godlike and all those apparent miracles and the rising from the dead are not real! Jesus was nothing more than a very well respected and influential teacher who apparently got himself stuck on a cross for offending the religious establishment—kind of like how Socrates got himself killed for upsetting the prominent citizens of Athens. Besides, you should not read those Bible accounts literally; I don't read the Bible literally, for those miracles defy the laws of science and nature. It simply is not reasonable to believe in a godlike Jesus who performed miracles. Not everything in the Bible is true, you know. Now, let us move on to chapter 4."

"So, you are saying that Jesus did not rise from the dead?" another classmate interjected.

Turning a bit red, Mr. Darby seemed to lose a bit of his professionalism. The tone of his voice changed as he said with almost an undercurrent of a growl, "Yes, that is what I am saying. God is dead, which means all your beliefs and traditions and morals are pointless. Because there is no God, your ideas are meaningless. Jesus was a historical figure—a man—no different than any of the other influential teachers of the past."

WHAT IF GOD IS DEAD?

In 1966, the front cover of *Time* magazine asked, "Is God Dead?" This provocative title certainly captured the spiritual climate of the sixties and even today. But let's think about that question: is God dead? If there is no existence of divine order to the universe, no divine plan, no outside force or God by which society is governed, and no supreme being to whom mankind is subject, what does this mean and where does this lead us? It means that we are the lone source of meaning and only as good as the strength, force, and wisdom we can muster up. We essentially take the place of God and then act like God for ourselves. While we were not built to operate this way, this is the typical mode of operation for our sinful nature. Since Adam and Eve, humankind has always tried to usurp God (see Genesis 3). We want to be master and commander of our own life, even though this breaks the First Commandment and runs contrary to our own limitations as created beings.

We know that God is not dead, though. We know this not because of some philosophical idea but because the tomb is empty. The God-man Jesus has risen from the tomb, ascended to the Father, and lives today.

After Mr. Darby's comments, everyone in the class knew that a nerve had been hit and that it would not be wise to push the topic any further, without the risk of severe homework repercussions. It was best just to move on to chapter 4 at that point.

About ten minutes into the discussion on chapter 4, it was noticeable that Mr. Darby's frustration had subdued. However, it was as if a melancholy cloud had descended upon him. I noticed his voice pitch dropped after each sentence, his eyes drooped downward on the sides, and his shoulders seemed to hang limply. Mr. Darby had gone from demonstrating antagonism to deeply rooted hatred to an empty sadness in less than ten minutes.

But why the sadness?

Looking back, I would say Mr. Darby was an individual who did not believe in the existence of God. He did not appreciate the miracles and supernatural aspects of Christianity. At the same time, he oddly admired the life and moral principles of Jesus, as told in the Gospel. It is worth noting at this point that Mr. Darby strangely and sincerely admired Jesus—you could hear it in his voice and see it in his mannerisms. When talking about Christianity, Christians, and God, he was tense. This was not the case while he talked about Jesus. He seemed to be drawn to Jesus and was not quite willing to write Him off completely. It was as if he could not fully commit to his atheistic tendencies for fear of what life would look like if the source of his childhood values—the apparent Sunday School lessons about Jesus that he was taught—dried up. Perhaps the reason for Mr. Darby's great sadness was that he could not bring himself to label the historical Jesus as a lunatic, even though he firmly held to the thought that Jesus was not divine.

The only Jesus Mr. Darby could fathom is our third false christ: the Good Teacher. This false christ is a good moral instructor and nothing more. Walking on water, healing the sick, and raising people from the dead—these things are not possible, for there is no such thing as God and no such thing as anything supernatural. At best, they are stories in the Bible that should not be taken literally, much like the well-intentioned yet exaggerated legends surrounding George Washington (e.g., that Washington could not tell a lie and that he threw a silver dollar across the Potomac River). In other words, there is no such thing as the God-man Jesus, but only the Good Teacher, who is all about that which is physical; the Good Teacher is a materialized false christ who simply was a good instructor and not the incarnate Divine Lord.

As in the cases of Jillian and Tamar, Mr. Darby has several presuppositions at work in his worldview that leads him to conceive of the Good Teacher. They are a bit different from Jillian and Tamar, though. These three presuppositions are (1) atheistic tendencies, (2) a magisterial use of reason, and (3) a rejection of reading the Bible literally.

The first thing we should address to understand Mr. Darby's false christ is his atheistic tendencies. I use the word *tendencies* because I could never tell if Mr. Darby was a committed atheist or a doubting agnostic or a confrontational secularist, because in his lectures his mind would sometimes drift back to his childhood years, resulting in him speaking warmly about going to church with his grandmother. In other words, at times he denied the existence of God outright, as an atheist would. Other times, he seemed a bit more generous and said we could never know for sure if there is a God, as an agnostic would. But then there were those times when Mr. Darby seemed to act like a

---

INCARNATION

The incarnation is the doctrine that Jesus came down from heaven and put on human flesh. Keep in mind that Jesus, the Son of God, is eternal. He is God of God, Light of Light—not made, meaning the Son of God took upon Himself full humanity and lived a true human life without losing His divine nature and without committing sin. Therefore, to assert that Jesus is nothing more than a good moral teacher is to deny Jesus' conception by the Holy Spirit and birth by the Virgin Mary—it is a denial of the incarnation. (See John 1:1-18 for details on the incarnation.)

secularist, meaning he just preferred that all conversations would be stripped of religious talk and religious symbolism.

These atheistic tendencies create a vastly different perspective of reality from that of the average Christian. For example, we Christians sometimes take for granted Genesis 1, which describes the creation of the world. However, if we examine these opening verses a bit more thoroughly, there is an important distinction Mr. Darby would adamantly reject: the "Creator versus created" distinction. Indeed, Genesis lays forth a world in which the Creator creates matter, time, and space.

ONTOLOGY—THE STUDY OF BEING

The word *ontology* is a rather unfamiliar term. Simply stated, it is a term that is used among philosophers to talk about the study of "being." For example, in order to teach differences in being, philosophers will compare a brick, a tree, a dog, and a human being. All four of these things are drastically different. A brick is simply matter; whereas a tree has matter, but is also alive. A dog has matter and is alive; however, the dog is aware of its surroundings. Humans, though, are more complex and are in a different ontological category from rocks, trees, and animals. Humans have matter, are alive, and are conscious; however, humans have the ability to engage in self-reflection on things such as the meaning of life and ethics. Humans can do this in a way that animals, trees, and bricks cannot.

Although the term *ontology* is a philosophical term, we Christians can certainly affirm that God has established differences in beings. Otherwise stated, even though bricks, trees, dogs, and humans can be classified as different types of being, they are all similar since they are all created things. Indeed, they are not in the same ontological category as our triune God. They have a beginning and are created, whereas God does not have a beginning and was not created. Therefore, Christians acknowledge the distinction between the Creator and the created. We see this distinction in being in many biblical metaphors such as the Shepherd and the sheep (John 10:1–18), the Potter and the clay (Isaiah 64:8), the Master and the servant (Matthew 25:14–30), and so forth.

This makes the Creator different from the universe and mankind. The Creator speaks the world into existence, which shows that the Creator—the triune God—has no beginning, whereas creation has a beginning and owes its status and being to God Himself. Mankind and creation are under and subject to God. It is this "Creator versus created" distinction that Mr. Darby could not embrace because of his atheistic tendencies. The professor could not fathom that matter, time, and space were dependent on a creator, for that would mean he would also be dependent on a creator.

By rejecting the "Creator versus created" distinction, Mr. Darby was ultimately rejecting the Creator—God Himself. He was attempting to remove what he perceived as an unrealistic higher authority. He was trying to isolate mankind as the sole source of meaning and insulate mankind as the highest being in the world. The well-educated teacher seemed to be organizing his views of Christianity to isolate mankind as the highest intellectual being in the world, so humans would be solely responsible for carrying the pressures of life on their own as well as defining their own meaning and working to actualize their own will to that meaning.

He was trying to isolate mankind as the sole source of meaning and insulate mankind as the highest being in the world.

What are the consequences of this reorganization of the Creator and created? Quite simply, if there is no Creator—if God does not exist—then the real Jesus is stripped of His divinity. If Jesus, our Savior,

IS MR. DARBY THE FIRST TO BELIEVE THAT JESUS WAS NOT DIVINE?

Very early on in Christianity there was a group of people called the Ebionites. The Ebionites were a Jewish-Christian movement that believed Jesus was the Messiah but certainly not divine and certainly not born of a virgin. As the writer of the Book of Ecclesiastes says, "What has been is what will be, and what has been done is what will be done, and there is nothing new under the sun" (1:9).

is not divine, there is no forgiveness of sins. If there is no forgiveness of sins, He is nothing more than a false christ, a false christ who teaches just like a professor. A false christ who Mr. Darby could comprehend, the Good Teacher.

Furthermore, if there is no such thing as God—if Jesus is not God in the flesh—then Jesus is no longer authoritative. In fact, all the miracles of Jesus and His rising from the dead, as evidence of His authority, are then deemed false by people like Mr. Darby.

We have met three false christs so far in this book, each vastly different. However, they are similar in that each has been created to satisfy the desires of a person's agenda and presuppositions. Jillian, Tamar, and Mr. Darby all change the testimony of the real biblical Jesus into a message that works for them. They will not and cannot let Jesus be who He is, but rather, they appeal to what we call a magisterial use of reason to place on Jesus what they want Him to be for themselves.

Within the Lutheran tradition, there are two important terms worth noting: (1) a *ministerial* use of reason, and (2) a *magisterial* use of reason. These two terms can be found in Martin Luther's writings, as well as in the writings of many contemporary Lutheran theologians. These terms help us understand how a person uses his or her own reason.

Simply put, a magisterial use of reason happens when our reason stands over and above the Word of God, like a magistrate (e.g., a judge). This makes God's Word captive to our reason. On the other hand, a ministerial use of reason occurs when our reason is shaped, formed, and held captive to God's Word. God's Word shapes and forms us rather than the other way around (2 Timothy 3:16).

Looking back to Jillian and Tamar, we could say that both of them have subordinated the real Jesus to a magisterial use of reason. More specifically, by rejecting God as the Creator, Mr. Darby is also denying a ministerial use of reason and upholding a magisterial use of reason. As a result, Mr. Darby is then able to reject Jesus' divinity, reject Jesus' miracles, and assert that the Bible should not be read literally. He does this on the authority of his reason, which he has lifted above Christianity.

As class was coming to a close that day, my classmates were packing up their books when from the back corner of the classroom another student quietly spoke, saying, "Mr. Darby, what did you mean when you said that you don't read the Bible literally? How do you read it then?"

This other student was not trying to be confrontational or rude, but rather, must have been really bothered throughout the whole class by Mr. Darby's statement not to take the Bible literally. As for myself, I could feel my entire body tense as this other student naively asked his question. I wanted to pack my backpack quickly and bolt out of the classroom; however, I also wanted to pretend to fumble through my books and listen. Instead of fleeing, I decided to stay and be a fly on the wall.

Mr. Darby, who was arranging the papers in his binder, paused, and then kept rifling through his belongings with his head down, saying, "Well, what I mean is that I am not a wingnut fundamentalist. It means that not everything in the Bible is true. That is what I mean."

The questioning classmate then said, "What parts are not true and how do you know they are not true?"

Closing his binder rather abruptly, Mr. Darby seemed to fight to keep his composure, for he had another class across the campus. The professor looked up and with a forced smile said, "Good day, sir."

What did Mr. Darby mean when he said, "I don't read the Bible literally"? Mr. Darby, as surprising as it may be, did not mean he was rejecting the basic rules of grammar used for literally reading the Bible. What Mr. Darby was essentially saying is that he did not read the Bible "authoritatively." In other words, when the phrase, "I don't read the Bible literally," is generally used, the person using this term does so to deconstruct traditional, objective, and conservative readings of the Bible. Although this may happen unintentionally, we must keep in mind that when a person says, "I don't read the Bible literally," they are essentially saying that what the Bible *means* to them is more important than what the Bible actually *says* to them.

When we review Mr. Darby's comments about the Bible, it is worth noting that he did not totally and blatantly reject the Bible. Instead of entirely dismissing the Bible like some committed atheists do, Mr. Darby was allowing himself some elbow room to deny the validity of the miraculous and morally uncomfortable aspects of the Bible. By doing this, he was allowing himself the option to find some nuggets of wisdom and truth throughout the Bible, which he felt applied to life today. He was leaving his options open as he deconstructed the Bible so something else could have the final authority—his reason. He was also not completely excusing the Bible because he kept his foot in the door as if he wanted to have some spiritual credibility. He said just enough in his statement to present himself as an expert on the Bible

HOW DO WE READ THE BIBLE LITERALLY?

The Bible is composed of sixty-six different books penned by some thirty-five different men of God. In these sixty-six books are various genres and literary devices: poetry, parables, history, revelations, apocalyptic literature, metaphors, similes, letters, and so forth. Therefore, in reading the Bible literally, a person allows the context of a Bible passage to dictate the genre. Then, the biblical text is read within the rules and characteristics of that particular genre. What this means is that the Bible cannot be flattened so every text is treated the same—like reading every text as if it were a parable when not every text is a parable.

We must also keep in mind that what makes the Bible different from other books is that the Bible is inspired by God, whereas other books are not. This means that the inspired Bible is true and free from error as originally given. Furthermore, the Holy Spirit is present with His power in the Bible to work through it. Therefore, when we read the Bible, we read it not only trusting that it is true but also knowing that it is the final authoritative word for faith and conduct.

without having to get involved in a religious discussion on the minute details of the Bible.

Just as Mr. Darby did not utterly and blatantly reject the Bible, he did the same with Jesus. In other words, according to Mr. Darby's non-literal and magisterial use of reason, Jesus was a good moral teacher but nothing more. Jesus was to be respected for certain aspects of his moral and philosophical authority—just like other religious leaders are respected—but not because of anything dealing with His divinity or what looked like the supernatural.

Responding to Mr. Darby

What is the main thing that drives and controls Mr. Darby's thoughts, logic, and decisions regarding Christianity and his views about Jesus? As we have learned, Mr. Darby subscribes to a magisterial use of reason. Therefore, Mr. Darby has subjected Christianity and Jesus to *his* reason. Like a judge, Mr. Darby has placed everything about Jesus and Christianity underneath his reason and his intellect, thus creating the Good Teacher.

When we respond to Mr. Darby—and others like him—it is important to ask what qualifies him as an expert on Jesus and Christianity to undermine his perceived superiority. In other words, it is common for individuals to implement a magisterial use of reason over Christianity, while having never put any effort or study into the subject itself. For example, Mr. Darby may assert something like, "We can't trust the Bible, for it is full of errors." In which case, we could respond, "That is very interesting. I would like to learn more about that. May I ask, what part of the Bible is in error and how do you know it is in error?" When we simply ask the question, "How do you know your assertion to be true?" we are forcing people like Mr. Darby who exercise a magisterial use of reason to show what they base their assertion upon. I have found that many people I have interacted with who make critical assertions against the Bible and Christianity, do so not on the basis of their personal research and investigations, but rather by simply repeating a talking point they have heard. Again, we must keep in mind that our goal is not to win the argument or force people into a debate submission, but instead, it is to provide an opportunity to not merely repeat Christian talking points but confess the timeless truths about the real Jesus Christ—a confession that can be spoken into their ears and hearts.

But what if Mr. Darby can answer the question above? What if he can "source" his assertions? If Mr. Darby can provide reasonable and well thought out answers to his bold assertions, then we can simply listen and learn a little more about him. If he provides some interesting things to ponder, that is certainly not to be considered a defeat or loss. Rather, it is an opportunity for us to learn more about the topic and continue the discussion at a future point. Furthermore, follow-up conversations with people like Mr. Darby provide wonderful opportunities for us to visit with our pastors beforehand and use the resources they possess to formulate respectful and well-researched questions and answers.

All of this stated, our conversation with Mr. Darby is twofold: we want to provide an adequate defense of the Christian faith (i.e., Christian apologetics) and we want to ultimately get to the point where we can confess the real Jesus—that the real Jesus went to Mount Calvary for Mr. Darby to die for his sins and to be raised for Mr. Darby's justification.

Will the Real Jesus Please Stand Up?

Mr. Darby had created a false christ through his mind of reason—one that did not exist. That is what happens when a person is not willing to fully reject the real Jesus and at the same time is not willing to fully accept the identity of the real Jesus. Indeed, denying the divinity of Jesus does nothing to change the reality of who Jesus is; it only creates a new false christ—a powerless idol named the Good Teacher, who does nothing for one's forgiveness, life, and salvation. Amazingly, this false christ strikingly resembles his creator—Mr. Darby.

On the other hand, the Son of God—the real Jesus—"became flesh and dwelt among us" (John 1:14)! This is remarkable. God Himself took on our poor and feeble human nature; He took on flesh. God is eternal, all-powerful and all-knowing, yet He descended from the heavenly throne and became true man (Philippians 2:6–8). Do you know what this means? This is not some theological nuance that is only important for theologians. Rather, it is extremely relevant to all people. The Son of God was made man so He could take our place on the sacrificial altar and die for our sins and the sins of the world (Galatians 4:4–5). Keep in mind that if Jesus were not true God and sinless, His life and death would be nothing and we would be lost and damned. If Jesus were not God, His life and death would have no power over sin, death, and the devil. On the other hand, if Jesus were not true man, how could He have kept the requirements of the Law and how could He have died? Indeed, in Jesus, we see true God and true man.

The false christ, the Good Teacher, could teach us many things but ultimately would not be able to save us with his knowledge, for the knowledge and ways of this false christ are not God's knowledge and ways (Isaiah 55:8). The real Jesus is indeed so much more.

Let's discuss the *Good Teacher*

1. What are Mr. Darby's main presuppositions that created the Good Teacher?

The questions below at first may seem disjointed and unrelated. However, as they are studied, it will be clear that these questions, with their verses, are showing that Jesus is not just a mere man (i.e., the Good Teacher), but God in the flesh who came into the midst of mankind.

2. Read Genesis 3:1–10. After Adam and Eve had sinned, it says that the Lord came to them in the midst of the garden. What is the significance of the Lord drawing near to Adam and Eve right after they sinned?

3. Read Exodus 25:8, 21–22 and 40:34–38. What was the purpose of the Old Testament tabernacle? Who would draw near the people of Israel in the tabernacle? What is the significance of this?

4. Read John 1:1–16. In these verses, we read about the Word and the True Light. Who is the Word and the True Light that is coming into (drawing near) the world?

5. According to John 1:14, how exactly did Jesus—the Word and True Light—draw near and live among the world?

6. Take a special note of the word *dwelt* in John 1:14. This word in the Bible's original language is technically *tabernacled*. It is a word that means to pitch a tent, tabernacle, dwell. What is the significance of this word *dwelt* regarding the person of Jesus? What is the significance of this word in regard to the Exodus passages in question 2?

7. Considering the verses from Genesis, Exodus, and the Gospel of John, what do we learn about Jesus? Is He just a mere man or more than a man? Who does Jesus draw near to?

8. What are ways that you can or have spoken the truth about Jesus to people who hold that He was only a Good Teacher? How can you utilize what we have just learned to help you in those conversations?

THE Therapist 4

Meet Wendy, the Life Coach

I waited for her text. I could tell she was typing. The message that appeared on my phone said, "Our next meeting is on Wednesday afternoon at 2:00 p.m. We meet at the public library. Hope you can come!"

Wendy was a vibrant and enthusiastic woman in her midfifties. She was a member of a prominent church in town and had garnered a reputation for being a Christian woman whom younger women looked up to. She had four adult kids: one was a doctor, one was a school teacher, one a stay-at-home mother, and the other was recently accepted to a prestigious university. Wendy also had a very loving husband, and though it was never said publicly, many envied their marriage. She was one of those people who seemed to have the right amount of joy in her life while still being able to gracefully handle her busy schedule.

Her schedule had become even busier as of late. She had just been certified as a life coach from an online educational institution that provided self-directed studies.

I first met Wendy at a local coffee shop. As I entered, I noticed one of my parishioners sitting at a table with a large group of women who were talking and laughing loudly. They were obviously having a very good time together. As I walked toward the front counter, I was immediately invited by my parishioner to the table and introduced to Wendy and her friends. While I visited with the women at the table, I soon realized it was an informal gathering in which Wendy was telling all the ladies about her weekly "Growing More" meetings.

"Oh, Pastor, you need to come to the next Growing More meeting. They are fantastic!" my parishioner said to me in front of the whole group.

Pastors typically receive about a dozen offers and invitations each year for new programs and ministry techniques that make grandiose ministry promises that frankly are not true. It is enough to make a pastor cynical. So, not wanting to look like a cynical curmudgeon before my parishioner, Wendy, and her friends regarding the Growing More meetings, I said, "I will have to see if my schedule permits."

Wendy immediately jumped in and told me, "We haven't finalized our next meeting yet, but I will surely send you a message about the details. I do hope you can make it, Pastor. It would be wonderful to have clergy present at our meetings. I was given your cell phone number off your church bulletin, so I will text you."

Wednesday came around and out of a sense of curiosity—and because I could not come up with a reasonable excuse—I decided to attend the Growing More meeting. The meeting was held at the local library. About thirty padded chairs were set out in rows, and coffee and donuts sat on a table in the back of the room. Wendy was talking to a group of women as I entered. As soon as she saw me, her face lit up with excitement and she immediately approached me with her hands extended for a hug.

When the Growing More meeting started, the group began by saying a pledge together. The pledge was a combination of what seemed to be an invocation combined with a mission statement. Wendy then walked over to a stool, sat down, set some notes on a nearby table, and intently gazed into the eyes of those in attendance—who happened to be all women except for me and another gentleman who looked as if he had been dragged to the meeting by his wife. After a longer pause, Wendy said, "You may have big obstacles in your life, things that you cannot seem to overcome on your own. The good news, though, is that you are not alone, for the most powerful one, Jesus, is at your side. If you truly yield yourself to Jesus and let go of your attempts at overcoming these obstacles, then Jesus will fill you and take you to a whole new level. Dear sisters—and brothers, empty yourselves so Jesus can fill you. Jesus will take you from being a carnal Christian to a spiritual Christian. Jesus has something better, something greater in store for you. With Jesus, you have a destiny to fulfill, something no one else can accomplish." Her mantra went on for a couple more minutes. As she continued to share, her voice became more and more inflected. With the increase in vocal inflection, the heads of the women in the room nodded more and more.

After Wendy's opening statement, there was a brief pause. Wendy looked over to her left and then said, "And now we are going to hear from Sue."

I quickly learned Sue was a founding member of the Growing More group. After she introduced herself, she began to share her faith story. She shared how she was "saved" at the age of ten while attending a Bible camp. She told of an evangelist who preached a powerful message at the camp, which resulted in her responding to an altar call and being baptized in a nearby lake. Sue shared, though, that it was not until she came to the Growing More meetings that she totally surrendered, let go, and emptied herself to Jesus. Sue lamented all the lost years of living in defeat but then rejoiced about her whole life being turned around when she surrendered to Jesus and found herself in what can only be explained as a higher and more victorious dimension. Jesus filled her, and Jesus got her from a defeated life to a victorious life, from a shallow life to a deeper life, from a fruitless life to a fruitful life, and from a joyless life to a joyful life.

As with Jillian (chapter 1), Tamar (chapter 2), and Mr. Darby (chapter 3), Wendy has bought into various presuppositions that have distorted the person and work of the real Jesus. Indeed, Wendy's presuppositions are twofold. First, she believes in a two-tiered Christianity system: carnal Christianity and spiritual Christianity. Second, in this two-tiered system, her false christ is a means to some other end. That is to say, her false christ is like a therapist who is only needed when personal problems arise. The false christ's primary purpose is to alleviate and improve bad marriages, parenting problems, unsatisfied sex, low self-esteem, and so on. This false christ is needed to help people journey from goodness to greatness, from mediocrity to excellence, and from ordinary to extraordinary.

Her false christ is like a therapist who is only needed when personal problems arise.

Looking closer at this two-tiered Christianity system of Wendy, we must note that this two-tiered system has a name: Keswick theology. Indeed, this two-tiered Christianity can be traced back to the Keswick Movement that originated in Great Britain and then came to the United States in the nineteenth-century. Keswick theology divides Christianity into two tiers as described above, and once one tier has been distinguished, it is the goal of each Christian (within Keswick theology) to move from the lower tier to the higher tier. This usually happens when the Christian surrenders or yields to the Lord.

HEARING KESWICK THEOLOGY IN TESTIMONIES

Maybe you have had a chance to hear what is called a "Testimony" in a church service. While there is nothing wrong with hearing people's faith stories, a good way to pick up on whether a person has been influenced by Keswick theology is to listen for a two-tiered Christianity. For example: "I was saved when I was nine years old and I yielded to Christ when I was nineteen."

Did you catch it? I was "saved" when I was nine (step 1); I "yielded" to Christ when I was nineteen (step 2). Jesus saved the person, but then the person surrendered, emptied him or herself, let go, and let God when they were nineteen. Typically, these testimonies end with how the person is now living in a completely different Christian dimension—higher and more victorious than they were before. Yes, indeed they were saved, but according to Keswick theology, they must also ascend to a higher level of victory and holiness.

A two-tiered Christianity should concern us because instead of returning a person to the real Jesus and His work for that person, Keswick theology shifts the focus away from the real Jesus. That is to say, instead of being returned to the real Jesus in repentance and faith, a Christian within Keswick theology is given directional language, by the teaching's beliefs, to go higher or to go deeper. It is claimed that as they go to this superior realm (second tier), they will become more spiritual, more victorious, and more fruitful. The harm in this is that this directional language to go higher or deeper essentially puts the focus on a supposed superior Christian life and not the real Jesus. Inadvertently and advertently this leads the Christian away from the real Jesus, because Jesus and His gifts no longer become the end goal of the Christian, but only something that is used by the Christian to get to a completely different goal. Without even knowing it, a Christian who falls victim to this can begin to feel that salvation is attained by their effort and how high they have ascended toward the second tier.

After Sue's testimony, there was a quiet, yet firm, clapping of hands as if the group was communicating that it was truly inspired. Wendy, nodding her head, approached the front again and positioned herself in a way that communicated that she was going to deliver the main address of the hour. She smiled and seemed to take right off with her opening statements saying, "Dear sisters, do not merely be a Sunday-only Christian! It is good to go to church, and it is good to attend on Sundays, but wouldn't you rather be more than an ordinary Christian? You don't want to be like all those other lazy and normal Christians—do you? You need to move beyond being saved. Leave the elementary doctrines of Christ and go on to maturity! Step out of your traditions and comfort. There is so much more waiting for you. Don't just merely abide, but blossom where you are planted. Furthermore, you don't want to have an ordinary marriage or an ordinary life—do you? Step out and let the Lord fill you so that you can be taken to a whole new level. You have greatness awaiting you; Jesus will take you there if you yield to Him this day."

We have already heard a bit about this fourth false christ; however, at this time let us officially meet the Therapist. This false christ is not the end or center of the Christian faith, but is a means to another end. And what end is that? The end located in the second tier that is supposedly better and greater for the Christian. This false christ is not about forgiveness, life, and salvation as an end, but about taking a person away from sadness, unfulfillment, stress, and averageness to better things (i.e., better marriages, improved parenting, more joy, a brighter future, greater maturity, etc.). In other words, like a therapist, this false christ is only needed when a person feels as if they are not meeting their full potential and desires to get to a higher level.

This false christ is only needed when a person feels as if they are not meeting their full potential and desires to get to a higher level.

feels as if they are not meeting their full potential and desires to get to a higher level. However, once a person arrives at the second tier, this false christ dismisses himself and then waits for a call at some later point when he is needed again.

In summary, two-tiered Christianity and a false christ who functions as a means to another end are the two characteristics of Wendy's theology and the heartbeat of Wendy's Growing More sessions.

It must be noted that nowhere in Scripture is Jesus spoken of as a "launching pad." Scripture does not indicate that we must somehow move beyond Jesus to a higher level. If I had to guess, I would say Wendy might not even realize her Growing More sessions call for women to go beyond Jesus. But she does believe there is another level of Christianity/happiness/faithfulness that believers can obtain by doing certain works. With that said, though, it must be maintained that salvation in Jesus is not a launching pad for greater and better, euphoric, mystic experiences. Jesus is not a metaphoric base that needs to be rounded before you get to home plate. Jesus is not a means to another end. No! He is *the* end. He is "the Alpha and the Omega, the first and the last, the beginning

Salvation in Jesus is not a launching pad for greater and better, euphoric, mystic experiences.

and the end" (Revelation 22:13). He is the "founder and perfecter of our faith" (Hebrews 12:2). We do not move beyond Jesus.

After Wendy's long motivational speech, there was light applause again from the women in the room. Wendy gave some concluding thoughts and then proceeded to ask everyone to take their chairs and arrange them in a circle for share time. Thankfully, the circle was not a perfectly round circle, which allowed me to place my chair off to the side in order not to be within the main area of group discussion. This share time was kind of like a group therapy meeting, where Wendy functioned like a therapist and all the individuals in the circle functioned like patients. For the next forty-five minutes, the women in the room shared about their ongoing stresses and their desires for a better Christian life. As each person shared, as they felt comfortable, Wendy would take notes and interject therapeutic pithy comments to acknowledge she had heard their discomfort and pain. Then she would declare there was hope for better times if they continued in the principles of the Growing More group.

Is Wendy wrong, though, to stress that the Christian should strive for a better marriage, more hope, more wisdom, better parenting, and so forth? No, she is not wrong, for there is nothing wrong with desiring these things. In fact, it is good to pray for better marriages, more wisdom, and stable jobs. It is good to gather together in prayer, and it is beneficial to have the Christian support of friends and neighbors. The problem with Wendy's goal of pushing Christians to a second tier is that it is wrong to make things other than the real Jesus the pinnacle and end-all of the Christian faith. By doing this, Wendy loses the real Jesus and goes the way of a false christ.

A prominent Lutheran theme is that we make progress in the Christian life by starting over again. That is to say, we are always beginning anew as Christians—dying to sin and being made alive by Jesus' saving work. Therefore, the solution to an unsatisfied marriage is not to call upon the Therapist to travel from an unsatisfied marriage in the

WHAT DOES THE BIBLE SAY ABOUT MOVING BEYOND JESUS?

Some people believe Jesus has saved them, but now they need to progress into living out of their Christian life—that they need to move beyond the basics of Jesus to more important things. Hebrews 6:1 says, "Therefore let us leave the elementary doctrine of Christ and go on to maturity." At first glance, it seems that the passage supports this view of maturity. However, is this so? Are we to "leave the elementary doctrine of Christ and go on to maturity"?

Let us look at this phrase in verse 1: "let us leave the elementary doctrine of Christ and go on to maturity." Now, for the sake of argument, eliminate the words "the elementary doctrine of." What's left? "Leave Christ and go on to maturity." Is that what the author of Hebrews wants us to do—to leave Christ? This is hardly the case. Rather, the author is calling for Christians to leave "the elementary doctrines" *of* Christ. In other words, the author of Hebrews is calling believers to leave the milk—the basic teachings such as contrition for sin and that it is by grace alone we are forgiven—so believers can go on to solid food which is more teaching about Jesus, such as Jesus being the everlasting Priest in the line of Melchizedek. It isn't that believers are to abandon these teachings, but that believers are to know them, believe them, and move on in maturity.

With that stated, where is this maturity into the solid food and what is this solid food? As we look to the remaining Scripture passages of Hebrews, we see that maturity goes beyond "the elementary doctrines of Christ" to the more mature doctrines of Christ. Hebrews 6 calls believers away from the elementary teachings (milk) to the mature teachings (solid food), but it does so teaching that both teachings are in/of Christ. In other words, the remainder of the Book of Hebrews plunges into the depths and riches of Jesus Christ from the perspective of the Old Testament, which is solid food.

What this means is that Jesus is not a mere starting point or a means to another end, but the beginning and the end of the Christian faith—the very center. Jesus is milk to the new believers and solid food for those who mature in the Christian faith. We can never outgrow or out-mature Jesus. In fact, the older we get and the more we understand our sinful nature, the more we will realize that we need Jesus. As it has been said before, when we grow and mature in the Christian life, we move from the lie that we are independent to the truth that we are dependent. Indeed, the more we mature in the Christian faith, the more we learn to be a beggar and receiver of the Lord and His gifts. Growing up in Christianity is realizing each day just how much more we need the Savior.

first tier to a satisfied marriage in a second tier. Rather, the solution to an unsatisfied marriage is to confess the sins that make the marriage unsatisfactory and to turn to the real Jesus for forgiveness, life, salvation, and strength. Truly, the Christian lives and grows in the Christian faith not by traveling upward to a second tier, but by returning to the Gospel of Jesus again and again and again.

We humans cannot produce holiness and righteousness for ourselves. We cannot overcome badness by climbing out of the badness pit to the second tier of glory. We cannot do this because we are the ones who are constantly jumping back into the pit. We are prone to wander and are prone to leave the God we love. We are prone to return to our own vomit like a dog (Proverbs 26:11). The problem is not that we Christians are not climbing hard enough to the second tier, but that we Christians constantly jump into the pit of sin, for we are infected with sin. Therefore, the constant solution is not a false christ that we use as some sort of ladder to climb out of the pit of sin—some lame false christ that hoists us up to some fake second level of victory. Rather, our constant solution is the real Jesus who continuously moves in on us to crucify us unto Himself, so that He might make us alive again and again and again (see Galatians 2:20). Indeed, God the Holy Spirit makes us alive—He creates in us a clean heart daily by the power of the Gospel (see Psalm 51:10). From our constant life in the real Jesus' Gospel, we are matured, continuously freed from sin, and empowered to walk by the Spirit. Frankly put, we cannot climb to a second tier because there is no such thing as a second tier. Our journey is not from mediocrity to a second level, but from our vices to the forgiveness, life, and salvation God obtained and gave to us for the sake of the real Jesus. This all might seem too simple for us because we live in a culture where we have to earn things: money, status, promotions, and so on. But with God, salvation in Jesus is free. There is no climbing, no huffing and puffing; rather, we are returned

We humans cannot produce holiness and righteousness for ourselves.

to this free salvation in repentance and faith daily. Despite our culture's focus on upward progression through pulling ourselves up by our bootstraps, we know from God's Word that it is only from and by faith in Jesus that we live and move and have our being. We indeed live this life by faith in the Son of God who loves us and gave Himself up for us (Galatians 2:20). We know that in this Christian life, "to draw near to listen [to God's Word] is better than to offer the sacrifice of fools" (Ecclesiastes 5:1).

On my way back to the church from the Growing More meeting, I could not help but feel a sense of despair for the women and myself. I soon realized that I had easily started to believe in the two-tiered system. I was plagued with the following questions: Was I completely satisfied? Was I ultimately victorious? Did I completely surrender to Jesus? Wouldn't it be nice to live in the second tier? Could things be better for me? These questions continued to haunt my thoughts for the remainder of the day until I was confronted with the reality that I was baptized. Indeed, in Jesus, there are no tiers, just Christ crucified for me. He came to me when I could not go to Him. He baptized me, claimed me, and made me His own. He did this all for me, and He did this for my parishioner attending that Growing More study, for Wendy, and for you, too.

Responding to Wendy

What is the main thing that drives and controls Wendy's thoughts, logic, and decisions regarding Christianity and her views about Jesus? As we have learned, Wendy has been ensnared by Keswick Theology. Therefore, Wendy has created a two-tier view of Christianity. This has led her to trust in the Therapist, a false christ who aids her in climbing to the second tier and keeping her Christian status.

So, when we respond to Wendy—and others like her—our main focus will be to address the two-tiered system. There are some ways to do this. We can simply ask questions that will cause Wendy to try and show from the Scriptures that there is such a thing as the two-tiered system (which she cannot do). Or, we can appeal to a non-Keswick theology, specifically our baptismal life in the real Jesus. We could ask Wendy the following questions, "Wendy, I have been buried and raised in Jesus by Baptism. Yes, Jesus has claimed me in Baptism because the Bible says that He loves me. He has forgiven me of my sins in His Supper. Paul says in Ephesians chapter 1 verse 3 that we have been blessed in Jesus 'with every spiritual blessing in the heavenly places.' Therefore, He is my hope, my joy, and my rest in the midst of this sinful world and in the midst of my failures of thought, word, and deed. Considering this, are you implying I need something more? Is Jesus and Jesus alone not good enough?" By going this route, we are gently forcing Wendy to contend with our assurance, which rests on Jesus' work, not our own.

Keep in mind, though, that Wendy is all about moving people from a lower tier to a higher tier, so she will most likely try to find a fault in our current assurance and then appeal to something grander and bigger on the higher tier. She will try to find some downfall in our current status and then paint a grander picture on the second tier as a way of trying to get us to move toward a higher spiritual realm. However, this is where our confession of Jesus can break her two-tier system! If we sense that we are being persuaded to a second tier or feel ashamed for something we lack, we can boldly respond that we do not need to move anywhere nor do we lack any spiritual blessing in the real Jesus! (In fact, when Christians typically try to go somewhere, it is usually away from Jesus and unfortunately toward sin.) So, we can confess to Wendy that the goal is to abide and remain with Jesus, as we hear in John 15:3: "Already you are clean because of the word that I have spoken to you." Think about this a moment—we can confess we have everything we spiritually need in Jesus (see Ephesians 1:3). We have received joy. In fact, our joy is complete in the real Jesus because Jesus is joy itself. Why would we need to move to any other tier? Confessing that we already are abiding with the real Jesus not only undercuts the two-tiered system but it is also a bold confession of the sufficiency of Jesus for everything we might possibly encounter in this life here on earth.

Will the Real Jesus Please Stand Up?

If we begin to believe that Jesus is not the beginning, center, and end of our Christian faith, and if we start to believe we are missing out on so much more if we settle for Jesus alone, then we will soon exchange the real Jesus for the Therapist and end up chasing shallow, empty, and temporal promises of greatness. Embracing the Therapist on our journey to the second tier takes us on a wild goose chase; it leads us to follow a carrot on a stick; it leads us to look for the treasure at the end of the rainbow. After all is said and done, though,—after all the chasing and climbing—there is no goose or carrot or treasure, just us alone abiding in our sin without Jesus, looking into the vast dark abyss of hell and damnation.

A false christ who is primarily for helping our children get on the honor roll, a false christ who is mainly for helping us run our businesses, or is chiefly for improving our marriages and sex lives, is powerless to deal with the real and most important issue of all: our sin.

Jesus is not a means to joy, wisdom, and peace; rather, Jesus is our joy, wisdom, and peace.

What this all means is that we are saved by the real Jesus, we are also sustained by the real Jesus, and we grow in the real Jesus (see Hebrews 12:1–2). Jesus is not a means to joy, wisdom, and peace; rather, Jesus is our joy, wisdom, and peace. Furthermore, we are not autonomous persons in the church body striving to build our individual second-tier empires of piety with a spiritual legacy conducted through our own clever devices. Rather, we are baptized Christians gathered back to Jesus and

His gifts so that we may daily receive the forgiveness of all our sin. It is not about getting to some second tier, but about being returned to Christ Jesus, our firm foundation (see 2 Peter 3:17–18). It is all about returning to Jesus' forgiveness, life, and salvation as delivered to us in Baptism, the Word, and the Sacrament of Communion.

Let's discuss the **Therapist**

1. What are Wendy's main presuppositions that created the Therapist?

The New Testament Church of Colossae was full of heresy (false teaching). One of the false ideas that had been spread throughout the Colossian Church was that the Gospel they had come to believe in was inadequate and lacking. False teachers were saying that the simple Christian message the Colossians embraced was not enough. The Colossians needed a higher understanding and great wisdom, which the false teachers were ready to give out.

Consider the following questions regarding the Colossian heresy and regarding ideologies presented by the Therapist in chapter 4. Read Colossians 2:6–15.

2. Consider Colossians 2:6. Since the Colossians already received Jesus, who are they to walk in (i.e., keep in line with)?

3. In what two ways are the Colossians to walk in the Lord continually? In what two ways are we Christians to walk in Jesus?

4. Where and of whom are the Colossians and the Christian complete? What does it mean to be complete?

5. How do these verses speak to Keswick theology and the idea that Jesus is some means to another end—some Therapist?

6. In keeping with the Eighth Commandment of not giving a false testimony against our neighbors, can you describe a situation (generically) in which you have experienced the Therapist?

7. Hypothetically, if you ended up in a situation where a group was presenting Jesus as the Therapist, how would you respond? What actions would you take?

Meet Jim and Stacy, the Blessed

I remember hearing the tragic news. I remember it like yesterday. Young Olivia Schneider had a brain tumor. I wanted to doubt this news at first, for Olivia was only seven years old at the time.

Several days later, it was confirmed that she had cancer—aggressive cancer. Our whole neighborhood was devastated and the community was shocked. The bouncy little freckle-faced girl who road her pink bike up and down the sidewalk was sick with cancer, which put the whole Schneider family onto a path that far too many others have had to walk.

The local churches, Rotary Clubs, and businesses immediately responded with emotional and financial support for the Schneider family. That is how it works in small-town USA. Expressions of shock, tears of compassion, and encouragements poured out over the next several weeks as the Schneider family explored treatment options.

Jim and Stacy Jaeger also lived on the same block as my family and the Schneider family. They were in their late forties, had older children, owned their own business, and attended the local non-denominational church in town. The Jaegers were longtime residents of the neighborhood and were fairly well respected in the greater community.

After hearing the news of Olivia's illness, the Jaeger family immediately became one of the Schneiders' biggest supporters. They organized meals, helped orchestrate several fund-raising benefits, and even began a prayer support group for the Schneiders. They rallied support for Olivia.

The local church I served at this time was also seriously impacted by Olivia's cancer, as she had attended the preschool held in our facility. The whole church was gripped by the Schneiders' predicament and seemed to be drawn into Olivia's fight against cancer. In fact, many of the members of the church became connected to the Jaegers' prayer group.

Throughout the next several months, we talked about Olivia after church and sometimes during Bible studies. As we talked about the sweet seven-year-old battling cancer, it was mainly to update information: how her treatments were going and how the family was holding up. With that said, though, every time Olivia was brought up in discussions, a unique spiritual narrative emerged and grew. That is to say, a specific spiritual story slowly developed over time and gradually became a part of the common discussion of the church. I can remember the first time I recognized it. One day a parishioner declared, "We all just need to feed our faith and then our fears will begin to starve to death." To this comment, another parishioner responded, "Yes, we need to stay positive about Olivia. We need to speak positive words about her being healed. We need to put these positive words into practice and plug them into the powerhouse of heaven with prayer. Olivia will be healed, oh yes; she will be healed because we have faith!"

These phrases used among church attendees were certainly different from how they had talked about faith in the past. In the past, church attendees talked about the reality of Olivia's condition and then commended it to the Lord's mercy by faith; however, this was not the case anymore. It was taboo to talk about the reality and challenges of Olivia's condition, and it was deemed lazy if one were to simply lay Olivia's condition before the Great Physician in prayer—no, one needed to speak about healing and in faith demand God to fix Olivia. What was bringing this about, though? The reality was that many of the members had been attending the Jaegers' prayer group. From what was reported to me, at the prayer group, Jim and Stacy Jaeger were doing more than praying petitions of healing for Olivia; they were teaching those in attendance about faith and healing. They were instructing the prayer group that their words were like seeds. The Jaegers shared with the group their belief that whatever Christians spoke would come back in the form of either positive or negative manifestations. Regarding Olivia, they were saying that it would be easy to become weary and give up, especially since the cancer was so aggressive. However, they pressed the prayer group to continue to speak toward Jesus with positive faith-filled words and to proclaim that healing was already on its way for Olivia. The positive faith-filled words declaring Olivia healed were deemed necessary for the Schneiders to see a breakthrough. The focus of the Jaegers' teaching was that Jesus came to give His followers the abundant life, and it only needed to be claimed.

Meet our fifth false christ: the Giver of Bling. This false christ is an Americanized prosperity idol, one who always grants health and wealth and success—bling!—to those whose faith in him reaches some undefined but satisfactory level. (Note: this level is typically never defined but functions like a carrot on the end of a stick. The false christ will never define the level of needed faith but will always keep the person striving for more, which results in the person always being in slavery to this false christ's demands.) The Giver of Bling promises abundance to his followers. He will release good things for the believer if they make a positive faith confession. In other words, according to this incorrect way of thinking, faith is a force within the Christian. Therefore, when the Christian speaks positive faith-filled words toward the Lord (declaring what one wants with confidence), then this positive confession will become a reality. It is as if the Lord will have no choice but to make the confident prayers come to pass. Conversely, though, this means that negative words or not being positive enough will form negative realities. This fifth false christ works hand-in-hand with what is called the Word-Faith Movement. Within this movement, there is an understanding that when positive faith-filled words are spoken, then the Giver of Bling is ready to dispense health, wealth, and success.

Regarding Olivia, the plan was simple for the Jaegers. Step one: gather people together in a prayer group. Step two: speak positive faith-filled words in prayer toward Jesus on Olivia's behalf, as a way of plugging into the powerhouse of heaven. Step three: witness Olivia receive the abundant healing the Lord Jesus Christ longs to give, for their positive confessions of faith will release Jesus' healing for Olivia.

I remember getting the news that Olivia had had some very successful treatments. The cancer had subsided. Olivia had also grown. She was now nine years old. Everyone seemed to breathe a sigh of relief. But little did everyone know that was only round one. Round two was about to begin.

CONSIDERING FAITH

The fundamental problem with the Word-Faith Movement is that it views faith as a self-generated work of mankind. This error occurs when we believe that God does His part in salvation, but then it is up to people to actualize their faith—to reach out in faith and seal the salvation deal.

Instead, as the Bible reveals, faith is God's work in us. God grants us faith—as a gift—so that it can be a passive instrument that receives salvation, like a child's open hand receiving the gift of candy. (See Romans 10:17 and Ephesians 2:8 where faith is described as a work of God.)

Faith is not created or strengthened by talking about faith, but rather, faith is created and strengthened when we hear about Jesus Christ dying for our sins. Faith is a fruit of the Gospel, not the determination of man's heart. Faith must always have an object that it clings to; that object is not mankind's willpower but Jesus Christ and His good gifts.

When Olivia's cancer pushed back, it was a mighty force. The treatments did impact the cancerous invasion; however, the disease was not willing to give up so easily. It was back in full force, which meant that the Schneider family was back to living out of suitcases in the hospital. The Jaeger prayer group was also back to regular meetings.

Soon, Olivia was not responding to the treatments the way everyone had hoped. The reports coming back from the hospital were that Olivia was slipping. Though nobody talked about it, many were thinking, "Is this little precious girl going to make it? Is she going to die?"

A conflict occurred one afternoon when Jim and Stacy Jaeger stopped by the church. Our church was working on another fund-raiser for the Schneider family, and the Jaegers were dropping off some sign-up sheets. After some administrative conversation, I brought up Olivia. I said, "Did you hear the most recent unfortunate news that Olivia is not responding to treatments? I pray she makes it. Lord, have mercy!" Stacy immediately smiled and lightheartedly replied, "There is nothing to worry about. Jesus will heal her. We have faith, don't we pastor?" I paused for a moment and gathered my thoughts and said, "Yes, Jesus will indeed heal Olivia. If she lives, she is healed. If she dies, Jesus will heal her by delivering her from this valley of tears unto Himself." Both Jim and Stacy's bodies recoiled at my words. They both took two steps back. Jim then leaned in with intensity and a finger raised saying, "Oh Pastor! Jesus is triumphant; we are triumphant. He has borne our diseases; by His stripes, we are healed. Victory is on its way for Olivia, which means we've gotta plan for the increase, restoration, and a comeback for Olivia's health and prosperity. You'd better get your faith in line with what Jesus says! There is no room for defeatist talk, especially right now. We need to claim the healing that already belongs to Olivia. Now is the time to have faith that is storming for heaven, not doubt."

Two more presuppositions emerged in the conversation above. First, the Jaegers have an over-realized eschatology presupposition (more on that in a moment). Second, they have an adverse reaction to suffering, resulting in them being unable to talk about the reality of suffering. Let us examine both of these presuppositions a bit more thoroughly.

Eschatology is a theological word that refers to the study of the eschaton, which is the end of the world according to the Lord's divine plan. It is the study of all the events that will take place when Jesus comes again—what will happen to the world, what happens to mankind, what eternity will be like. With that stated, when a person has an

COMEDY OR TRAGEDY?

My wife's parents used to own a movie theater, which meant that my wife and I became movie critics when we were dating during high school. One of the things that we would often speculate about was whether the movie we were about to watch would be a tragedy or a comedy. In theatrical terminology, tragedies are movies that begin with joy, success, and happiness and then end with sorrow, pain, and sadness. On the other hand, comedies are movies that begin with sorrow, pain, and sadness and then end with joy, success, and happiness.

With that said, Christianity is a comedy, not a tragedy. We are born into this life and live in the vale of tears; we live with tribulations and struggles as Christians. We know that we are constantly attacked and plagued by the devil, the world, and our sinful nature. However, we do not live as if we do not have hope. Indeed, the Christian's hope is that no matter how bad it gets, we know that when Jesus comes back again, everything will be made right—no more tears, no more pain, no more sin, renewed bodies, a new heaven and earth.

An over-realized eschatology, however, rejects this comedic view of Christianity. It avoids the current suffering of the here and now. An over-realized eschatology metaphorically fast-forwards through the suffering portions of a movie to watch the end; it immediately turns to the back pages of a book in order to get to the joy, success, and happiness. An over-realized eschatology is essentially in denial of the current sufferings and trials occurring for the Christian as he or she lives in this vale of tears.

over-realized eschatology, they are looking to the future blessings and promises of Jesus and then pulling these future blessings and promises into the present context. That which is promised to happen for the Christian at some future point, after Jesus' second coming, is applied to the present time when the Christian can claim it by positive words of faith.

An over-realized eschatology is another characteristic of the Giver of Bling. The future promises and blessings of the real Jesus are dislodged from their future framework and then relocated with the Giver of Bling in the present time. If a person wants a future blessing now, they believe they cannot get it with the real Jesus, so they exchange Him for a false christ. The false christ will then supposedly dispense new heaven and new earth triumphant blessings and eternal victorious prosperity before the great eschaton.

The Realities of Suffering

The Jaegers were not able to deal with the realities of suffering. Talking about or admitting to suffering was considered negative talk that would most assuredly undercut the effect of the positive faith words. Suffering has a way of undercutting the so-called power of positive thinking. But more than all of this, suffering was not and is not compatible with the Giver of Bling.

The Giver of Bling and suffering mix as poorly as oil and water. Suffering exposes this false christ. It exposes this false christ's gospel of prosperity, which is no gospel at all. A prosperity gospel teaches that health, wealth, and success are the will of God for Christians, whereas God never grants suffering or poverty. That is to say, suffering is not from God but is always a part of sin and Satan. What this means is that a person who is suffering is suffering because they have not made the decision to resist the sickness. If it is not God's will for them to be sick, then they should choose to have Satan defeated by using the mighty power of their faith—as a powerful force—to obtain God's will of health, wealth, and personal success.

Consider the ramifications of the message of the Giver of Bling when someone experiences suffering. To the person who prays to the Giver of Bling, the loss of a job, bankruptcy, sickness, or depression means that a person's faith is not strong enough. The prosperity gospel would not allow a person to believe that the Giver of Bling is not all-powerful, so according to the prosperity gospel, a person would need to conclude that he or she is limited, not fully using their power, or is bound up in the kingdom of darkness. Therefore, to recover from the suffering, he or she must seize and claim health, wealth, and success by the powerful force of their own faith to have a breakthrough of success. If there are problems obtaining success, though, then the person would be directed to have more faith.

Several months after my conversation at the church with the Jaegers, I received the news that Olivia had died. Her fragile body did not have enough energy to continue the fight against the beast of cancer. The Schneider family was devastated; the whole community was distraught.

We continued to talk about precious Olivia in our neighborhood, as well as in the church and community long after the day of her funeral. One day after Sunday services, I was sitting at a table having a conversation with a group of people while enjoying some refreshments

TROUBLES WITH THE PROSPERITY GOSPEL

What the prosperity gospel teaching fails to realize is that sometimes, instead of solving our problems and giving us our wildest dreams, the Lord may allow our problems to remain. He may choose to have us suffer a hardship for a time, even as He provides us with the power to stand. See 2 Corinthians 12:7–9. This, also, is the Lord's loving care. Rather than supplying what we need for our problem, the Lord may choose in His wisdom to remove us. In other words, He may take us to Himself in heaven, where all troubles cease.

in the fellowship hall. I became aware of a group of people discussing Olivia at the other end of the table. It was one of those conversations where a person is not a part of it but can inadvertently hear everything being discussed. As this group was discussing the events leading up to Olivia's death, one parishioner—who was a part of the Jaeger prayer groups—asked a question to prove a point, "We do know the real reason why Olivia died, right?" In which several people in the group dropped their heads and mumbled the word, "Cancer." The parishioner paused, shook his head as if to show disrespect toward the group's answer, and then said, "I believe the reason why Olivia died is that we did not have enough faith. Yes, if we would've just had more faith, if we would've prayed so much that God would've answered just to shut us up, I don't believe Olivia would've died." There was a heavy silence in the group as members of the group anxiously shuffled in their chairs. There was even awkwardness on my end of the table, as many individuals—whom I was sitting with—heard this too but kept talking in their conversations. Most often in Midwestern American culture, uncomfortable subjects are dismissed by changing the subject when they become too painful. And once the conversation has been changed to another subject, it is rude to bring up the uncomfortable subject again. So, after a few seconds of awkwardness, the subject was changed at the other end of the table to the Minnesota Vikings' football game that would soon be starting later that afternoon. In other words, it was easier to talk about the Vikings' losing season than the possibility that we had caused little Olivia's death through our lack of faith.

The following week, I heard a common phrase emerge in the community: "Olivia died because we did not have enough faith." As it turns out, the Jaegers had held a follow-up prayer meeting shortly after the funeral where it was concluded by the Jaegers and the prayer group that individuals in the community did not have enough faith—as they had—and that was the reason for Olivia's death. It was as if the Giver of Bling would have gladly kept her alive had our words been more direct, our prayers more fervent, our hearts more devoted—if we would have been "real" Christians and not some subpar second-class Christians. I slammed my door to my office in disgust. A righteous anger toward this message of prosperity burned in my soul. After the anger subsided, I realized that this subject would need to be addressed in the church. It could not be addressed through an aggressive direct confrontation but through a thorough and patient study of God's Word in the church. More specifically, this wretched theology would need to be reproved and rebuked with patient teaching and proclamation of God's Word from books like the Old Testament Book of Job.

The fundamental problems regarding the Giver of Bling is that this false christ and its shameful theology not only have an over-realized eschatology, an incorrect view of faith, and the inability to address the realities of suffering, but it also positions mankind and the Lord into an "if-then" relationship. In other words, when we put conditions on the Lord through the "if-then" ideology, mankind assumes the active role, spiritually speaking. This "if-then" arrangement shifts our attention to how well mankind is performing the "if's" toward the Lord, rather than what the Lord is doing and has done for mankind. It attempts to put the Lord in debt to mankind's actions: "Jesus, I have done these things, now You owe me and must respond to me!" (For an example of this if-then ideology, see Job 11:13–18.)

All of these views or ideas result in the tragedy set before us with the Jaegers' assertions that we must have more faith. That is, when a person speaks their faith-filled words in prayer, and the "then" portion of the equation does not come true, these persons are left with only two options: either the Lord does not care about their needs (i.e., the Lord did not care about Olivia), or the individual lacks faith (i.e., if the person really had enough faith, Olivia would not have died). If it is the former, then the Lord's character is flawed beyond repair. If it is the latter, then the person might not be a Christian, for they do not have enough faith.

Responding to Jim and Stacy

What is the main thing that drives and controls Jim and Stacy's thoughts, logic, and decisions regarding Christianity and their views about Jesus? As we have learned, Jim and Stacy have bought into a prosperity Gospel, which sees faith as something that mankind must generate and actualize to get the Giver of Bling to dispense success.

Consequently, when we respond to Jim and Stacy—and others like them—we need to address their prosperity theology. However, to expose their prosperity theology it would be best to avoid talking about health, wealth, and success, and rather instead focus on the topic of faith. Keep in mind that the Jaegers see faith as a self-generated work of mankind; they see faith-filled words as the key to unlocking, seizing, and obtaining prosperity. Why is this important? It is important because the Jaegers have linked faith and prosperity together in a cause-and-effect-relationship. Positive faith-filled words result in a positive reality, whereas, a lack of faith and negative words result in a negative reality.

A helpful approach to exposing this false system is to ask personal questions that demonstrate the downfall in the cause and effects of daily life. Their theology needs to be gently turned around and applied to them. For example, a powerful, yet applicable, question for Jim would be to ask him why he wears glasses. Yes, his prosperity theology needs to be turned around and applied to ailments and struggles in his own life. And for Stacy, we need to ask her why she has not received that promotion at work, for she has been at the same place of work for the last eight years and hasn't advanced. In other words, if the Lord will have no choice but to make the confident prayers and positive confessions a reality, why is it that the Jaegers, who tout a glorious life based on their own shining examples of spirituality, do not have fulfilled, complete, and total health, wealth, and success? Is it that they have not noticed their struggles and failings? If so, they better get busy praying and speaking positive words of faith—they should be healed of bad eyesight and should be getting those job promotions. If they are aware of their bad eyesight and lack of job promotions and have been praying for this, they need to be asked if they do not have enough faith.

It may seem a bit harsh to turn the Jaegers' prosperity theology back on them, but frankly, this would be one of the best things we could do. You see, it is easy to apply theology to someone else, but it is more difficult to apply it to ourselves. For the Jaegers, they need to be brought to the end of themselves—they need to be shown that their self-generated faith is useless in acquiring prosperity. The Jaegers need to apply their prosperity theology to *all* aspects of their lives. Then, only when their prosperity theology bankrupts them, can they hear the message of the real Jesus who comes to poor miserable sinners with forgiveness, life, and salvation. Indeed, Jesus is not coerced to come to people who have superstar faith, but He graciously comes to create and sustain faith in those who cry out saying, "Lord have mercy on me, the sinner."

Will the Real Jesus Please Stand Up?

The temptation to follow the Giver of Bling is based on craving his fake glory. We are attracted to this false christ's health, wealth, and success; we want his comfort, honor, prestige, special handouts, and respect. We want only to be blessed at all times. This is not real glory at all; this is not what makes the real Jesus glorious. The promises of the real Jesus do not begin with us at all.

The promises of the real Jesus do not begin with us at all.

What makes the real Jesus glorious is not that He overcame and destroyed the Roman Empire, but rather, Jesus was beaten, bloodied, and destroyed on a Roman execution cross. Jesus' glory is not Him correcting a crooked justice system, but Him standing obediently before a kangaroo court that is enacting perverted justice upon Him. What Jesus' glory looks like is not a halo, but rather a crown of thorns. Indeed, the real Jesus in His full glory is not a radiant king sitting on a golden throne dispensing glittery accolades, but rather the Suffering Servant spit upon, beaten, and crucified. Jesus' glory is seen in His crucifixion, a crucifixion that does not carry any renown, honor, beauty, respect, delight, splendor, or adoration. (See Isaiah 53:2–12 which talks about the suffering servant—Jesus.)

But how can this be glory? It does not look like glory. It does not sound like glory. It does not feel like glory.

When the real Jesus was lifted up on the cross—after being spit upon, bloodied, mocked, betrayed, and forsaken—the Scriptures say that He drew "all people to Himself" (John 12:32–33). Yes, in what seems to be an anti-glorious place on the cross—in this dark, ugly, low place of shame and death—Jesus drags and pulls the weight of sin from the whole world unto Himself.

Are we now able to begin to understand why the cross is the quintessential place of glory?

Olivia's Jesus, the real Jesus, chose the crown of thorns—for Olivia and you. He chose the hammer and nails—for Olivia and you. He went into the darkness—for Olivia and you. He chose the cross—for Olivia and you. He drank the cup of wrath as He dragged and pulled the weight of sin, Olivia's sin and our sin, unto Himself to be our sin-bearer. First John 3:16a says it well, "By this we know love, that he laid down his life for us."

So, whether we live or die, whether we are rich or poor, whether we are healthy or sick, or whether we are happy or sad, we already have glory. We have glory because we have Jesus crucified for our sins upon the cross. The cross is Jesus' glory, accomplished for Olivia and for me and for you. Glory that we boast about. Indeed, as Paul says in Galatians 6:14, "Far be it from [us] to boast, except in the cross of our Lord Jesus Christ."

Let's discuss the *Giver of Bling*

1. What are the main presuppositions of the Jaegers that make up the Giver of Bling?

In the Old Testament Book of Job, we read about the afflictions of a man named Job. Job was pronounced as blameless three times in the first two chapters of the book; however, as we read through this book we hear about the decline in Job's health, the loss of his property, and the loss of his children. In the story, we hear about Job's three friends and their attempts to make sense of Job's disasters. The following questions will show us that there is nothing new under the sun, regarding the false ideology that makes up the Giver of Bling.

2. Read Job 11:13–20. Take note of the "if-then" construct. What things does Zophar say that Job should do in verses 13–14?

3. If Job does the things mentioned in verses 13–14, what does Zophar say will happen to him? See verses 15–19.

4. Consider verse 20 for a moment. Zophar assumes that the wicked will fall and that they will have no hope. Is this always the case? Do bad things happen to bad people only and good things happen to good people only? Why or why not?

5. Is Zophar saying that Job can change his suffering and condition if he changes his behavior and puts away his sin? How is this problematic?

6. How do these questions and the verses shed light on the Giver of Bling?

7. Maybe more than any other false christ today, do we experience the Giver of Bling in our day-to-day interactions. How can or do you share the truth of Christ-crucified for your sins to people who hold to this idol?

NATIONAL PATRIOT

6

Meet Jack, the Theocratic American

It was a late Saturday night. I had forgotten a book in my office at the church. Instead of waiting until the next morning, I decided it was worth the trip back to have the book I needed.

As I entered the church around 9:00 p.m., I noticed that the security system had been deactivated. This was puzzling. Who else would be here so late at night on a Saturday?

I walked down the hall and noticed a light on in the sanctuary. Strange, for our custodian typically worked in the early morning hours, not at night.

I peeked into the sanctuary only to find that it appeared empty. However, as I turned around to shut the lights off, I heard some mumbling coming from the front. I paused, turned around, and noticed two women from the church kneeling at the left side of the altar.

Were they praying? Were they okay? Was one of them hurt?

"Is everything okay?" I said with firmness, while still expressing compassion.

Both of the ladies' heads lifted up immediately to the sound of my voice. A blank look came over their faces. They looked at each other and looked back at me.

I walked toward them and asked again, "Is everything okay?"

"Oh, Pastor . . . it is you. Hmm, yeah. It's good to see you."

After seeing and hearing that they were not in any danger, I then asked them, "What on earth are you doing?"

With some hesitancy in her voice, one of the ladies, named Susan, said, "Pastor Larry asked us to move the United States flag two inches away from the altar every week."

This made absolutely no sense to me. What were they talking about? I can imagine my confusion was clearly discernible on my face.

The other woman, Jan, smiled and clarified, "It's because of Jack."

"What does Jack have to do with the flag and you moving it two inches?" I said, with my voice a bit strained, for I was very mixed up at this point.

Jan continued, "Pastor Larry had been a little uncomfortable with how close the American flag was in proximity to the altar and decided to move it to the corner of the sanctuary. This was a couple of months ago. When Jack came in one Sunday morning and saw that the American flag had been moved, he stormed out of the church and sat in his car for the whole service. His poor wife had to sit by herself in the pew. As he left the building, he threatened not to come back into the church unless the flag was returned to its original spot next to the altar."

"Oh, I did hear something about that. But what does that have to do with you two being on the floor of the sanctuary on a Saturday night?" I said.

Susan responded, "Well, Pastor Larry immediately moved the flag back next to the altar to calm Jack down; however, Pastor Larry talked to us privately and asked us to move the flag two inches away from the altar every time we set things up for Sunday communion. Pastor Larry wanted the flag away from the altar and figured he could accomplish this without Jack noticing it if we moved it two inches every week . . ."

Jan could hardly contain her laughter. A giggle erupted out of her mouth as she interrupted Susan saying, "Oh Pastor Matt, you should've heard Jack. He was furious! He was yelling that moving the flag was unpatriotic and that America was a Christian nation, possibly God's new Israel. He said that Jesus had a special blessing for America, so we shouldn't be concerned about the altar being so close to the flag."

I took a deep breath and sighed.

Jan continued, "Jack sure let Pastor Larry have it in the fellowship hall; he said that Pastor Larry was unpatriotic and un-American and that he was falling prey to the atheistic agenda to secularize our country. As Jack left the building, he mumbled something about the flag always being a part of the church's décor and that he could not figure out why anyone would want to change this."

Even though this is a somewhat humorous story to think about, it does bring forth a serious question of why Pastor Larry wanted to move the American flag away from the altar. Why the concern? Later that week, I found out that Pastor Larry was concerned that the American flag was overshadowing the altar. From the right side of the sanctuary seating, the flag was blocking the people's sight of the communion elements that were placed on the altar. Furthermore, Pastor Larry wanted to make sure that the congregation understood there was a difference between the realm of the church and the realm of the state (i.e., government). He wanted to make sure the parishioners knew they

THEOCRACY

Medieval European history has shown us that the distinctions between the Roman Emperor and the Catholic Pope were often blurred. In fact, the church slowly began to be the prominent institution during that time. This resulted in the clergy having both political and ecclesiastical authority. Such subordination of the civil government to the church—into one institution—is what is called a theocracy.

Generally speaking, Israel functioned as a theocracy from the time of Moses until the destruction of Jerusalem in 586 BC. After 586 BC, though, Israel ceased being a theocracy and the people were ruled by foreign governments, such as the Babylonians, Persians, and Romans.

did not live in what is called a theocracy, where the realms of the church and the state are merged into one realm.

Jack, on the other hand, found the new location of the American flag to be very upsetting. He could not figure out why Pastor Larry wanted to move the flag. For Jack, an altar without the American flag meant Christianity separated from America. He could not fathom America and the church in two distinct and separate categories, for God blessed America, and, according to Jack, America was a theocracy just like Israel was in the Old Testament. In other words, the separation of America from Christianity—for Jack—was the destruction of the manifest destiny of America being a new Israel—an America that had a special divine favor from God. To separate America (i.e., the state) and Christianity (i.e., the church) would be equal to denying that America had God's special divine favor. Furthermore, if the state and the church were in two separate spheres, Jack may feel like he would have to choose between his allegiances with America and Christianity.

If we can think about the altar as representing the church (i.e., right-hand kingdom) and the American flag as representing the state

WHAT IS MEANT BY TWO KINGDOMS?

God has established both the state and the church. They are two separate and distinct kingdoms. The kingdom on the left (i.e., the state consisting of civil authorities such as the president, senators, judges, policemen, etc.) serves mankind to keep order and protect (see Romans 13:1-7, which speaks of the left-hand kingdom). It operates by coercion, laws, and force—the sword. On the other hand, the kingdom on the right (i.e., the church) operates by the good news of love, mercy, and grace—the sword of the Word and the blessed Sacraments (see John 18:33–37, where we hear about the two kingdoms). It is evident that both kingdoms are different, yet work together. The left-hand kingdom keeps order, safety, and peace, while the church proclaims forgiveness, life, and salvation.

(i.e., left-hand kingdom), should Jack cling to the altar or the flag? Where is a Christian's allegiance: the church or the state?

This either-or choice was a very similar choice the real Jesus faced some two thousand years ago, as two groups called the Herodians and the Pharisees attempted to trap Him between having to choose God or Caesar. In Matthew 22:15–22, we read about the religious leaders approaching Jesus and asking Him, "Tell us, then, what You think. Is it lawful to pay taxes to Caesar, or not?" In other words, this question was attempting to trap Jesus. If Jesus would have said, "Yes, it is lawful to pay taxes to Caesar, to the Roman Empire!" then Jesus would have been aligned with the Roman Empire, an empire that most people despised during that day and age. If Jesus would have said, "No, it is not lawful to pay taxes to Caesar, to the Roman Empire!" the religious leaders would have then conveniently reported Jesus to the Roman Empire as one who was attempting to promote insurrectionist ideas against Rome, which would have gotten Jesus arrested.

The religious leaders attempted to pit the realms of the church and state against each other and tried to make Jesus choose one or the other. This is a tactic known as an "either-or logical fallacy." By posing a question this way, the hearer feels the need to choose just one response. We can see this type of logic in the situation with Jack as well. When the altar and the flag were distinguished as different—not one and the same—Jack reacted strongly and subsequently refused to come back into the church until the flag and altar were joined back together again. More specifically, what Jack and the first-century religious leaders did not understand was that there are two separate realms—the state and the church—and that both the realm of the state and the realm of the church are from God; they are both instituted by Him. Simply put, the flag and the altar are different, yet they both belong to the Lord and are under the Lord's authority. Jack did not want to separate the two realms; the religious leaders attempted to separate the realms and pit them against each other. Both misunderstood the kingdoms of the state and the church.

Several weeks later, Jack returned to the church services satisfied that the American flag had been returned to its place next to the altar. Only a few in the congregation knew that the flag was being stealthily moved without his knowledge.

I was the Associate Pastor to youth, and since the church was rather large, I had limited contact with Jack. I was, however, an attentive fly on the wall whenever Jack was in my vicinity. What I gleaned from the casual interactions was that Jack and several others in the church had a significant resistance to distinguishing the Lord's two kingdoms. This may not seem like anything substantial; however, what this tragically resulted in was Jack inadvertently creating a false christ for himself. This false christ was a sanctifier of Jack's political party, political beliefs, and an advocate for the culture of America. In other words, the ideology of this false christ conveniently matched up to and supported the views of Jack's political party, as well as the American Dream; this false christ was not consistent with the actual teachings of the real Jesus in the Bible.

A FALSE DILEMMA?

Imagine a world where you had to choose either peanut butter or jelly for your sandwiches. No middle road; one or the other! Furthermore, imagine a world where all your friends advocated for peanut butter and scorned jelly. Besides this being a tragedy to sandwich lovers, this is an example of a false dilemma or what can also be called an "either-or logical fallacy." In other words, a false dilemma is created when two things are pitted against each other when they do not need to be. In the case of peanut butter and jelly, we do not have binary oppositions like heaven and hell, but two things that are equally good and can both be embraced. To place peanut butter and jelly against each other is to create a false binary, when it is obviously not needed.

Meet our next false christ: the National Patriot. This false christ appears when God's ordained right- and left-hand kingdoms are not adequately distinguished—for example, when the church forgets her identity and tries to take the place of the state. In that scenario, Jesus is viewed mainly as a patriot giving His all for the national cause, which creates the false christ—the National Patriot. In this scenario, the National Patriot rules not by the Word and Sacraments, but by laws, policies, economics strategies, and military tactics. When the two kingdoms of God are mixed, everything in the Christian faith is twisted and corrupted. Law and Gospel are convoluted, and the identity, work, and mission of the real Jesus are redefined into a false christ. Instead of the identity, work, and mission of the real Jesus being about forgiveness, life, and salvation, this false christ makes everything about life, liberty, and the pursuit of happiness. The American Dream becomes the main mission.

In the case of Jack, since he did not distinguish between the two kingdoms, he ended up blurring the characteristics of the state and church together, thus creating a false christ that was mainly about the American ideals of individualism, independence, innovation, democracy, capitalism, opportunity, and the freedom of choice. Indeed, the National Patriot exchanges the corporate nature of the church in favor

DISTINGUISHING LAW AND GOSPEL

God has two words; two distinct teachings in the Bible: God's yes and God's no. God's no is known as His Law. The Law says "do." It tells us what God's will is—what we should do and what we should not do. The Law condemns by revealing sin. The Gospel, though, is God's yes. The Gospel says "done." It tells us about what Jesus has done for sinners—how forgiveness, life, and salvation have been accomplished for mankind. The Gospel absolves by revealing Christ-crucified. Like the doctrine of the two kingdoms, Law and Gospel cannot be balanced or mixed, for they are two separate words of God with different effects, yet the same aim of salvation.

of individualism. He replaces childlike dependence with self-made independence. The rich heritage of the church is forsaken by this false christ for the sake of innovation. A patriot of the nation need not focus on the forgiveness of sins, so this false christ rather promotes opportunity and options and therefore exchanges God's sovereignty for mankind's freedom of choice.

The National Patriot exchanges the corporate nature of the church in favor of individualism.

Furthermore, Jack's false christ was not about being a crucified savior for poor miserable sinners, but rather was a powerful ruler who was establishing a new Israel-like-theocracy where heretics, atheistic infidels, and unpatriotic anti-nationalists were branded as enemies. Indeed, the National Patriot would stand against anyone who opposed America as a Christianized utopian dream and would be against anyone who distinguished the differences between the right- and left-hand kingdoms.

Responding to Jack

What is the main thing that drives and controls Jack's thoughts, logic, and decisions regarding Christianity and his views about Jesus? As we have learned, Jack is unable to distinguish between the right- and the left-hand kingdoms. As a result, Jack has allowed characteristics of the left-hand kingdom to bleed into the realm of the church and the person/work of Jesus.

So, when we respond to Jack—and others like him—our main objective is to help clarify between the two kingdoms. By pointing out the different realms of the state and the church, we are helping Jack create two categories for him to process his views of Christianity and his understanding of Jesus. Frankly, this will likely be a rather radical concept for Jack, for he has long processed everything in the one category of a combined church-state.

Revealing the idea of the two kingdoms to Jack will not rip anything away from him. We are simply helping him add a distinction. We are not telling him that he cannot be patriotic and we are not telling him that he cannot be devoted to Jesus; rather we are showing him that we are citizens of both earth and heaven, two different kingdoms.

As is often the case when an idol is taken away, a person may get very defensive. Removing an idol can cause a great amount of insecurity and leave a person feeling vulnerable. With the Patriot, though, we are not taking anything away, but showing that this false christ emerges from a misunderstanding of the right- and left-hand kingdoms. Jack's passion for his country is directly tied to his spirituality. God and country have become one. As a way of example, we may gently expose Jack's misunderstanding by pointing out the tasks of those serving in the military.

> *Removing an idol can cause a great amount of insecurity and leave a person feeling vulnerable.*

In the military, soldiers are called to lay down their lives and pay the ultimate sacrifice to defend their county from threats. This action and service are dependent upon soldiers who are governed by laws that dictate proper order and distinguish right and wrong and hierarchy. This is how a good government works to protect its citizens from harm. This is something we can affirm for Jack. We, too, are thankful that God has ordained governments to execute law and order. We, too, are thankful for soldiers who lay down their lives for our freedom.

Then we can ask Jack to think of God's kingdom of heaven. Who does the act of sacrifice? We only see the real Jesus our Lord laying down his life as a ransom for many. He alone bleeds and dies on our behalf on the battlefield against sin, death, and the devil. His kingdom rests solely on His body and blood. What this means is that when we lay these two kingdoms side by side, we can then see the importance of distinguishing and valuing each of them for the gift that they are. We can, by God's grace, implore Jack to direct his passion for his country to civic duty and his passion for his Savior to faithfully receiving that which was won for him on Mount Calvary.

Some possible verses to consider in visiting with Jack over this distinction are 1 Peter 2:13–17; Titus 3:1; 1 Timothy 2:1–2; and Matthew 20:20–28.

Will the Real Jesus Please Stand Up?

Right before Jesus' crucifixion, when He was present before the Roman governor of Judea, Jesus said that His kingdom was not of this world (John 18:33–40). With these simple words, Jesus rejected any political goals within the left-hand kingdom before Pontius Pilate. Jesus clarified this further by stating that if He had political aspirations, His followers would be fighting for His freedom—which they were not. Truly, Jesus' kingdom is not of this world.

Although Jesus' kingdom is not of this world, His kingdom comes into the world. Consider for a moment the whole of Jesus' ministry. By sending Jesus into the world, the Father ripped open the heavens. The kingdom of God invaded the world as Jesus was born in a manger and, as our Savior, journeyed toward the cross (Matthew 1:18–23). God was doing something that He had not done before, but something that was promised long ago. God was sending His only Son to live a perfect life and then die on behalf of sinful mankind—accomplishing salvation for the entire world (John 3:16).

This means that Jesus' kingship in the right-hand kingdom is not derived from the left-hand kingdom or dependent on the world's affairs. It is completely foreign (or separate). Furthermore, this right-hand kingdom brings and gives forgiveness, regardless of which political party is in control and regardless of the condition of the state (i.e., government).

Jesus' right-hand kingdom is ruled by the power of the Gospel not the force of the sword. It seeks repentance and faith not legal punishment and civil justice. Therefore, as Christians, we give unto Caesar what is Caesar's and to God what is God's. We engage within the realm of the left-hand kingdom as American citizens, as citizens with the understanding that we are also citizens of heaven, who are blood-bought and baptized into Jesus.

Ideally, the altar and the flag, the state and the church, are two different realms in which we live. They both must be sharply distinguished, while also affirming that they do not contradict. They both find their origin, operation, and essence in the Lord. They work harmoniously, side by side. They are two separate kingdoms—two realms—but ultimately servants of the real Jesus Christ. (See Romans 13:1–2 where Paul states that governing authorities have been instituted by God.)

Let's discuss the **National Patriot**

1. What is the main presupposition of Jack that makes up the National Patriot?

Perhaps no better passage of Scripture shows the confusion of the two kingdoms than Matthew 20:20–28. Read these verses and consider the following questions.

2. What was the request by the mother of the sons of Zebedee? (See vv. 20–21.) Why did she ask what she did?

3. Did the mother and her two sons truly understand what they were asking by sitting at the right- and left-hand of Jesus? (See vv. 22–23.) What were they thinking when they asked?

4. How does Jesus contrast His kingdom of grace with the kingdom of power? (See vv. 24–28.)

5. As a way to summarize, how do these questions and the verses shed light on the National Patriot?

6. In the United States, it can be challenging to address the false christ, the Patriot. We have such national pride ingrained into our DNA. How can we lovingly teach about the true Jesus and challenge the false one?

SOCIAL JUSTICE *Warrior*

7

Meet Simon, the Liberation Activist

The sirens sounded. The dikes were breached. Water began to flow. Twelve-foot-tall waves of mighty water came pouring into the heart of the city at thirty to forty miles per hour for about five weeks. This mighty water showed no mercy; it destroyed houses, memories, and livelihoods. It was a level five catastrophe that evacuated twelve thousand people from their homes to nearby shelters.

In the weeks that followed, hundreds of people came to the aid of this traumatized city. Since the church I was serving was only three hours away, a group of men organized to go and help in the disaster relief. About six of us packed up our boots, hammers, overalls, and tool belts, and traveled to the center of the devastation.

When we arrived, we were assigned a house to work on that had been flooded. It had to be stripped down to the bare studs—the basic framework of the house.

"So, what organization are you here with?" Simon asked with a pleasant smile. Simon and I were partnered together to pull nails from the inside of the house after the drywall had been removed. He was in his late twenties, with a long beard, an East Coast accent, and glasses.

"I am a part of the Lutheran Church; the congregation I serve is due west of here about three hours," I responded.

There were a few moments of silence as we started to work side by side. Simon seemed to be gathering his thoughts. He pulled some more nails out of a beam of wood, paused, and said, "Wasn't the founder of the Lutherans, Martin Luther, alive at the same time as those other guys named John Calvin and John Wesley . . . and that one other theologian, I forget his name . . . hmm . . . is it, Zwingli?"

I was rather impressed Simon knew of these theologians' names. Nodding my head, I said, "Yes, Calvin and Zwingli lived about the same time as Luther; however, they were French and Swiss theologians, not German like Luther. And John Wesley was not around until about two hundred years after the Reformation."

After about an hour of small talk, Simon stepped away from the wall, leaned in a bit toward me, and said, "I don't mean you any offense, but I think these guys were limited in their understanding of things."

My face must have scrunched up because Simon reached out his hand as if to gesture he was not trying to hurt me or insult me. He continued, "What I'm saying is that these guys were restricted in their thinking and would not be able to deal with the social injustices that we have going on right now."

"What do you mean by that, Simon?" I asked.

Simon leaned in again toward me with a bit of enthusiasm, saying, "Well, they would not be able to speak to the social injustices we are experiencing, not because they were wrong ethically, but because they were wrong theologically."

At this point, it was obvious Simon was fairly well-read and articulate on the subject of theology and social injustice.

Since we had several more hours to pull nails, I said, "Tell me more."

At this point we returned to pulling nails out of the wood and eventually found a rhythm of pulling out nails and interjecting conversation between the motion and noise of our hammers. Simon seemed to pour his passion into his work as well as his words. He continued, "If Luther and Calvin were alive today, they would not be able to deal with the issues we are facing in our society—things like gender inequality, racism, poverty, homosexual bigotry, a women's right to choose, transgender rights, and global warming. They could not speak to these modern issues because they were wrong theologically."

I was confused at this point, and the conversation was cordial enough, so I replied by saying, "How were they wrong theologically?"

Wiping sweat away with the back of his hand, Simon continued, "Well, they failed to listen to the Bible with openness and they did not read the Bible through the eyes of the victim being oppressed—" A crash of drywall hitting the floor in another room interrupted Simon. He paused a moment and then continued, "They didn't get Jesus, what He was really about. They did not understand that He was about liberating people from unjust powerful systems; that He was about standing against the inhumanity of those who oppressed the poor and struggling. It is a sad irony that Jesus got crucified by these oppressive monsters—those Pharisees and Sadducees."

Meet our seventh false christ: the Social Justice Warrior. This false christ is a warrior who fights for victims—those who have been socially, economically, and politically oppressed. He is embraced for his exemplary fight for the deprived and outcast of society and revered simultaneously for his fighting against powerfully oppressive people and powerfully oppressive systems. Since this false christ died on the cross at the hands of oppressive religious leaders, he also is an excellent icon of comfort for those who are also underneath heavy-handed social, spiritual, economic, and political systems. Salvation from this false christ is not deliverance from the condemnation of sin, but rather it is liberation from unjust economic, political, spiritual, or social conditions.

Keep in mind that the Social Justice Warrior false christ is not the Savior who died for the sins of all people, for that would make all of humankind enemies of God; rather, in Simon's view, the Social Justice Warrior is an advocate for only a selected group of oppressed people, typically people whom Simon deems as victims. Therefore, Simon has rejected the real Jesus, the one crucified for *all* of sinful humanity, and instead created a false christ who is a social justice warrior advocating for only a portion of humanity. He has created a false christ who damns the privileged and fights for the disadvantaged.

"So, what if a person happens to believe the same way as these old theologians?" I said with a bit of pushback and curiosity.

Simon turned his eyes away from me, focusing on the nails in the wall. "It's like this, brother: if we do not recognize who is being oppressed, we can't recognize who is oppressing them. And if we can't recognize who the oppressor is, then we won't know who to challenge, for our task as the church is to challenge these oppressors. We need to challenge these persecutors and their systems that are sinning against the least of society."

WHAT IS LIBERATION THEOLOGY?

Liberation theology came forth in the twentieth-century in Latin American Roman Catholicism. It teaches that the Church must stand on the side of the poor and the needy and, if necessary, overcome any systems that contribute to impoverishment and oppression of people.

Liberation theology has a lot of similarities with the ideology of the nineteenth-century philosopher Karl Marx. Marx essentially divided society into two categories, the oppressor (i.e., the privileged) and the oppressed (i.e., the disadvantaged). The oppressor-oppressed distinction is used for analyzing a society and then allowing individuals to identify what must be changed through offensive action.

In the case of Simon, he most definitely subscribes to liberation theology and Marxist ideology as he uses the categories of "oppressor/privileged" and "oppressed/disadvantaged" within his views on Jesus and culture in general.

"So, if a person is not a victim, then they are either part of the problem or part of the solution? And if a person does not act, then they are a part of the problem?" I asked.

Simon then looked back at me, "Yes! To love God is to love those who are persecuted. To serve God is to work to bring about a change in the systems that abuse. To be Christian is to be like Jesus and to fight for a just society. A person can't simply stand on the sidelines; they must get alongside those being oppressed and make a difference, changing people's attitudes and hearts! Only when these abusive systems and tyrannical oppressors are overcome by Christian action is a victimized person made whole."

It was all starting to make sense to me, "Simon, am I right to assume that you are very involved in activism then?"

"Absolutely! That is why I am here helping these flood victims. The guy who bought this house was charged a boat load of interest and given no flood insurance. Now he is stuck with a messed up house and a six-figure debt that is payable to some fat businessman who exploited him!"

I could tell Simon was getting worked up by our conversation. His hammer was being swung a bit more forcefully as he continued, "Several weeks ago in St. Paul, some friends and I protested at the State Utility Commission at the Metro Square Building. We've been trying to stop the pipeline that runs from Clearbrook to the Twin Cities. Last month I was at the Capital and Loring Park fighting for same-sex couples, for their right to marry. The way I look at it, following Jesus is not about retracing Jesus' path, but re-creating His path in our twenty-first-century by fighting against the injustices of this world."

It is important to stop at this point and take note of three things.

First, the Social Justice Warrior is created in the mind of individuals like Simon when certain presuppositions are held. The primary presupposition behind this false christ is that society is divided into two categories: oppressor and oppressed. Jesus and His followers are then viewed as rescuers, liberators from whatever is placing the oppressed in bondage. This creates a false christ and a social-based form of Christianity—a pseudo-Christianity.

DEEDS, NOT CREEDS?

"PREACH THE GOSPEL AT ALL TIMES. USE WORDS IF NECESSARY."

You have probably heard the previous quote that has been attributed to St. Francis of Assisi. This quote has been frequently used in many circles, as we are encouraged to focus on deeds, not creeds. The surprising thing, though, is that this quote is not literally from St. Francis.

Even though the popular quote is not directly from Francis, only derived, it is still simply wrong. For example, we need to keep in mind that there is a large difference between the Great Commandment (Matthew 22:36–40) and the Great Commission (Matthew 28:16–20). Too often Christians are confusing the Great Commission with the Great Commandment.

- The Great Commandment is about serving neighbors through loving works.
- The Great Commission is about making disciples through the Word and Sacraments.
- The Great Commandment consists of good deeds we do for our neighbor.
- The Great Commission consists of what God did for the world by sending His only Son.

What does this mean for the quote above? It means that our deeds do not atone for sin; they are simply deeds that are a worshipful response to Jesus' atonement for us. Our deeds are a response to the message of the Gospel; our deeds are not the Gospel itself. Our deeds do not bring about salvation but only love toward our neighbor, whereas the Good News of the Gospel is that which creates, sustains, and delivers forgiveness, life, and salvation.

Second, what Simon is advocating for is not to feed the hungry, give drink to the thirsty, clothe the naked, give shelter to the homeless, visit the sick, protect transgender persons from violence, and give proper burials for the dead; rather, he is seeking to identify who is responsible for the hunger, thirst, nakedness, homelessness, sickness, assaults, and death, and then stand up against the responsible parties. For only when liberation from oppression and injustice occurs—according to Simon—is there true wholeness, that is to say, salvation.

Third, for liberation to effectively happen in a social justice situation, what is needed are deeds, not creeds. In other words, it is not merely enough to explain what is going on. Instead, the task of people who follow the Social Justice Warrior is to change society with movements, protests, marches, picketing, sit-ins, petition drives, etc. This means that the church and the Christian faith are a means for bringing about deliverance, typically through deeds and not creeds. Theologians and Christians are to be practitioners.

Responding to Simon

What is the main thing that drives and controls Simon's thoughts, logic, and decisions regarding Christianity and his views about Jesus? As we have learned, Simon classifies everyone into the categories of oppressor and oppressed. This results in Simon trying to rescue and fight against the oppressors to save the oppressed.

Therefore, when we respond to Simon—and others like him—we must certainly commend him for his compassion for the poor and downtrodden. However, we cannot ignore the fact that by embracing an oppressor-oppressed view of humanity, he has created a false christ who focuses on liberating only a portion of the population. By placing people into the categories of oppressor and oppressed, Simon has positioned the oppressors outside of salvation—perhaps unintentionally, but that is the inevitable outcome. Therefore, this problem is what needs to be shown to Simon. He needs to be shown that Christianity does not divide humanity into the categories of oppressor and oppressed; rather, there are only sinners who have sinned against the Lord in thought, word, and deed and the Lord Jesus Christ.

More specifically, when we talk to Simon, we must make sure to affirm that people are indeed oppressed by evil institutions and corrupt systems in the world; however, being oppressed does not make a person any less in need of the Lord's forgiveness, life, and salvation. Being a victim—as painful as that is—does not make one automatically righteous, for Romans 3:10–12 says, "None is righteous, no, not one; no one understands; no one seeks for God. All have turned aside; together they have become worthless; no one does good, not even one." Indeed, Christianity classifies all humanity within the category of "sinner" and it understands mankind's sin as the "main" problem. This means that the real Jesus confronts *both* the oppressor and the oppressed as sinners. This is the most certain truth that Simon must come to understand: the real Jesus confronts all sinful humanity by calling everyone to repentance—the oppressors and the oppressed. The real Jesus confronts all sinful humanity at the cross of Calvary, where He is made to be sin so that in Him all people might become the righteousness of God (2 Corinthians 5:20).

Will the Real Jesus Please Stand Up?

The real Jesus was not a social justice warrior who ultimately was martyred on the cross while fighting against his oppressors. He was not dragged as a victim to the cross. He chose to go right toward death, not to merely die a physical death but to sacrificially die for sin (John 10:18). Yes, Jesus chose the crown of thorns. He chose the hammer and nails. He knowingly went into the darkness. He chose the cross. He drank the cup of wrath, He dragged and pulled the weight of sin—your sin and mine—into the anti-glorious place, called Golgotha, where sin was put to death and defeated.

While the real Jesus undeniably extended compassion to the poor, sick, and downtrodden, certainly healing many of them, we must recognize that Jesus' solution to the less fortunate was not to topple the Romans, Pharisees, and Sadducees. Jesus' solution to society's ills was for these individuals to be brought to repentance through the Law and to be given faith in Him by the Gospel. To put it another way, salvation is not found in the liberation of people from an oppressive system; it is found in people's liberation from the condemnation of their sin through the proclamation of the Gospel and the administration of the Sacraments. (See Romans 6:18 and 8:1 where Paul speaks of the impact of the Gospel—freedom from sin's condemnation.)

Although there are times when peaceful petitions and marches are necessary to raise awareness about certain abuses in culture, Jesus Christ's Church cannot forget that her main focus is proclaiming the Word of God, baptizing, teaching, communing, and burying in the name of Jesus. These are the Church's priorities. Jesus is not a warrior positioned against only certain segments of culture, but rather, He is the one who came to earth to be the Savior of all sinners—those who are oppressed and those who oppress others (Romans 3:23–24). The goal is not to topple political, economic, and religious systems, but for *everyone's* sinful hearts to be toppled—for *all* people to be brought to repentance and given faith in Jesus, for it is only Jesus who forgives the oppressive sinful heart within us all. (See Romans 6:6.)

Let's discuss the **Social Justice Warrior**

1. What are the main presuppositions of Simon that make up the Social Justice Warrior?

Jesus Christ did not go to the cross to die for victims; He went to the cross to die for sinners who sinned against God in thought, word, and deed. Furthermore, even though He could have called down twelve legions of angels—countless angels—to stop the actions of the ruthless Romans and sly religious leaders, He chose the cross instead. Read Isaiah 52:13–53:12 and Matthew 26:47–54, and then consider the following questions.

2. Applying the oppressed/oppressor construct to the verses in Isaiah, who is the oppressor and who is the oppressed? What are the implications of Isaiah 53 upon the Social Justice Warrior false christ?

3. In considering the verses in Matthew's Gospel, a great crowd with swords and clubs approached Jesus. This said, who were the oppressors and who was the oppressed? Who had the upper hand? Why did Jesus do what He did?

4. Did Jesus have any other choice but to be the suffering servant (i.e., the ultimate oppressed one suffering for the sins of the world); did Jesus have the ability to usurp the powerful systems that brought about His crucifixion and death on a cross? How would someone like Simon respond to the real Jesus Christ?

5. Consider John 10:17–18 and Mark 10:45. What was the mission of Jesus Christ? How was His mission different from a mission to topple oppressive political, economic, and religious systems?

6. Is there a time and place to work for change against abusive and oppressive systems? If so, consider what we learned about the left-hand kingdom in chapter 6.

7. As we consider the Social Justice Warrior, how do we take what we have just learned and challenge the worldview of that false christ?

The Moral Example

8

Meet Ruby, the Moralist

When I was called to a previous church, it was a part of my pastoral duties to lead a chapel service for a women's group that met at least once a month—if not more. This women's group consisted of a dozen ladies from a local assisted living community, as well as another fifteen women from my church. The interesting dynamic to this group was that many had various denominational backgrounds. Therefore, it was not uncommon for some theological tension to develop between my chapel sermons and the women who listened to the sermon.

One Wednesday morning, after the chapel service had ended at the assisted living community center, I pushed the moveable pulpit back to its spot because the room we were in functioned as a chapel and also a dining room. After I returned the moveable pulpit to its storage location, Ruby came up to me and said, "But why not go on Pastor? We get that Jesus died for our sins; we've all heard that. So, let's go on and focus on how Jesus lived as a source of inspiration! We need to live a life of obedience, a life modeling the life of Jesus." Ruby was not a member of my local parish but frequented our Sunday morning church services. Other than being loosely acquainted with the church I served, Ruby was very involved in this assisted living group. As we can hear from her suggestion above, she was one of those women who often struggled with my sermons. In fact, it had become a common occurrence for her to visit with me after my monthly assisted living chapel service with questions and concerns.

"Ruby, what do you mean when you say, 'I should go on?'" I asked. In talking with people who disagree with my teaching, I always try my best not to sound too defensive. To be honest, though, it's not always easy!

Ruby sighed, "Pastor, what I mean is that you are not giving us enough practical examples so we can be like Christ. You are good at talking about justification by faith; however, you need to move on to Christian living. We are not hearing the full Gospel."

My body language must have betrayed just how startled I was. In all honesty, I was a bit offended, too, because I had clearly proclaimed the full Gospel in the sermon. Thus, I quickly inquired back, "What do you mean you are not hearing the *full* Gospel?"

Instead of backing down, Ruby met my response with an elevated pitch and a slight strain of her vocal chords, "We are new creations in Jesus, which means we have divine responsibilities. These divine responsibilities mean that we *must* follow Jesus as our example, living by every Word of God. We *must* love the Lord with all our heart. We *must* choose this day whom we will serve. You have told us about forgiveness, but that is not the full Gospel, you *must* go on to God's Law and Jesus' patterns so we can respond to these divine responsibilities set before us. We *must* commit ourselves to acts of determined consecration."

Lowering my voice a bit, I said, "With all due respect, Ruby, didn't I preach the Law and the Gospel this morning in the chapel service?"

"Well, yes, you did, but the Law was too negative, and you seem to be too hard on us women because when you preached the Law, you made it sound like we can't fulfill the Law. As far as the Gospel, well, the Gospel was incomplete too. You told us about Jesus' death on the cross, but you did not teach us completely about Jesus' obedient life. How are we to know what sin to throw off and how to walk in obedience unless we can model our lives after Jesus?"

Without any further ado, meet our eighth false christ: the Moral Example. This false christ is exactly what he says he is: a moral example which people are to emulate and copy. This false christ grudgingly acknowledges the suffering, crucifixion, and death of the real Jesus at Mount Calvary, but, like the Therapist false christ of chapter 4, the Moral Example attempts to move people away from what the real Jesus accomplished at Mount Calvary toward what mankind should do to either obtain or sustain righteousness by following his example. Simply stated, the Moral Example takes the focus away from what the real Jesus did and puts it upon what the Christian must do for righteousness, which inadvertently undercuts everything accomplished at Mount Calvary. The real Jesus' suffering and death, which happened at Mount Calvary to accomplish salvation, are only useful for a person's conversion at some point in the past, which results in the cross being spoken of as a past event. To this false christ, what matters at the present time is not a bleeding-dying-forgiving-savior, but rather a moral example Christians must exemplify for moralistic living—living in a way that somehow obtains or sustains salvation.

Scripture does say that Jesus is an example for us to follow (see 1 Peter 2:21); however He is not *exclusively* an example. Furthermore, Jesus is an example for us to follow, but not at the expense of denying, conditioning, or diminishing what happened at Mount Calvary. We do not follow the real Jesus as an example in order to earn or sustain salvation, but rather, we look to Jesus' example to know love as stated in 1 John 3:16: "By this we know love, that he laid down his life for us, and we ought to lay down our lives for the brothers." Furthermore, 1 Peter 2:21 talks specifically about following in the footsteps of Jesus' cross—that we are to bear our crosses of suffering in this life. The Moral Example, though, tells us that he has done his best and now we must do the rest.

> The Moral Example, though, tells us that he has done his best and now we must do the rest.

There are several rather large presuppositions at work in individuals like Ruby that lead them to construct the false christ known as the Moral Example. Indeed, like the other false christs we have examined so far, Ruby has several unique ideas about Christianity—a set of presuppositions that are very definable.

The first presupposition is that Ruby does not fully understand original sin and its "continued" implications for Christians. Ruby likely understands that sin originated from the fall when Adam and Eve disobeyed God in the Garden of Eden. Their sin resulted in the sin of all mankind; we are all born with the fear of God. However, Ruby would discontinue original sin "after" conversion; she limits original sin to before she became a believer only.

Let us examine Ruby's first presupposition a bit more thoroughly.

JUSTIFICATION

Imagine for a moment standing before a judge. You are guilty. The evidence has been presented and jail awaits you—possibly even the death penalty. The judge then delivers the verdict, "Not guilty." People in the courtroom erupt in anger saying, "How is this so?!" The judge calls for order in the court, slams his gavel down, and says, "The defendant is justified—he is righteous! He is not guilty and is free to go!"

Considering this scenario, even though you are guilty, the judge has declared you righteous in the eyes of the law and he has the final say. Because of the judge's declaration, it is as if you have never committed a crime—you really are not guilty. This is what it means to be justified.

Regarding Christianity, we are justified for the sake of Jesus Christ. In the eyes of the Father, the reality is that we are not guilty, but completely righteous; it is as if we have never sinned. Keep in mind, though, that we cannot be justified before God by our own strength, merit, or works. Rather, this justification is delivered to us personally through the Word and Sacraments and received through faith.

It is true that when a person is converted (i.e., baptized/becomes a Christian) that the "guilt" and "condemnation" of original sin are removed; that is to say, the person is justified. However, it is important to note that sin itself, with its desires, remains after conversion in the life of the Christian. (See Romans 7:7–25 as an example of what the life of a Christian looks like.) Therefore, since Ruby discontinues original sin and its ongoing desires at conversion, she essentially has no place for ongoing justification—for Ruby, justification is confined only to the point of conversion. Keep in mind that she does not reject justification, but rather, holds to justification as something that is placed in her past. For Ruby, justification and Baptism happened when she was converted; they are not present realities. It is the same with original sin. She *was* a sinner, and she *was* saved—both past tenses. She would not say, "I *am* baptized, and I *am* saved," but would say, "I *was* baptized, and I *was* saved." As a result of these presuppositions, the real Jesus is important for Ruby's past conversion of making her a Christian, but not for her ongoing daily life; therefore, she acknowledges the real Jesus as a part of her past justification, but then inadvertently turns her back on the real Jesus toward the Moral Example for her daily living.

A HIGH VIEW OF MANKIND LEADS TO A LOW VIEW OF JESUS

When we fail to clearly see or underestimate the depravity of mankind, the person of Jesus suffers. What kind of Savior is needed if mankind is only hindered or struggling? If mankind is viewed as basically good with some bad habits, then Jesus becomes a helper, or worse, a life coach or a mere example. Conversely, when we assess mankind in light of the Scriptures, we see that mankind's nature is always much darker than we usually believe it to be. True, mankind is created in the image of God; however, the fall of mankind in Genesis 3 marred the image, making man not "mostly dead" in sin, but "dead-dead" in sin. A mere life coach, moral example, and helper are not sufficient with this view of man. Rather an all-powerful, all-knowing, sufficient savior is needed to deliver mankind from their sin and death.

Second, by diminishing original sin and its effects, Ruby thinks of sin as a series of separate naughty events, avoidable with some effort in following the Moral Example. Heartbreakingly, Ruby has downplayed the seriousness of sin because she not only underestimates the depravity of mankind but has resorted to embracing an overinflated view of mankind's abilities. On the one hand, this means Ruby understands sin as either silly choices or temporary struggles that can be ultimately avoided with acts of determination with the help of the Moral Example. On the other hand, this means Ruby believes that if a person is struggling with sin, they are either not trying hard enough or they have forgotten to look upon the Moral Example for guidance in their Christian obedience. In summary of Ruby's second presupposition, sin is not a condition of the heart, but only external actions that can be monitored, curbed, controlled, and managed.

Third, by underestimating the problem of ongoing sin and inadvertently inflating the abilities of the Christian, Ruby mistakenly develops a low view

WHAT DOES PERFECT OBEDIENCE LOOK LIKE?

It is easy to believe that a person is obedient to the Law of God when they do not steal their neighbor's speed boat or sleep with their neighbor's wife or murder their neighbor. However, God's Law does not merely call for external perfection. Jesus teaches us in Matthew 5 that if we lust in our hearts toward our neighbor's wife or hate our neighbor in our heart, we have committed adultery and murder (vv. 21–30). Indeed, a drunk may give up his drinking, a womanizer may stop his fornication, and a gossip may tame his tongue . . . and all still go to hell. In Matthew 5:48, Jesus calls us to be perfect as His heavenly Father is perfect. This means complete perfection—in that which is external and that which is internal. And because we cannot truly fear, love, and trust God, and because we cannot love our neighbors as ourselves, we need the real Jesus to forgive us of our sins. We need to be created anew daily—strengthened in faith toward God and strengthened in love toward our neighbor.

of God's Law (e.g., God's Law as expressed in the Ten Commandments). It would seem that someone like Ruby has a great deal of respect for God's Law; however, this could not be further from the truth. And here's why: a high view of the Law demolishes all ideas that we can successfully live a perfect upright moral life, whereas a low view of the Law causes us to believe that the upright moral life is attainable by our own spiritual powers. For Ruby, the Law must not be too severe, but rather, it must function in a way that it can be within our reach and ability to fulfill. This means Ruby will not embrace the real Jesus, who calls for 100 percent perfect obedience in thought, word, and deed (Matthew 5:48) and who says, "Unless your righteousness exceeds that of the scribes and Pharisees, you will never enter the kingdom of heaven" (Matthew 5:20). Rather, Ruby will embrace a false christ who lowers the bar of God's Law just enough for mankind to jump over it and fulfill it. The Law must be low enough so it can be reachable. The Law must be stripped of its stern demands of perfect holiness and changed into mere guidelines that can be implemented. This is a law that says "you can do it!"

THE CIVIL WAR WITHIN

The harsh reality is that we have this sinful old nature until the day we die. As our Lutheran Fathers used to say, we carry the old Adam around our necks from birth to death. Yes, even we Christians have this sinful nature, for we are simultaneously sinners and saints (sinners by birth; saints by our baptismal rebirth). This means we are at war with ourselves—an inner civil war that causes us to struggle between the old Adam and the new life we have in Jesus. Indeed, from the time we are joined to Jesus in Baptism until the day we die, we will always be in conflict with ourselves. The civil war within will never end, which means we will always need the real Jesus. It means we will always be people of prayer, praying against our sinful nature. It means we will always seek the Lord's Supper because we are always sinning in thought, word, and deed. We are sin-sick, which means we will always need Jesus and the medicine of the forgiveness of sins.

With this stated, we must pause to note that the Moral Example never teaches and preaches a law that is unachievable or impossible to fulfill (i.e., the biblical Law of the Bible that calls for perfect obedience of actions and thoughts). The Moral Example never demands "complete" perfection of a person's heart but will offer achievable suggestions, guidelines, and principles for words, deeds, and attitudes. Like the Mascot in chapter 1, this false christ is also lawless, for he rejects the real Law of the Bible, but does so by watering it down.

There was an awkward silence after Ruby's comments. I contemplated whether I should respond more or if this conversation was one of those that should be left for another time. Ultimately, I found myself engaging in the conversation once again, "Ruby, you said that the Gospel was incomplete. Are you saying that Jesus' death and resurrection were incomplete?"

"Of course not! What I am saying is that you are focusing too much on justification by faith. You are preaching too much about grace. You need to move on to the Christian life and focus more on what we Christians are to do. If you don't tell us how to be like Christ, you will be giving the impression that people have a license to sin or you will be giving false assurance!" Ruby responded.

As we have already heard, Ruby downplays original sin in the life of the Christian, softens the seriousness of sin, and also embraces a weakened form of God's Law. In her comments above, we can further learn about her fourth presupposition: she believes lawlessness springs forth from too much grace. Somewhere in her thinking, she has rationalized that if the Gospel is presented as "too free or too unconditional" that the result will be lax morality, loose living, and lawlessness. It is as if she believes that the freeing message of the Gospel produces, encourages, and grants people a license to sin. Because of this rationalization, she seems to want to strap, hold, and attach restrictions to the Gospel so she might

According to Ruby, a Jesus that forgives unconditionally is a promoter of sin.

DO CHRISTIANS DO GOOD WORKS?

In John 15:1–6, we read the parable of the Vine and the branches: "I am the true vine, and my Father is the vinedresser. Every branch in me that does not bear fruit He takes away, and every branch that does bear fruit He prunes, that it may bear more fruit. Already you are clean because of the word that I have spoken to you. Abide in Me, and I in you. As the branch cannot bear fruit by itself, unless it abides in the vine, neither can you, unless you abide in Me. I am the vine; you are the branches. Whoever abides in Me and I in him, he it is that bears much fruit, for apart from Me you can do nothing. If anyone does not abide in Me he is thrown away like a branch and withers; and the branches are gathered, thrown into the fire, and burned."

In this parable, Jesus is the Vine and believers are the branches. It is certainly obvious from this parable that Jesus deserves all the credit in declaring us clean and connecting us to Him. As dead helpless branches, we have been forgiven and grafted into the true living vine by the power of the Lord's Word and promise pronounced upon us. Once connected to Jesus, though, notice that our calling is not for us to work toward becoming more connected or more grafted into Jesus, but to abide and remain. Thus, we can confidently know that we have been cleansed and are fully and completely grafted into the Vine because of Jesus.

Being completely grafted into the Vine also means that it is not up to the branch to try and produce fruit (that is, good works) as a bargaining tool for continuing connection to the vine or as a payment for the status of being declared clean. Rather, the Vine (Jesus) is the source of all our good works (fruit) that the forgiven Christian gets to bear. The implications of this reality are clear. The good works we do have no power to make us more clean or more connected to the Vine. They are simply the result—not the cause—of us being connected to Jesus by the Word and faith.

As branches, we are not the source of good works. The Vine is. What this means is that we don't produce good works, but bear good works as Ephesians 2:10 tells us, "We are his workmanship, created in Jesus for good works, which God prepared beforehand, that we should walk in them." Indeed, God prepares good works for us. We don't do good works to become Christians—we do them because we are already Christians. God not only prepares good works but also gives us the opportunity to serve our neighbor with them in our callings. Our daily tasks are opportunities God gives us to bear fruit.

prevent or limit lawlessness. According to Ruby, a Jesus that forgives unconditionally is a promoter of sin. Like the argument presented by the Apostle Paul in Romans 6:1–2, Ruby fears that a person will hear the Gospel and abuse it by ignoring God's will and intentionally sinning, knowing that God will forgive. She fears that the Gospel will allow a person to continue in sin in order that grace may abound.

Everyone's sinful nature loves the weakened law and conditioned gospel the Moral Example proclaims. Why? Because a weakened law and a conditioned gospel mean that our sinful nature is not confronted with the Law unto repentance and not swallowed up by the Gospel through faith. Weakened law does not bring us to the point of understanding that we are poor miserable sinners in our thoughts, words, and deeds. A conditioned gospel conditions forgiveness, life, and salvation upon some man-made prerequisite or codified response, thus making the Gospel about what both Jesus *and* mankind does. Rather, our sinful nature and desires are given plenty of room to play within a faulty spiritual system. And this is exactly what Ruby desires. Since

IS JESUS A PROMOTER OF SIN?

In Galatians 2:17, Paul says, "But if, in our endeavor to be justified in Jesus, we too were found to be sinners, is Jesus then a servant of sin? Certainly not!" In this verse, the apostle Paul shows us that it is not a fair conclusion to link lawlessness to the freeing message of the Gospel. To put it in another way, the proper effect of the Gospel of Jesus (i.e., justification by faith alone) does not grant a license to sin nor lead us to lawlessness. The Gospel is not and cannot be held responsible for lawlessness. For if lawlessness did come about by the preaching and teaching of the Gospel, then that would make Jesus Christ a promoter, supporter, and distributor of sin and rebellion! In other words, Paul is declaring, "God forbid this rationalization!" If lawlessness and a license to sin exist, then these perverted freedoms can be traced back to something else other than the Gospel of Jesus Christ, namely our sinful nature that takes advantage of and twists the Gospel of Grace.

she underestimates her own depravity (rejects the ongoing effects of original sin), she desires to be in the driver's seat of her spirituality. Her false christ is simply there to be an example she can follow when she wants, similar to a push-button navigation system. Indeed, when she successfully walks in the patterns and examples laid forth by the Moral Example, she can then congratulate herself that she has evidenced her faith through obedience.

There is a certain kind of relief for people when their sinful nature is not confronted by the full force of the Law and when they are allowed to participate with the Gospel (meaning, they have a part in accomplishing their salvation, even if it is only a small part). The reason why? The full force of the Law condemns—exposing sin, stopping self-justifications, and rendering a person dead in sins. Furthermore, an unconditional Gospel does not allow people any claim to salvation—it ascribes everything to the real Jesus and excludes their works, acts of determined consecration, as a merit for salvation. The full force of the Law and an unconditional Gospel destroy the sinful nature, they crucify the old Adam and raise the person anew into Jesus. The sinful old Adam cannot stand this, for the old Adam demands to be in control and desires to rule.

"Ruby, who am I giving false assurance to?" I asked, a bit confused. "Isn't that the purpose of preaching, to grant assurance in Jesus?"

Ruby bristled and said, "If you preach too much grace, you're going to make a bunch of lazy Christians who won't try their best for God.

WHY BOTH LAW AND GOSPEL ARE NEEDED

Both Law and Gospel are needed: the Law of Mt. Sinai in its full sternness and the Gospel of Mt. Calvary in its full sweetness. The reason why: the Law reveals sin; the Gospel absolves sin. Tragically though, Law without Gospel opens the door to legalism; Gospel without Law opens the door to lawlessness.

They won't walk according to the example of Jesus but will think that they are okay and then do whatever they want!"

Lastly, Ruby has a very big presupposition—a foundational idea—that dictates a completely different view of Jesus and the Christian faith. Because of her overinflated view of mankind and a diminishing or downplaying of original sin, she understands herself and other Christians to be in a neutral state where sin and righteousness are laid out as two equal choices. Therefore, if she and others hear too much grace, they may be led to become lazy and complacent with sin. At this point, this sounds very reasonable. She believes she is essentially free to sin or not to sin, which then leads her to want to keep her freedom in check. (See "The Myth of Free Will" in the Introduction.) This is why the Moral Example is so needed. The Moral Example demonstrates to Ruby what the best decision is, then she can choose righteousness and avoid sin; the Moral Example helps keep this freedom to sin or not sin in check. For Ruby, the real Jesus with His unconditional Gospel does not solve the problem of her freedom, but actually, makes things worse for her.

With this stated, we must pause again and ask ourselves a brief question: is the real Jesus needed to bind supposed freedom or is He needed to set free those who are bound? You see, when we go the way of Ruby's thinking, believing original sin is no longer a concern once

TO BE LIKE JESUS?

If a person has faith in Jesus, they are conformed to Jesus! Conformity does not happen by mankind trying to imitate Jesus by trying to be super pious, for this goes by the way of mankind's efforts and doings. Rather, conformity to Jesus happens by faith, when we receive Jesus and His gifts. The Holy Spirit, through the Word and Sacraments, mortifies our sinful nature and regenerates us, making us to be Christlike. To be like Jesus is a work of the Spirit through the Word and Sacraments, not a work of man.

we are converted to Christianity, then a false moralistic christ is needed to tighten up the reigns of freedom; however, if we rightly see mankind as bound in sin, then a bleeding-dying-rising Savior is needed to free the sinner who is bound. In other words, we Christians do not need some sort of moral example set before us who we can supposedly emulate through our own strength. We cannot be the real Jesus; we are not the real Jesus. Rather, we need the stern force of the Law to reveal just how ensnared we are to the ongoing effects of original sin. Once our sin is revealed, we do not need to compensate for our sin by trying to dig our way out of it, for virtue is not the opposite of sin. We need the bleeding-dying-rising Savior—the real Jesus—to forgive, free, and renew us. We need the Holy Spirit to create a clean heart in us and renew a right spirit within us so we may walk by faith in the Son of God who gave Himself for us.

Tragically, Ruby's assumption that she is basically free from the effects of original sin cause her to reject the real Jesus and exchange him for the Moral Example, thus living by her own perceived abilities.

WHAT DOES IT MEAN TO COOPERATE?

In the Lutheran Confessions, we come across the word *cooperation* in regard to living out the Christian life. Considering this word, the Solid Declaration (part II) of the Formula of Concord (in the Lutheran Book of Concord) helps us understand that we do not cooperate alongside the Holy Spirit in the way two horses draw a wagon together. In other words, after the Holy Spirit has begun His work of rebirth in us—through the Word and Holy Sacraments—we do not cooperate with Him as if He exerts 50 percent and we do the remaining 50 percent. Rather, it is necessary to understand that we cooperate when we are made instruments and tools in conversion. Indeed, as instruments and tools of God the Holy Spirit, we only do good to the extent that He rules, leads, and guides us. If He would withdraw His gracious hand—if we ceased to be direct objects of His actions to and through us—we could not for one moment remain in the faith, let alone bear good fruit.

Responding to Ruby

What is the main thing that drives and controls Ruby's thoughts, logic, and decisions regarding Christianity and her views about Jesus? As we have learned, Ruby is a rather complex person who has several presuppositions at work. Out of all of these presuppositions, the main one at work in Ruby is her failure to see the continued implications of original sin in the life of the Christian.

When we respond to Ruby—and others like her—our main goal is to help her see a more realistic and biblical view of the life of the Christian. Since Ruby views her Christian life as basically good with some bad habits, she really sees no ongoing need for the real Jesus and exchanges Him for the Moral Example. Sadly, Ruby thinks she has no need for the real Jesus in her Christian life, for He was only needed to convert her into a Christian. Now, she believes she is doing quite all right with the Moral Example.

But how will we help Ruby come to a more realistic and biblical view of the life of the Christian? Though it will immediately reveal Ruby's presuppositions and may lead to a heated controversy, a key passage to read is Romans 7:7–25. We could start by saying, "Ruby, I've heard it said before that the life of the Christian is best explained in Romans 7 where Paul speaks as a believer struggling with the war against sin." After saying this, we need to be prepared for Ruby to get rather defensive. Ruby will most likely respond by saying that Romans 7 is not speaking about Paul as a Christian but about Paul before being a Christian. To this, we can point out that in verses 7–23 that the apostle Paul switches to the present tense. In other words, the apostle Paul is not speaking in the past tense as in the previous verses. He switches in verses 7–23 to describe his present life as a Christian. The apostle Paul says in verses 15 and 19, "For I do not do what I want, but the very thing I hate. . . . For I have the desire to do what is right, but not the ability to carry it out." We can accentuate that this great man who furthered the Kingdom of God is in fact confessing a daily struggle with sin.

Keep in mind that by going to Romans 7, we are doing so to help Ruby see the civil war present in the life of every Christian, which will hopefully result in her recognizing that she needs more than the Moral Example. Even though she will try to rationalize away this section of Scripture—saying again that Paul was talking about himself before becoming a Christian—Ruby will still need to contend with other passages in Scripture. For example, 1 John 1:8 says, "If we say that we have no sin, we deceive ourselves, and the truth is not in us." It is very difficult to dethrone the Moral Example, for followers have built up years of their own righteous works to convince themselves they are safe from sin. We need to point out that they have indeed built walls, but those walls are in fact caging them in with their own sin. As painful as it may be, we need to be willing to confess our own sins and gently point out theirs so as to crumble their defense and make way for proclamation of the real Jesus.

We pray that Ruby hears God's Law and Gospel and comes to the conclusion that the only one to save her—even as a Christian—from this body of death is the real Jesus.

Will the Real Jesus Please Stand Up?

The Moral Example is a false christ who is created when original sin and its effects are diminished or not understood as the Bible teaches it. As a result of tragic presuppositions, this false christ promotes a watered-down version of the Law with absolutely no Gospel—or, at best, a conditioned Gospel, which is still not the Gospel. Sadly, even when a watered-down law is presented without the Gospel, not only is a person distorting the real Jesus, but they are also essentially making things worse, not better. You see, the Law without Gospel leads only to two options: pride or despair. When Law is preached without the

Gospel, it leads the hearer to the realization that they cannot follow it, so they reason in their mind that they might as well quit trying to be a Christian and become a pagan. They reason in their mind that it is better to live as a pagan and be condemned than to try and be a Christian and be condemned as well. This is the despair of a soul who realizes they cannot keep up appearances. On the other hand, instead of resorting to despair, others increase their determination to model Jesus, thinking they can fix the problem of sin by simply modeling Jesus' life. In doing so, however, they are simply resorting to pride in the areas in which they feel they are excelling. Alas, both of these options, despair and pride, lead us away from the real Jesus.

Sin is not canceled out by living lawfully. And Christian hope is not found in a pool of despair. We do not answer mankind's bondage-to-sin-problem with the solution of more weakened law from the Moral Example, and we do not answer it properly by leaving a person in condemning despair. Keep in mind that the Law does reveal sin, but it does not absolve it. (See Romans 7:7–12 where Paul explains that he would not know sin if it wasn't for the Law.) The Law does show what godly living looks like but it cannot motivate it, as we know from Galatians 3:21b, "For if a law had been given that could give life, then righteousness would indeed be by the law." That belongs to the blessed and divine Gospel! The Gospel absolves. The Gospel forgives. The Gospel justifies. The Gospel sanctifies. This proper distinction of Law and Gospel—Law to reveal sin and Gospel to forgive sin—is only found in the real Jesus, not the pseudo-moralistic false christ named the Moral Example.

Let's discuss the *Moral Example*

1. What are the main presuppositions of Ruby that allow her to embrace and sponsor the Moral Example?

Perhaps no better portion of Scripture captures the life of a Christian than Romans 7, where we read about the struggle between the new man created at Baptism and the old Adam that remains. They are at constant war.

Consider the following questions on Romans 7 and how the apostle Paul speaks about himself and the person of Jesus.

2. Read Romans 7:14–23. Is the apostle Paul speaking about himself in the past tense or present tense? What is the significance of knowing this difference?

3. According to these verses, does the struggle against sin continue after conversion and Baptism?

4. Does the apostle Paul see his sin as avoidable? Does he have power to overcome sin by his strength?

5. Through the Law (7:7), Paul's sin is revealed to him. Furthermore, Paul acknowledges that the good that he wants to do, he does not do. And the evil that he despises, he keeps on doing. All of this said, he cries out, "Wretched man that I am! Who will deliver me from this body of death?" What kind of action does Paul cry out for? What doesn't he cry out for? Why is this significant regarding this chapter's false christ?

6. Read Romans 7:25-8:1. Who rescues Paul and what is done for him?

7. As a way to summarize, how do these questions and the verses in Romans help us better understand the Moral Example?

8. When you cross paths with this false christ, how can or do you respond?

Meet Walter, the Legalist

It was about 74 degrees out with a slight breeze. Laughter and pleasant conversation floated on the afternoon breeze. The smell of hamburgers cooking on the grill also filled my nostrils. This was my church's annual potluck in the park.

Each year on the second Sunday of July, my church family had a mid-summer fellowship gathering. We gathered in the morning around 10:00 for the service and communion. After the service, everyone went home for several hours and then drove to the city park around 2:00 p.m. to eat food, visit, watch kids play on the playground, and participate in various games such as horseshoes, lawn darts, and bocce ball.

This get-together was typically well attended. Furthermore, since it occurred in the lazy days of summer, the potluck reflected the easy-going atmosphere. No talk of the church budget or the struggles with Sunday School. Just good ole fashioned Midwest fellowship. Everything seemed to be going fine that afternoon, at least until Walter showed up.

Walter was a semi-retired businessman in town. He had a big smile and always had a joke to share. He was one of those guys who people liked to be around—he filled in those awkward group silences with quick-witted comments and typically had his arm jovially around someone's neck while talking with a loud vibrato voice.

WILL THE REAL JESUS PLEASE STAND UP?

This day, however, Walter had a completely different disposition. His lips were in a snarl, and his jaw was tightened, the tension clearly visible on his face. He walked right up to me when I was getting a refill of my lemonade and said in a harsh whisper, "You won't believe what I saw. I almost can't bring myself to talk about it."

Not knowing if he was upset with me or something else, I forced a smile through my anxiety and said, "How about we take a walk."

With my lemonade in hand, we began to walk. About six steps away from the lemonade cooler, Walter stopped, turned to me, and shook his head in disgust, "It's Ted!"

Thoughts raced through my mind. Did Ted die? Was there an accident?

Raising his voice, Walter said, "It's worse than you think, Pastor. I just minded my own business walking in the alley on my way to this here potluck. And lo and behold I happened to look off to my right, and there is Ted finishing mowing his lawn and . . . a cold one. Yes, he was drinking a beer."

I was having a tough time connecting the dots at this point. Thinking Ted had died, I was relieved he was alive. With a sigh of relief, I said, "Wow, for a moment there I thought that something serious had happened to Ted."

A red flush crept up Walter's neck and face. He was clearly upset by my apparent lack of concern. "But it *is* serious Pastor! He was drinking, and I saw him. Others probably saw him too. What do you think his neighbors think of him and our church? After all, he is our Chairman."

"Ted was drunk and making a scene? If he was, then this is clearly contrary to everything that we teach and are about as a church," I responded.

Walter stuttered, "Well, no, I do not think he was drunk, but that is beside the point. He's our Chairman. Any Christian—especially a leader—should never appear to endorse alcohol. The idea that we expect Jesus to smile along with us as we drink in moderation, knowing that other people are watching us and potentially copying us, is reprehensible! Let me ask you, Pastor, what does this teach people about what it means to be a Christian? What does it teach our youth? If anyone saw Ted drinking, they could conclude that there is no harm in drinking and that it is an acceptable thing for Christians, so if they are at a party they will get drunk because they saw Ted drinking, and then they begin the downward spiral with drugs, cigarettes, porn, and everything else in the same category. We can't justify this! You and I know Jesus would not approve of Christians drinking. Ted needs to stop. He is not acting the way a Christian should act; he should know better."

Walter has introduced us to our ninth false christ: the New Moses. This false christ is a lawgiver like Moses; however, this false christ is about giving new laws, developed according to his followers' desires. This means the message of the New Moses will change, depending on what his followers deem right and wrong. Furthermore, with this false christ, there is no Gospel, just new obscure laws used for legalistic salvation and spiritual abuse.

To understand Walter's presuppositions, it is best to examine the Gospel of Mark. In Mark 7:1–13, we read about first-century Pharisees who followed certain man-made traditions that were not in the Old Testament Scriptures. They elevated these man-made traditions to the status of God's Law, as if God prescribed them Himself, when He actually did not. To make things even worse, the Pharisees enforced these man-made traditions upon the people as if they were God's binding Word, which resulted in people following the traditions of man rather than the Word of God. People were doubly damned: bound in man-made traditions without God's real Word. When we exchange God's Word for the word of man, we not only damn people by our man-made traditions but we also withhold God's Word of forgiveness—doubly damning people. This was also the case with Walter. Several man-made traditions stemmed from his spiritual upbringing, which led him to create new laws that supposedly came from Jesus, and it was these man-made standards he used to judge people like Ted.

Every group of people has their own traditions and practices; they have their own ways of doing things. Every group of people has certain personalities, moods, and outlooks too. Their traditions and practices are formed over time and become embedded within specific cultures. For example, Minnesota Norwegians love dried cod soaked in lye, which is called lutefisk, while Manitoban Canadians like French fries covered with gravy, and Californians cannot get enough of In-N-Out Burgers. The point being, the personality, mood, and outlook—what is inherent to the culture—shapes and forms traditions and practices. These traditions and practices can become very powerful forces indeed. They are repeated and solidified from generation to generation. They

ANTI-TRADITION?

The sixteenth-century Reformers rejected traditions made by human beings for the purposes of appeasing God and earning grace, for these eliminated the need for the bleeding Savior. That's right, they excluded traditions that were contrary to the Gospel and that were contrary to the teachings of the Christian faith. That said, Martin Luther and the Reformers were not anti-tradition; rather, they intentionally rejected many of the Roman Catholic Church's traditions that obstructed the Gospel from reaching the people and wrongfully obscured the Word of God. However, we must—I repeat—we must keep in mind that the Reformers did not abolish every single tradition of the time. Why not? Because many of the traditions and ceremonies actually did serve the purpose of teaching people what they needed to know about Jesus; many of the traditions did lead people to confess their sins and uphold the Gospel. These good faith traditions and ceremonies were preserved by the Reformers! It would have been foolish to toss these out, for they were noble, good, and true. They served the saints of the church by bringing them to Jesus and His Word.

are often held in reverence and passed down to youth. The traditions and practices can be harmless at times; however, what happens when they conflict with the Word of God or when they become more revered than the Word of God? This is what is occurring regarding Walter. His reaction to Ted holding a beer has more to do with a Midwestern temperance tradition than any teaching from God's Word.

At this point, we must keep in mind that the Bible clearly condemns drunkenness, a sin that must be avoided and repented of when committed (1 Corinthians 6:9–10). Furthermore, drinking under age is a sin, as it violates the Fourth Commandment, which calls Christians to respect the governing authorities and laws of the left-hand kingdom. However, drunkenness is not the same as a person of legal age having a drink—in moderation—in the privacy of their backyard. Walter, though, glossed over the Bible's teaching on this to promote a new law coming from a false christ—a law based on his own cultural traditions of it being unacceptable for a person to have the smallest drop of alcohol on the tongue or be anywhere near a container with alcohol.

"Walter, we need to be careful we don't insinuate that Ted was drunk!" I said.

Walter cringed, "But that is beside the point pastor! He had a beer in his hands! Whether he was drunk, drinking, or just holding the bottle, he is still out of line. Jesus would not approve. Ted should know better, for what kind of example is he setting for his kids and for others in our church?"

"Walter, are you saying Ted has sinned?"

Raising his voice a bit, Walter said, "I am saying he needs to stop what he is doing and live the respectable life of a Christian—he needs to get back onto the straight and narrow. By drinking, he's testing how far he can bring Jesus down with him in his sinful ways, rather than being a shining light. He is our Chairman! He should know Jesus would not approve. This must stop; he mustn't drink. Pastor, what does this say about Ted's Christian faith?"

Whether Walter realized it or not, he was not able to bluntly assert that Ted had sinned but certainly was questioning the validity of his Christian faith. Was this because he subconsciously knew his judgment against Ted was based on a cultural tradition and not the Word of God? I do not believe so. Rather, Walter was not interested in sin being confessed and repented of; he was interested in seeing some kind of external moral change in Ted's life or what he perceived as needed justice.

Like the Moral Example in chapter 8, the New Moses is also not interested in sin being exposed under the Law and then forgiven in the Gospel. Remember, the New Moses is about giving new laws not in the Bible—according to his followers' desires—that will enforce a cultural tradition and not the real Law of the Bible. This false christ is an artificial authority used to uphold man-made traditions that serve as the basis of salvation.

Walter desires for Ted to change his ways—not to line up with Holy Scripture but to line up with Walter's traditions and practices, as prescribed by his false christ. Walter sees Ted living with a vice, and he wants him to turn to the virtues prescribed by the New Moses. For Walter, being a Christian and being a part of the church is not based on a common confession of sin in light of God's objective Law and

WHAT IS STRAIGHT AND NARROW WAY OF LIFE?

Doing bad things is often ascribed to the way of the wide gate and doing pious good things is often ascribed to the way of the straight and narrow. However, this is not what Jesus was getting at in Matthew 7:13–14. In other words, the wide gate is the gate of self-effort along with all mankind's spiritual resumes, scorecards, trophies, virtues and vices; whereas, the narrow gate is the gate for those who are tired, worn out, beggarly, and beating their breast saying, "God have mercy on me the sinner." The narrow gate is for those with empty hands who say, "I am helpless, God help me!" In other words, the straight and narrow way of life is not religious perfection—walking on a straight line—but it is the narrow gate of grace through faith.

the reception of the Word and Sacraments, but instead, upon a common visible cultural lifestyle or a preset list of socially acceptable norms.

Walter looks at Ted and sees him in need of being converted from a vice to virtue. Once Ted adheres to Walter's specified set of standards and exhibits the proper fruit, he will be justified in the sight of Walter and Walter's false christ, the New Moses.

Walter looks at Ted and sees him in need of being converted from a vice to virtue.

What has just been described in Walter's actions and words is what is commonly called legalism. Both legalism and lawlessness are like ditches people can easily fall into.

Someone who rejects God's Law and embraces free, unrestricted living has fallen into the ditch of lawlessness. Legalism is on the other side of the road and is a deep abyss full of man-made rules, cultural practices, and traditions used to judge oneself and others. Since the rules, traditions, and practices are typically based upon man-made customs and not God's Holy Law, a legalist is typically successful in living up to his or her own standards. A legalist is all about looking good on

SIN: CELEBRATE, CONCEAL, OR CONFESS?

A libertine (someone who embraces lawlessness) typically "celebrates" sin. Their glory is in their shame. A legalist typically does the exact opposite; they conceal their sin and find glory in supposed successes of triumph over sin. And while libertines and legalists might seem like polar opposites, they have more in common than meets the eye. Neither acknowledge and own their sin; nor do they remorsefully confess their sins; they either celebrate them or conceal them. Thus, the truth is not in them, as we hear from 1 John 1:8. Christianity, though, goes the way of "confessing" sin, which is radically different from celebrating or concealing it. Sin is confessed before the Lord, and the Lord does not despise a broken and contrite heart. Rather, He is near to the brokenhearted and saves the crushed in Spirit (see Psalm 34:18). When we confess our sins, the Lord is faithful and just to forgive and cleanse us (see 1 John 1:9).

the outside (i.e., words and deeds), while not giving much attention to that which is hidden (i.e., thoughts). Jesus says in Matthew 23:27 that legalists, "Are like whitewashed tombs, which outwardly appear beautiful, but within are full of dead people's bones and all uncleanness." Jesus goes on to say in verse 28 that legalists, "outwardly appear righteous to others, but within . . . are full of hypocrisy and lawlessness."

It is important to note that a legalist lives according to his flesh and not by the Spirit. Furthermore, he is living by his own self-imposed religious system. This begs the question: how does a legalist feel about himself when he successfully fulfills his religious customs, practices, and traditions? How does he feel about those who do not successfully fulfill their religious customs, practices, and traditions, especially those in his own church family?

Interrupting Walter, I said, "Walter, I need to ask you a question: has Ted sinned?"

Walter shuffled back and forth and ground out his answer through clenched teeth, "Well like I said, this is not appropriate, especially for a leader."

RIGHTEOUSNESS: DEVELOPED OR RECEIVED?

In seminary, I had a professor who would say, "Gentlemen, we do not do good works to become a Christian, but we do good works because we already are Christians." This professor was teaching us that our righteousness before God is not advanced by our virtuous acts, as if the practice and improvement of our virtuous deeds somehow develop righteousness before God, like earning brownie points with God. Rather, as Christians, it is the Holy Spirit working through the Word who gives us holy impulses, impulses that lead us to love our neighbor. Indeed, for Christians, good works have been created in advance for us to walk in (Ephesians 2:10) and the Holy Spirit gives us spiritual impulses to walk in these works, neither for the glory of ourselves, nor for the purpose of acquiring salvation by works, but for the love of our neighbor and the glory of the Lord. (See Galatians 5:16–26.)

Pushing back, I asked, "Appropriate according to whom and appropriate according to what, Walter? I am not trying to be confrontational, but we need to determine whether Ted has sinned. If he sinned, then we need to go to him and help restore him gently. If not, well. . . ."

"Pastor, it is offensive, you see!" Walter spat the words out rather forcefully. "It is beneath our standards as a church, for we are Christians after all! The Lord in His mercy probably allowed me to see this so I could warn you and others about this; however, if this is the kind of church we are, then I want nothing to do with it!"

It has been said that the greatest needs of mankind are money, sex, and power. People will lie, cheat, and steal to acquire money. Marriages are destroyed, families are ruined, and jobs are lost as a

LOVING A WEAKER BROTHER?

When the Bible speaks of sin, God gives only one option for Christians: to confess their sins and receive forgiveness of sin in Jesus. However, there are things in the lives of Christians that the Bible neither mandates nor forbids, such as whether it's okay to enjoy an alcoholic beverage. In such cases, there can be conflict over degrees of piety. In Romans 14:1-4, we read that some people are weak in faith and only eat vegetables, whereas those who are stronger in faith will eat all food. As we can imagine, this caused conflict for the church in Rome, since the Bible neither commanded nor forbade on this topic. For the sake of peace, though, the apostle Paul says in verse 3, "Let not the one who eats despise the one who abstains, and let not the one who abstains pass judgment on the one who eats." In other words, those stronger in the faith must not despise the weaker brother *and* the weaker brother must not pass judgment upon the stronger brother when dealing with issues that are not black and white, wrong or right. By not despising and not judging, weaker and stronger brothers can live together in peace and harmony. Regarding this chapter and Walter, we can see how he was judging Ted on an issue that was neither commanded nor forbidden in Scripture.

result of sexual affairs or pornography consumption. Physical fights, threatening letters, and intimidation tactics are engaged to keep another person underneath a thumb. But none of these things are truly the greatest need of mankind, for that need is the need to be justified, to be considered right.

For Walter, he had accumulated traditions and practices in which he was considered right; therefore, he saw himself as self-justified. However, as soon as his self-justification was challenged, he became defensive. This is how it goes when a person lives by means of self-imposed law. That to which our self-justification is connected will need to be maintained, upheld, and defended at all costs. The New Moses needs protecting when others do not uphold the same traditions, customs, and practices. The New Moses sees these "others" as threats to self-imposed law and, as a result, they are often ostracized or kept at bay. They are viewed as "unsaved" because of their rejection of this false christ.

It becomes apparent that if a person clings to their keeping of their own traditions, practices, or customs as the basis of being justified, then the need for the real Jesus is eliminated. What is needed is a false christ that will not only support a particular tradition or practice but will actually be credited with mandating it.

Not really knowing how to respond to Walter, I paused and then quietly said, "Walter, what do you want to do about Ted? Is this something Ted needs to repent of or not? Where did he violate God's Law? Where do we go from here?"

"Pastor, I've told you already, it's just not right. This is not the way a good Christian should act; it isn't how Jesus would want us to be and live," Walter said, his voice now deflated and his head and shoulders dropped in a combination of disgust, confusion, and sorrow.

We can feel sorry for Walter at this point. We can also feel sorry for Ted as well because no sin was pinpointed on the basis of Holy Scripture, which means no sin can be repented of; however, Walter's condemnation still hovers over Ted. Whether Walter realizes it or not, he is oppressing the soul of Ted and his false christ is passing judgment as well.

Whereas the real Jesus Christ desires sin to be identified by means of the Law, so it can be repented of and forgiven in the Gospel, the New Moses is the exact opposite. Instead of offering forgiveness, this false christ oppresses souls. This false christ condemns certain actions and practices according to the desires of his followers, but does not label these actions and practices as sin. Once condemned, the only relief is for the person to try and correct their actions according to vague traditions and practices. Often this leads to utter despair, for even if an individual is successful for a time, the tradition or legalistic practice could change without notice.

People who subscribe to the New Moses do so to self-justify themselves by not doing certain things they deem wrong, and also by getting others in line with the man-made traditions and practices they like and have created for themselves. Not only does this give followers of the New Moses satisfaction in converting others, but it also gives them satisfaction in their prescribed traditions and practices used as a basis for their self-justification.

OPPRESSING THE SOUL?

People's souls are oppressed when they are not given the opportunity to repent of sin and are left under condemnation. This is typically the way of the evil one. The sly serpent continually condemns not unto repentance and ultimate forgiveness but unto despair. The Holy Spirit, though, will indeed convict Christians of sin but will do so in order that sin might be absolved/forgiven in Jesus. In summary, oppression of the soul is a condemnation of non-sinful acts unto despair, whereas Godly sorrow is condemnation of sinful acts unto forgiveness.

Responding to Walter

What is the main thing that drives and controls Walter's thoughts, logic, and decisions regarding Christianity and his views about Jesus? As we have learned, Walter elevates his man-made traditions to the level of Holy Scripture. The New Moses then affirms these traditions as being authoritative. All of this is done to justify himself.

When we respond to Walter—and others like him—our aim is to help Walter distinguish between his man-made traditions and God's Law. But how shall we do this? If Walter were a new Christian who struggled to understand that a person is completely justified by faith and not by the traditions of men, we would need to be extremely careful. Why? Because when dealing with new Christians, we must remember they act the way they do because their faith is weak. Therefore, we must be patient and gentle with new Christians as they learn that their justification is not in their works but solely in Jesus. (According to this way of thinking, the Apostle Paul had Timothy circumcised in Acts 16:3.) On the other hand, because Walter is not a new Christian and is quite adamant about his views, to the point of attacking other Christians, he must be opposed. Indeed, instead of honoring his traditions, we must demonstrate that his legalism is a blatant error. We are not to be intentionally confrontational with Walter by any means, but rather, we must make sure we do not comply with Walter so as not to give the impression that his faulty legalism and his false christ are legitimate. This may seem unloving, but it is actually what the Apostle Paul does in Galatians 2:3 when he refuses to have Titus circumcised when some of the legalistic leaders insisted he should. By opposing the legalists in Galatia, Paul actually stood up for the Gospel, to prevent the Legalists from destroying the Gospel by adding to it.

This can all present a difficult challenge, for it might be hard to distinguish the differences between those weak in the faith and those who are legalistic. A telltale sign is that those who are weak in the faith—generally speaking—will have a grieved disposition when their traditions are cast aside for the sufficiency of the real Jesus. They will lament, put their head down, and retreat to an area of safety. Legalists, however, will go the way of Cain. (Due to his uncontrollable jealously and hatred, Cain killed his brother Abel, a direct result of God rejecting his self-generated righteousness. See Genesis 4.) Having the spirit of Cain, legalists will do everything possible to validate their man-made traditions to preserve their self-justification. When the real Jesus is proclaimed, those who are wounded by their sin will be healed, those weak in the faith will become grieved, and the self-righteous will get angry. This pattern of legalists getting angry and attacking is evident throughout history: Cain killed Abel; the Pharisees crucified Jesus; the sixteenth-century Roman Catholic Church pronounced the death sentence on Martin Luther, and entire books have been written on the martyrs. In fact, if we examine the history of the Church, we will find a trail of the martyrs' blood leading us back to the first stone used by Cain to kill his brother Abel. The same sordid motivation, that hatred of grace that we refer to as the spirit of Cain, is responsible for inflicting mortal wounds. Indeed, the spirit of Cain will always attack those who profess justification by grace through faith—alone.

Just as we certainly draw near to those who are weak in faith, for they will need compassion and further teaching in the matters of the faith, we also need to understand that people like Walter will seek us out. Indeed, Walter will not come to us with the intent of redeeming his neighbor from a violation of God's Law, but with the intent of retaliating against his neighbor for a violation of his self-made pseudo-law. He will proclaim authority from the New Moses, whose wrath and fury knows no limits.

In our discussions with the Walters in our life, we can take comfort in the fact that when attacks come on the basis of who the real Jesus is and on the message of the Gospel of Christ-crucified, we are truly blessed. (See Matthew 5:11.) Blessed? Yes! For it is in moments like those when we remember the suffering of our Lord Jesus Christ, who told us to expect persecution. For the world has hated our Lord first, and we can take comfort that He has indeed died for that hatred as well. What can mere man do to us? The Gospel is truly the power of God unto salvation, for us, and we pray also for the Walters we may encounter.

Will the Real Jesus Please Stand Up?

The real Jesus is not a new lawgiver. He neither expands the Law given to Moses nor does He reinterpret it, for there is only one divine Law, and He fulfills it. Indeed, in the words of the Apostle Paul, Jesus was "born under the law, to redeem those who were under the law, so that we might receive adoption as sons" (Galatians 4:4–5). He is the only one who kept it perfectly, which resulted in "the many being made righteous" (Romans 5:19).

The real Jesus is not used to reinforce a person's own attempts to self-justify.

The real Jesus does not oppress the soul unto despair but convicts unto repentance.

The real Jesus calls for real sin to be revealed so that repentance can happen. This repentance results in our condemnation being met with His absolving Gospel. Ultimately, this leads to the Christian's justification being found in the real Jesus and not within the person or his religious traditions. (See Romans 3:21–24.) When a person's justification is located in the real Jesus and not somewhere else, then faith and assurance are produced, and unbelief and uncertainty are cast aside. (See John 20:26–28.)

Let's discuss the **New Moses**

1. What are the main presuppositions of Walter that allow him to embrace and sponsor the New Moses?

The real Jesus and His followers did not follow the traditions of the Pharisees. Mark 7:1–13 records the confrontation that resulted from their conflict. Read Mark 7:1–13 and consider the following questions.

2. In verse 7, Jesus quotes Isaiah the prophet. According to verse 7, what are the Pharisees doing with the commandments of men?

3. Consider verses 8–13. Once the Pharisees raised the commandments of man up to the level of God's divine commandments, what resulted?

4. What happens if a person goes the way of the Pharisees and elevates the traditions of mankind, rejects God's divine commands, and then validates all of this in the name of Jesus Christ?

In chapter 8 we met the Moral Example and here we met the New Moses, false christs who both go the way of works-righteousness. They also tend to see sin as something external and goodness as something inherently internal. In light of this, consider the following question regarding Mark 7:20–23.

5. Both Ruby (chapter 8) and Walter not only keep up good external appearances but also tend to see sin as something outside of themselves. However, where does the real Jesus locate the problem of sin? What are the implications of where Jesus locates the problem of sin?

6. To summarize, how do these questions and Mark 7 shed light on the New Moses?

7. How can we help address the Law/Gospel confusion people have when they follow the New Moses?

10

Meet Zach, Mindy, and Stephanie, the Mystic Pietists

There was a large couch, a love seat, and a recliner chair in a cozy semi-circle in front of a fireplace where a fire crackled and popped. Several kitchen chairs were also scattered about the room. The smell of appetizers and freshly brewed coffee lingered in the air.

My wife and I had been invited to Zach and Mindy's house for a small group Bible study. It was a Bible study hosted by a church not affiliated with the congregation we were attending at the time, but some of our close friends had invited us to the study and we decided to attend out of curiosity.

The hosts, Zach and Mindy, were a very kind and loving couple who graciously hosted this weekly Bible study at their house for younger families. They had been hosting the Bible study for the last two months and were working through chapters in "Joining with God," a popular young family study series. This Bible study series was the current trend among young Christian couples, and the local Christian bookstore, in which one of my relatives worked at, seemed to barely be able to keep up with the demand for them.

About five minutes before seven o'clock, all of us worked our way from the kitchen to the living room with our study Bibles, highlighters, and the study series booklets. As we came into the room, the noise level increased as we chatted among ourselves.

As everyone was finding a place to sit, Mindy spoke up loud enough to be heard, "I believe we left off with chapter 6. So, if you have your workbook, please turn to page 34."

After everyone located the correct page, the sound in the room decreased and Zach read the opening question, which contained a couple of verses from the Epistle of James. After a brief moment of silence, Zach said, "Now that we have read our opening question, what do these verses mean to you?"

We must pause here and examine something that may be easily overlooked, and that is Zach's question. Where does Zach's question take the group? If you and I were asked this question, how does it impact the way we think? Note that Zach did not ask, "What are these verses saying?" Rather, he asks, "What do these verses mean *to you*?" In other words, Zach's question to this group immediately takes the conversation out of an objective sphere and places it within a subjective personal sphere—the question causes a person to look inward.

After Zach's question, several faces scrunched up as people were contemplating Zach's question and what the verses meant for them.

Right about the time when the silence made everyone feel uncomfortable, Mindy leaned forward and said, "I once had a direct encounter with the Lord that sort of awakened me to the inner freedom to let go of some of the ways that the church has limited Jesus. I came to know Jesus dwelling behind all the rituals and doctrines, and I came to know

MYSTICISM

When a person claims to have a direct connection/communication with the Lord, they are a mystic. Typically, a mystic's connection/communication with the Lord occurs directly; they claim to receive some sort of unique, personal, and direct communication with the Lord, and it is not through the Bible. However, the Holy Spirit always works through the Gospel to call, enlighten, sanctify, and keep people in the true faith (SC II).

Him through that still small voice within. I saw Him through the eyes of my heart!"

As Mindy was talking, several people began to nod their heads and mumble in agreement. It was a quiet mumble that made a humming noise, like a cross between the word *Amen* and a hushed sigh. This amen-hushed-sigh not only expressed affirmation with what Mindy said, but it also expressed encouragement.

Brady, another person in the group, responded to Mindy, "I have been unable to identify the voice of the Shepherd. I have desired a deeper intimacy with God, but I can't seem to find it. So much of the time I feel empty and worried."

Mindy nodded her head and said, "Yes, I know what you mean! If you are feeling empty, you should dwell in Jesus' love, for He delights to meet you and refuel you. Learn to focus and know what to listen for when Jesus speaks to you."

ENTHUSIASTS

Adam and Eve were the first enthusiasts because they were the first sinners. They were given the Lord's Word in Genesis chapter 3, to not eat of the fruit of the tree that is in the middle of the garden; however, when Eve saw that the tree was good for food and that it was a delight to her eyes, she ate it and gave it to Adam to eat as well. In other words, Adam and Eve departed from God's clear external Word; the judgment from their own rationale and the desires of the heart persuaded them that it was okay to eat the fruit. Enthusiasts, like Adam and Eve, won't take God's external Word as is, but will take God's Word inside of them. The Word will go inside and become an internal matter. Once the Word of God is taken inside, the enthusiast goes to work on God's Word—deconstructing God's Word, swallowing up parts of God's Word and spitting out new interpretations. The point being, an enthusiast understands God's Word only through his or her own inner workings of the heart. An enthusiast will always ask, "What does this mean to me?" and will not ask, "What does this say to me?"

With eagerness in his voice, Zach jumped into the conversation and said, "I have found that Jesus' voice comes not in an audible voice, but as a spontaneous thought. Not just any old spontaneous thought, but a thought that seems to light up the inner soul. For example, just the other day I was thinking about praying for a person who had been struggling, and lo and behold, two minutes later they called me on the phone to simply see how I was doing. Now, you better believe it, that was Jesus telling me to pray. That was a Godcedence!"

Meet our tenth false christ: the Mystical Friend. This false christ is very personal and close to the heart, so close that he lives deep down in the heart of experiences and emotions as a spiritualized being. This false christ is also separated from the external Word and Sacraments—that is, the Bible, Baptism, and Communion. Rather than speaking through the Word, this false christ whispers sentiments in that still small voice from the caverns of the heart. This false christ exalts signs, wonders, emotions, and experiences above the Word of

MATERIAL AND SPIRITUAL?

The ancient philosopher Plato held to two different realms. He held to a spiritual, or nonphysical, realm and also to a material realm. For the most part, Plato got this right since mankind is both body and soul—we believe in all things visible and invisible. However, where Plato goes terribly wrong is that he considers the spiritual realm right, true, and perfect, but the material realm as changing, flawed, and a mere shadow. As a result, Plato taught that it was the goal of mankind to escape their evil and flawed bodies. Simply stated, Plato considered the soul as good and material things as bad. This material versus spiritual dualism is what sets the stage for an Early Church heresy called Gnosticism. Gnosticism didn't like the material world but favored the spiritual world. This became especially troubling when Gnostics began to teach that Jesus did not have a body. They believed that it only *seemed* that Jesus had a body. This is problematic, for if Jesus was not fully man, then salvation is not fully possible.

God and is always communicating through tingly and moving experiential feelings for assurance.

As with all the other people we have met so far in the previous chapters, Zach and Mindy's presuppositions create a false christ that functions within their already preconceived notions. More specifically, though, what are their presuppositions?

First, Zach and Mindy tend to look inward regarding the things of faith. This was easy to identify by Zach's question of "what do these verses mean to you." Furthermore, Zach and Mindy identify the Lord's voice as coming to them not through the external Word and Sacraments, but through spontaneous ideas or the eyes of the heart. Their spirituality is focused inward: the Mystical Friend speaks from within as spontaneous thoughts, is seen with the inward eyes of the heart, and refuels a person if they look inward where this friend dwells.

But what does it mean to look inward? Where is one looking when they look inward? This inward realm is not a physical inward dimension but an inward spiritual dimension of the soul—it is the person's private inner space. Therefore, what this means for Zach and Mindy is that the Lord does not mainly speak through external and physical things like written words from the Bible or physical puffs of air coming from a pastor preaching the Scriptures. For Zach and Mindy, the Lord primarily speaks to them in this inward dimension of the soul apart from the written and spoken Word in the Bible, and this apparent inward voice of God must be identified with the eyes of the heart or by the result of an ignition of the soul.

There is a second aspect to this inwardness as well. Zach and Mindy are not only looking internally to this inner self of the soul, but they believe that the soul—the inward invisible dimension—is more special and more holy than things in the external material world. Things like preached words, water, bread, and wine are earthly external material things that are essentially inferior to the inward soul. To them, these external material things do not have power over the soul so they are not respected. How can they have power? To Zach and Mindy, they are merely examples or signals of the inner workings of salvation in the interior soul. For Zach and Mindy, the deep inner soul is where the Christian faith really comes alive; it is where the "real" action occurs, not outwardly on Mt. Calvary or in God's Word and Sacraments that are delivered to sinners.

But what about their false christ, the Mystical Friend? Zach and Mindy have created an idol who dwells in this inward realm of their souls. Keep in mind that this inward realm of Zach and Mindy's souls is not big enough to house the real Jesus who has a body; therefore, Zach and Mindy recreate a false christ by stripping away the body and making their false christ into an ethereal apparition that can fit within the inward realm of their soul. That stated, it is important to pause here to differentiate Zach and Mindy's Mystical Friend from the real Jesus. The real Jesus truly dwells in the Christian's heart *through* the Holy Spirit who comes to us in Baptism and God's Word. Furthermore, the real Jesus is also cemented to the Christian by faith; it is as if the

JESUS IN US?

Is Jesus in us or not? If we say that Jesus does not dwell in us, we risk making Jesus into some abstract ideological content—an impersonal idea. On the other hand, if we say that Jesus dwells in our hearts, we risk making Him into some bodiless mystical being. The only way out of this predicament is to understand that Jesus dwells sacramentally in believers by communion. Indeed, Jesus is in, with, and under the bread and wine of Communion—the body and blood that we eat and drink. Furthermore, we must recognize that Jesus is in believers through the Holy Spirit. Truly, the indwelling of Jesus through the Spirit is the whole Jesus—the God-man—who is received by faith. Jesus by the Spirit is really present in believers! (See John 14:15–20.) And finally, we must also remember that no one receives the Holy Spirit without the external Word of the Gospel.

Christian and Jesus are as one person by faith. And, finally, as Christians eat the real Jesus' body and drink His blood in the Lord's Supper, they can know Jesus is truly present within them to forgive, renew, and strengthen them. Zach and Mindy, though, do not believe this because they have stripped away the human nature of Jesus and recreated the real Jesus to be the Mystical Friend, to be a mystical spiritualized false christ. Indeed, they are holding to a bodiless false christ who has not bodily ascended and is not seated at the right hand of God the Father but is a waiflike being buried deep in the caverns of their heart. To make things worse, since Zach and Mindy's mystical spiritualized false christ does not have a human nature, the physical shed blood of the cross does not have any dramatic contribution or relevance to their version of Christianity. That is to say, Zach and Mindy neither look to what Jesus accomplished on Mount Calvary nor do they look to the Word and Sacraments to receive Jesus and His gifts. Instead, Zach and Mindy look and listen to the inward soul for the mystical spiritualized false christ to impart divinely-inspired messages, messages that are many times contrary to God's Word in the Bible.

After Zach mentioned his "Godcedence" moment, Brady seemed a bit excited yet still perplexed. He started to speak then paused. Eventually, he admitted, "I totally understand what you are saying, but, uh, I struggle in identifying Jesus' voice."

Nodding her head with a tender smile, Mindy continued, "We must keep in mind that this is a communication that happens through thoughts, impressions, and visions, not analytical thoughts. We are talking about spontaneous impressions and visions of goodness. They will come to you, Brady, as you go to a quiet place and still your own thoughts and emotions so you can hear the voice of the Lord. If you are not still, you will sense only your own thoughts."

Somewhat interrupting Mindy, Brady said, "So, here is what I am struggling with. This is the reason why I am asking this question . . . "

The whole small group seemed to perk up with interest. It was as if we were all interested in what Brady was going to bear—for it's always invigorating to a group when someone lets down his guard and allows his authentic, transparent self out.

"As you all know, I have been at the same job since college; however, I have been presented with another job opportunity. My current job is okay but the other job is a super opportunity. But I don't know if I should take it." Brady said with a great deal of frustration in his voice.

Zach looked around at the entire group and then said to Brady, "Brady, if it would be okay with you, could we pray for you right now?"

"Yes, I would like that," Brady said.

Zach bowed his head and prayed, "Dear Lord, we just come before you this day for our brother Brady. He has been presented a new job and does not know if he should take it. We just pray that you show him which job is your will. Give him dreams; quiet his heart so he can hear the still small voice. Lord, Brady needs your help. Also, Lord, we are going to lay down a bunch of fleeces, and we demand that you boldly answer our prayers. And Lord, we just pray for a hedge of protection around Brady as we lift him up to you. And all of God's people say, Amen." (Note: While it is good to pray to the Lord for

---

KNOWING THE LORD'S WILL

As we Christians make decisions in our everyday lives, we do so in light of God's moral will of love—we are to love the Lord our God with all our heart and all our soul and with all our mind, and to love our neighbor as ourselves (see Matthew 22:37–38). However, what does this love specifically look like? This love is not a mysterious love, but rather is very evident. It is evident in God's commands. In other words, every command of the Scriptures is a specific expression of the command to love. For example: the Ten Commandments are a specific expression of God's moral will of love; they are God's will for mankind. (See Romans 13:8–10.)

wisdom and guidance in life's events, it is actually wrong to assume that God will reveal His will through dreams and a supposed still small voice in the heart—dreams and voices that are apart from God's Word. As we will see a bit later, God's will is best known from His revealed Word—the Bible.)

After the small group meeting had finished, several of us decided to hang out. Some went outside, while others went into the kitchen to visit. I ended up outside talking to Brady. I was a bit curious about his situation, so I asked him a question, "So, Brady, you and your wife have a young child, right?"

Brady smiled with complete joy, "Yes, Isaac is two. And we are just starting to tell people that we are expecting our second child!"

I gave him one of those proud guy handshakes to congratulate him, and we exchanged some small talk about the excitement and fear of him being a dad of two.

After several minutes, I changed the subject back to his question, "So, with the possible job—if you don't mind me asking—is it a lot more money than your current job? Are you able to make it on your current job's salary?"

Brady said, "I don't mind you asking at all. The pay at the possible new job is a quite a bit more. And yes, my current job is supporting us fine; it makes for a nice living."

"How about the job description; same kind of duties or different? Will it be more or fewer hours?" I said.

"Well, it will be a lot more traveling for the possible new job. It will require me to do a lot of flying around the Midwest and a lot of driving, and some hotel stays here and there. And the hours will be considerably more." Brady said.

"And how does your wife feel about that?" I asked.

Brady paused and shuffled his feet a bit, "She isn't too happy about that part of it. She says we aren't spending enough time together as a family already."

Brady looked down. It was apparent that he was rather stressed out about this decision. He said, "I have wished that the Lord would just reveal to me what I should do. I have been praying like crazy and have been getting nothing. However, while we were praying tonight, I think the Lord told me to take this new job."

Not sure if I was going to offend Brady, I gently asserted to him, "Let me make sure that I hear you right. You are looking to take another job that would take you away from home more, while your current job is meeting your financial needs and while your wife is pregnant and while you are currently struggling to spend enough time with your family already?"

Brady nodded his head with a bit of confusion, "Yeah, that is pretty much it."

I then asked him, "So, why do you think it is the Lord's will for you to take this new job, when all of your circumstances point that you should not?" Thankfully, Brady did not seem agitated by my comments. So I continued, "Brady, how is this the Lord's will? The Lord's will from the Bible is that you are called to be the spiritual head of your family, to be there for your children, and be there for your wife. If you were struggling financially, this job change might make sense, but you are doing fine. If you were to take this new position, would you do a better job fulfilling your role as a husband and father, or a worse job?"

Brady's job crisis demonstrates another presupposition of this false christ. The Mystical Friend is separated from the clear teachings of the Lord's will in the Bible and speaks instead through signs, wonders, emotions, and experiences. In other words, the Lord's will for Brady's situation is very clear in the Bible: he is called to the vocation of father and husband, in which he is called to serve his family. If Brady's family were short on finances, it would make sense for him to take the new job, even though the excessive traveling might be a sacrifice to the whole family. However, this was not the case. Yes, he would be paid more for the new job, and yes, it would be a job promotion; however, this new job was not financially necessary. In other words, this corporate promotion was not God's will, for it was not necessary and would be detrimental to Brady's vocation as a husband and father. It would be harmful to his family.

It is important to note that the Lord's will for mankind is not some floaty, intangible, and unknowable thing that is only discovered through mystical encounters in the heart. Rather, the Lord's will for mankind is expressed in the Word—the Bible. We must keep in mind that the Bible is all about Jesus—He is the focus. Jesus says in Luke 24:44, "Everything written about me in the Law of Moses and the Prophets and the Psalms must be fulfilled." Furthermore, Jesus is the everlasting Word, which means He is the author of all the Scriptures (see John 1:1). This means we do not have to search our inner emotions to discern the Lord's will for our lives; we can simply look to the Bible.

It was about nine o'clock, and it was announced that the events of the evening were coming to a close. I went into the living room to

THE MEANS OF GRACE

Jesus died and rose from the grave in AD 32—salvation accomplished! However, unless we have a time machine, we cannot go back and obtain this accomplished salvation in AD 32. Therefore, the Lord needs to deliver this salvation to mankind throughout every generation and throughout every continent. How does this happen? The Lord uses tools or instruments to create and sustain the faith of the believer; the Lord works through the Means of Grace to give the Holy Spirit. These Means of Grace are the Word and Sacraments.

The Word of God delivers forgiveness, creates faith, and sustains faith in the believer when it is spoken, read, sung, pictured, preached, and so on. The Sacraments of Baptism and Communion deliver forgiveness, create faith, and sustain faith as well. The Sacraments are sometimes denoted as the visible Means of Grace, because something visible (i.e., water, bread, and wine) are joined with the Word.

retrieve my Bible and then went with my wife to the kitchen to say thank you to the hosts.

When we entered the kitchen, everyone was standing in a circle with their belongings in their hands. Stephanie, another member, was sharing her appreciation for the small group. As I walked up to the circle, I heard her saying, "I never could hear from Jesus in the church. I wanted His peace but did not find it in the church. But here in this group, I have found peace."

A person from the group interjected, "Where do you attend church?"

Stephanie smiled, "This is my new church, here with you all! The Sunday sermons at my old church were okay, I guess, but not exactly what I needed."

Mindy leaned in and touched Stephanie's arm, "I know exactly what you mean. I got so tired of that dead letter preaching. What is really important is doing life together with Jesus and that is what this small group helps us with. We are here to give each other grace."

PIETISM

Pietism was a movement from the seventeenth-century that originated in Lutheranism. Pietism no longer exists as a movement but its views and ethos live on.

According to church historians, we learn that Pietism accentuated the significance of personal piety, while putting the emphasis on the subjective heart. It stressed "Christ in us" more than "Christ for us." Furthermore, it underscored the changed life as the mark of the Church rather than the Word and Sacraments. It made religious experiences more vital than doctrine. Finally, it stressed sanctified living more than the forgiveness of sins.

Every major Christian denomination has aspects of pietism in some form or fashion, for it is so incredibly easy to put the main focus on the Christian and not the real Jesus. Furthermore, it is most definitely at work in Zach and Mindy's small group study.

"I totally agree with Mindy!" Stephanie said. "I guess I got tired of taking Communion with so many people who were not even trying to live the Christian life. It's nice to be here with the truly regenerative people! This group has been more of a real church to me than anything that I've ever experienced in my previous church. Jesus is certainly present here with us."

We can learn two more things from Stephanie and Mindy's interaction. Just like Brady, who separated God's will from the Bible, Stephanie and Mindy have separated Jesus and His grace from the proclaimed Word and the blessed Sacraments of Baptism and Communion. They have subscribed to a false mystical spiritualized christ in the caverns of their heart, which then results in this false christ only delivering grace to others "through" people like Mindy and Stephanie. Let us examine Mindy and Stephanie's views on this a bit more thoroughly.

Through the internal workings of the Mystical Friend, Mindy and Stephanie believe that they are granted a "real and living" faith that becomes recognizable through their love for each other. Then from this love, Mindy and Stephanie can give each other grace, support, and

WHAT IS THE CHURCH?

What makes a church a church is not a mission statement, its polity, its tax-exempt status, its programs, the building, the celebrity-ness personality of the pastor, or the piety of the parishioners. No, may this never be, for these are all fallible marks—man-centered. Rather, the church is defined as anywhere the Gospel is purely taught and the Sacraments are correctly administered to believers. This means two things. First, the church is not founded upon the strength of the believers, but upon the mighty Word and Sacraments, which are for the believers. Second, we do not go to church to give our best to God, but we go to receive God's best for us. We do not go to be strengthened by our neighbor, but we go with our neighbors to be strengthened in faith toward the Lord and strengthened in fervent love toward one another by the Lord's Word and Sacraments.

consolation. What this means is that Jesus' grace does not come through the external Word and Sacraments to Mindy and Stephanie, but rather, Jesus and His grace come through Christians giving grace to one another. Mindy and Stephanie have exchanged "Christ for them in the Word and Sacraments" for a false mystical spiritualized christ who is "in them," resulting in Mindy and Stephanie believing that Christians are a "means of grace" to one another. Tragically, this makes Christians into some kind of sacrament—it is up to the Christian person to uphold the church and other Christians. According to this way of thinking, Jesus and His grace are not present in the preached Word or Baptism or the bread and wine, but are only present in the experiences and pious living of Christians.

There is another tragedy to this line of thinking as well. According to this outlook, the local church is no longer needed or valued. Instead of the church being identified by the preaching of Jesus' Word and the administration of Jesus' Sacraments, everything is changed to the church being where the false sacrament of right living is present—namely in a small group.

Responding to Zach, Mindy, and Stephanie

What are the main things that drive and control Zach, Mindy, and Stephanie's thoughts, logic, and decisions regarding Christianity and their views about Jesus? Throughout this chapter, we have learned quite a few things about them; however, one key characteristic worth investigating is that Zach, Mindy, and Stephanie locate their spirituality internally in the caverns of their hearts—it is located in the subjective person. In other words, when we ask Zach, Mindy, and Stephanie about their assurance of salvation, they do not look to the external Word and the Sacraments, but look inward to the attitudes of their hearts and its innermost workings. For example, Zach, Mindy, and Stephanie's assurance of salvation can be defined more by peace in the heart than an objective peace with God the Father through the substitutionary death of the real Jesus. Or, if Zach, Mindy, and Stephanie were asked how they know Jesus lives, they would not point to the empty tomb but would say that they know Jesus lives because he lives in their hearts. And if asked how they were made Christians, they would not point to their baptisms, where the Lord washed them, but would speak of a decision that they made with their whole internal beings to become Christians.

Because of this inward focus, Zach, Mindy, and Stephanie will subconsciously develop an unhealthy pattern of looking inward to the heart for hope and solutions, while inadvertently seeing sin as something external and outside of them. While it is true that the enemies of the world and the devil exist outside of us, we must take note that the closest threat of sin is not lurking nearby in a tree, but within all of our human hearts. The prophet Jeremiah accurately laments in 17:9, "The heart is deceitful above all things, and desperately sick; who can understand it?"

When we respond to Zach, Mindy, Stephanie, and others like them, our intention should be to challenge their dependence on their own internal spiritual status. As it has been said before, we do not challenge individuals to be confrontational or divisive, but rather, we do this in love to help reveal the inadequacy and folly of their misplaced trust in a false christ, which in this case is the Mystical Friend. We challenge Zach, Mindy, and Stephanie's inward-focused spirituality by simply pushing their limits a bit, asking, "When you don't feel peace, do you ever worry that you don't have peace with God?" Or we can ask, "Has your resolute internal decision to follow Jesus remained steadfast all these years? If it has not, do you fear you may have fallen out of God's grace?" By asking these questions we will no doubt push Zach, Mindy, and Stephanie even more inward to examine their hearts. However, as we push them, we do so in order that they might have to experience the bankruptcy of their Mystical Friend who leads them inward toward self rather than lifting their eyes to the author and perfector of their faith, the real and true Jesus.

If we are fortunate enough to witness Zach, Mindy, and Stephanie realize the problems of their Mystical Friend, we can rejoice, for they now need to hear a message outside of themselves. They need the Lord—from outside of themselves—to put forgiveness, life, and salvation into their ears in the Word of the Gospel: "Jesus Christ forgives you of all your sins." They need to hear that the Lord puts forgiveness, life, and salvation upon their heads in Baptism: "I baptize you in the name of the Father and of the Son and of the Holy Spirit." They need to hear that the Lord puts forgiveness, life, and salvation upon their lips and on their tongues and in their bellies in communion: "Take and eat, this is My body; take and drink, this is My blood which is shed for you for the forgiveness of your sins."

Zach, Mindy, and Stephanie need to be turned inside out. They need to hear that assurance and objective certainty are found outside of them in the real Jesus, not in themselves or in the quality of their internalized spirituality. They need to hear that certainty is found in Jesus' perfect life, not theirs. They need to realize that Christianity is not about them, but about the real Jesus who is for them. Zach, Mindy, and Stephanie need to realize that the Lord works from the outside to the inside—that He comes to all of us in the Word and Sacraments, thus our faith never digs around in the caverns of our heart but always looks to, longs for, and receives the real Jesus and His good gifts that come to us from the outside. He truly is the lifter of our heads. We pray that He would fix our eyes continually on Him and Him alone.

Will the Real Jesus Please Stand Up?

The real Jesus has a body, for He was crucified, died, and was buried. He also rose from the dead again on the third day and ascended bodily into the heavens. The real Jesus is the God-man who rules over the whole universe. He is not some fairy-like creature without a body that mysteriously dwells in mankind's heart. (See 1 Corinthians 15:3–9, where the apostle Paul talks about Jesus rising bodily.)

Furthermore, the real Jesus does not distribute forgiveness, life, and salvation to mankind from within mankind's heart, as if mankind must turn inward to find Jesus and His gifts. Rather, Jesus comes to us with Himself and His gifts through the external Means of Grace. In other words, even though Jesus has ascended to the right hand of the Father and exercises His divine power over the whole universe, He has promised specifically to deliver Himself in the Word and Sacraments to mankind. He is in our ears through the preaching of the Word: "Faith comes from hearing, and hearing through the word of Christ." (Romans 10:17). He is upon our head and hearts in Baptism: "Go therefore make disciples of all nations, baptizing them in the name of the Father and of the Son and of the Holy Spirit" (Matthew 28:19). And He is upon our mouths, tongues, and in our bellies in the Lord's Supper: "Drink of it, all of you, for this is my blood of the covenant, which is poured out for many for the forgiveness of sins" (Matthew 26:27b–28). It is from receiving these external Means of Grace that we are strengthened, refreshed in faith toward God and in love toward our neighbor. We do not receive these gifts through digging around in our hearts, by leaning upon the experiences of others, or by mystic dreams and signs.

Let's discuss the **Mystical Friend**

1. What are the central presuppositions of Zach, Mindy, and Stephanie that allow them to embrace and sponsor the Mystical Friend?

As a way of review, consider these comments about Gnosticism in regard to the following questions:

In the Early Church, there was a heresy called Gnosticism. Gnosticism didn't like the material world but favored the spiritual world. This became especially troubling when Gnostics began to teach that Jesus did not have a body. They believed that it only seemed that Jesus had a body. This becomes problematic, for if Jesus was not fully man, then salvation is not possible.

2. Read 1 John 1:1. What three human senses does John talk about? What do these senses have to do with Jesus?

3. Read Acts 1:6–11. What do these verses teach us about where Jesus is now?

4. If Jesus is at the right hand of the Father—bodily—is He somehow confined or restricted to a particular place in heaven so that in His body He can't be present with mankind? Examine Jesus' Words of Institution in Matthew 26:26–28. What does Jesus promise in the Lord's Supper?

5. Read the following verses in the order they follow: Romans 10:17; 1 Corinthians 1:21; 1 Peter 1:23; Hebrews 4:12; and 2 Timothy 3:16. What do these verses teach us about the Word of God?

6. How do these questions and the verses shed light on the Mystical Friend?

7. If one of your friends said to you: "I don't need to go to church anymore because I am getting everything I spiritually need in the joy I experience in my small group," how would you respond?

Meet Eva, the Feminist

It was obvious that the bride, Melissa, and her maid of honor, Eva, were best friends. They had been friends since the first grade, sharing so many memories together. They attended the same grade school, the same high school, and then decided to be college roommates. After college, they had planned to move from the Midwest to the East Coast together to pursue their careers in business and political science. This all changed, though, when Melissa met Scott.

When Scott came into Melissa's life, Eva watched Melissa's dreams and professional goals morph into other things. Melissa no longer dreamed of a high-rise apartment and Wall Street, but of a house, children, and a quieter life in the suburbs. Needless to say, this changed things between Eva and Melissa, as Eva still had her heart set on the East Coast. Regardless of the changes in their lives, Eva was pleased to be the maid of honor in Melissa and Scott's wedding.

I was the officiant for this wedding and had been invited to the reception and dance as well. The reception was at an old winery, which made for a calm and relaxing atmosphere as we enjoyed a delicious meal and conversation with the people at our tables. Well, it was relaxing for most.

"Hey, Rev, things went well, nobody fainted during the service," Eva said with a smile.

"Thank you," I said loudly over the reception music and the talking in the background.

Balancing her drink in one hand and leaning forward as if she was trying to speak through the noise, Eva said, "Quick question, though. In your message you mentioned Ephesians 5—the part about submission, and before the vows you talked about Melissa submitting to Scott. You weren't pushing that old-fashioned male-dominance marriage structure where Melissa is expected to be a doormat, were you?"

I must confess that I was taken aback by the question. Furthermore, I was not totally sure if I heard what she said. So, I got up from my spot at the table and moved over a couple of chairs toward Eva. It looked like several others around her had taken an interest in her comments and questions, since everybody at the table had finished eating and were patiently waiting for the dance to begin. They were leaning in with curiosity to tune into the conversation that was about to unfold.

"Sorry Eva, what were you saying?" I asked.

"Your sermon and the vows implied that Melissa needs to submit to Scott. Melissa has given up so much already; you are not suggesting she be some doormat to Scott or imprisoned by this marriage?" Eva asked.

Still a bit confused, I responded, "I was sharing from the apostle Paul in Ephesians 5, where he talks about mutual submission in marriage, out of the reverence for Christ—a marriage of trust and sacrifice."

Nodding her head, Eva said, "I've heard Ephesians 5 before; I am just wondering if you expect Melissa to submit to Scott like women did centuries ago. You're not advocating a repressive male-dominance structure, are you?"

Not quite sure if I was being set up with a trick question, I asked her, "What are you trying to get at, Eva? What do you mean by a repressive structure?"

Looking a bit frustrated, Eva reacted with a bit of a strain in her voice, "Are you one of those Lutherans who allows women to be pastors or are you one of those other Lutherans that 'only' allow male pastors?"

"The denomination that I am a part of only ordains men, but I don't think I am following you," I said, trying to follow her train of thought.

Leaning back with a slight look of disgust, Eva said, "It's okay, it all makes sense to me now."

What is going on in this conversation with Eva? As we take the time to examine this interaction, we can begin to piece things together, recognizing that Eva is what is known as an egalitarian feminist. As an egalitarian, she does not see any differences in the sexes. In fact, she is rather repulsed by gender roles. More specifically, as a feminist, she is reacting to the word *submit* in Ephesians chapter 5. But why such a concern over the word *submit*, since Ephesians 5 is talking about the mutual submission of the husband and wife—the husband shall love his wife as Christ loved His church and the wife ought to submit to her husband as the Church submits to Jesus? The answer is that Eva was triggered by the word *submit* and was attempting to see if I was promoting an oppressive male-dominated structure—where men treat women like objects, rule with a harsh heavy hand, and give women

---

WHAT IS MARRIAGE?

Remember the Mascot from chapter 1? Oftentimes when talking about marriage, the Mascot will emerge with the Feminized false christ (who you'll meet in the following pages) and they will redefine what marriage is. In other words, the real Jesus, quoting from the Old Testament in Matthew 19:3-6, teaches that marriage is the union of a male and female in heart, body, and mind for the sake of creating a family and the procreation of children. However, the Feminized will attempt to erase the male and female distinctions, while the Mascot will then step in and say that marriage is a loving emotional bond of two persons that is distinguished from other relationships by its passion, glee, and pleasure. As a result, same-sex marriage emerges as a so-called viable marriage, while biblical marriage—with its view of male and female being sexually compatible for the procreation of children—is dismissed.

crumbs of emotional attention. To confirm her suspicion of possible oppressiveness toward women, she asked whether or not my denomination ordains women pastors. Upon hearing that the denomination I am a part of does not ordain women, she was not only offended as an egalitarian, but she was extremely agitated as a feminist, for my denomination's stance on not ordaining women confirmed her suspicions of an apparent abusive male-dominance structure.

It is important at this time to take a brief excursus to mention that there are three different types of feminism—different kinds that are each unique, yet they build off one another. Like waves, the most recent feminist movement builds off the previous wave's momentum; like the second movement built off the first. However, that is not to say every previous movement buys into the ideologies of the ones that come after.

The first wave of feminism occurred in the late nineteenth century and early twentieth century, focusing on women's suffrage (i.e., women's right to vote, as well as women receiving property rights). The second wave of feminism started in the 1960s and continued into the 1980s. Its focus was on things such as equal pay and equal opportunity (i.e., closing the wage gap and allowing for equal career opportunities). Currently, we are in the third wave of feminism, which began in the 1990s. This wave is a continuation of the unfinished work of the second

EGALITARIANISM

Egalitarianism is mostly the way liberal western culture understands male and female interactions. Men and women are equal, and vocations (other than those necessitating the use of male or female biology and physiology in childbearing) are pretty much interchangeable. For egalitarians, there really is no difference between the sexes in most situations, and every effort should be made to level the playing field and downplay differences. Egalitarianism is generally considered our modern culture's emerging viewpoint on the attributes and interactions of males and females.

wave, and its focus is not so much on changing laws, but changing people's opinions and language, and overhauling social constructs that are oppressive to women.

The reason for mentioning these three waves of feminism is to make clear that Eva is a third wave feminist (i.e., she supports all three waves, but is especially drawn to the third). Even though there are plenty of political battles in the court of law to be fought, she is more concerned with the way people think about women and how women are perceived in society. Her focus is not so much on a continued fight for equal pay or unfair maternity leave policies or upholding *Roe v. Wade* (maintaining abortion rights), but rather, her focus is on abolishing gender role expectations, removing stereotypical gender roles, and toppling oppressive male structures. She is about deconstructing traditional patriarchal language that she believes is used to suppress the roles of women.

"Sorry Eva, not sure what you are trying to say," I shared with a bit of concern in my voice.

"I work with a non-profit group on the east coast, and our goal is to free women from male-dominated corporations and institutions.

WHAT ARE SOCIAL CONSTRUCTS?

Social constructs are ideas and roles created and accepted by a particular society. They are ideas of behavior and of how people relate to one another in social groups. Considering this, since they are created and accepted by people in a society, they can be deconstructed and torn down.

While there is truth to the fact that some social constructs exist due to the needs, values, and interests of a particular culture, it is not true that everything is a social construct. Fashions, political systems, and social classes are examples of social constructs; however, things like marriage and gender are not—they belong to the realm of the created order of things. (See Genesis 1–3 for the created order.)

We have accomplished so much, and it's just upsetting to see that the church is stuck with male sexism! It's frustrating to see that Christianity is so entrenched in the old European male-dominance structure. It is a continued injustice that girls and women are facing inside the walls of the church. It all needs to be torn down!" Eva asserted with an articulate tact.

I was still trying to catch up to Eva's concern, "Are you struggling with today's marriage ceremony? Are you struggling with marriage being an earthly image of Christ and His bride, the church?"

"Yes, actually I am. That nuptial imagery certainly is problematic to women," Eva answered.

"How so?" I asked.

"Well, if we hold to the idea that Jesus does it all for His Bride, the Church, we are reinforcing passivity, dependence, and submission, which is detrimental to a woman's well-being. Furthermore, it is a bad metaphor because it develops the idea that the woman brings nothing to the marriage except sin, death, and damnation, like Eve did in the Book of Genesis. Everybody knows how majorly Eve screwed up in the garden and men have been blaming her ever since," Eva responded.

PATRIARCHALISM

Patriarchalism is mostly the way conservative western culture understands male and female interactions. Men are to be ultra-manly-men and women are to be ultra-feminine. Primary roles for each arise out of the idealized nuclear family structure where the male is the head of house (i.e., in charge of wife and children), breadwinner, slayer of wild beasts, lifter of heavy objects, opener of pickle jars, etc. and the female has a docile heart, making her subservient to her husband's authority. She is the bearer of children and the manager of the home. Patriarchalism is generally considered the traditional viewpoint by our modern culture on the attributes and interactions of males and females.

"So, you see this nuptial metaphor of Christ the groom and His Bride, the Church, as reinforcing the subordination of women?" I asked.

"Yes, it is completely sexist, if you think about it. These gender roles lock women up. Furthermore, this whole idea of God becoming a 'man' is fundamentally sexist and opens the floodgates of oppression," Eva answered.

At this point, I was rather taken aback—again—by her comments. I must have had a look of confusion when I said, "Are you saying Jesus should not have been a man?"

"What I am saying is that the maleness of Jesus should be separated from His divinity. Jesus was divine, but not divinely male. We shouldn't have to understand Jesus in terms of male leadership, male power, and male-domination. Instead, he is a person who goes to the downtrodden to give them encouragement and compassion in the face of oppression," Eva responded.

Meet our eleventh false christ: the Feminized. This false christ is meek, mild, soft, and gentle with longer feathered hair and a perfect complexion. He spends His time cuddling little lambs and catering to our emotions.

Not only is Eva drifting toward some of the aspects of the Social Justice Warrior and Liberation Theology (chapter 7), but Eva is enforcing several presuppositions upon the person of Jesus which makes this tenth false christ slightly different from the Social Justice Warrior.

Eva wants to separate the two genders of male and female. In other words, as an egalitarian, she does not want males and females grouped together or compared and contrasted—she wants to detach male and female from each other. The reason why? Eva wants to eliminate gender distinctions to ensure females are not dependent upon or submissive to males. For Eva, eliminating gender distinctions is a way of diminishing gender differences, which ultimately reduces traditional gender roles—roles she believes are oppressive to women. This ultimately is intended to give women autonomy and freedom from oppressive men and an oppressive patriarchal social construct that promotes supposed male dominance over females.

Once Eva has eradicated the traditional gender roles of male and female, she then, as a third wave feminist, works to remove any traditional masculine aspects that are supposedly consistent with a male-dominance structure. This is most evident in how Eva removes traditional masculine features from Jesus, such as gritty strength, fearlessness, leadership, and authority. Again, Eva believes that by eliminating traditional masculine characteristics from Jesus, she is removing features that are supposedly consistent with the male-dominance structure she accuses Christianity of promoting. Simply stated, a male savior who has masculine characteristics essentially beckons, supports, and strengthens notions of male superiority, which is contrary to Eva's third wave feministic objectives.

As a result of Eva trying to eliminate a male-dominance structure in Christianity, she inadvertently strains out everything ascribed to traditional masculinity, leaving not a neutral Jesus but a Jesus characterized by traditional feminine attributes. This false christ is the reason for so many contemporary praise and worship love songs, touchy-feely sermons, and effeminate pastors. Furthermore, this false christ exalts emotions, experiences, and opinions above sound teaching. This false

WHAT IS A GENDER BINARY?

Males and females are opposite sides to the same coin. Males and females are two genders that form what is called a gender binary. Simply stated, if I say male, you say female. If you say female, I will complete the thought by saying male. Regarding both male and female, they are usually set off against each other. This is most noticeable when a person goes to public restrooms. If the two restrooms are labeled "men" and "women," a gender binary exists. However, if there are two restrooms and there are no "men" or "women" signs on the door, there is no gender binary present but two bathrooms.

christ is only about encouraging the downtrodden and giving sweet, sentimental nurturing care to those who are oppressed.

The chances are that you have met this false christ before. Simply do an image search on Google for the words, "Jesus Good Shepherd." What are the top image search results? The majority of the pictures on the internet portray Jesus by having Him holding and embracing little lambs. In other words, what makes the Good Shepherd good? He shows compassion to the little lambs by holding them and even cuddling them as if they were a fluffy cat or a small dog. However, is this how the Bible talks about Jesus as a Good Shepherd? Let us examine John 10:10–18 to learn a bit more.

> The thief comes only to steal and kill and destroy. I came that they may have life and have it abundantly. I am the good shepherd. The good shepherd lays down his life for the sheep. He who is a hired hand and not a shepherd, who does not own the sheep, sees the wolf coming and leaves the sheep and flees, and the wolf snatches them and scatters them. He flees because he is a hired hand and cares nothing for the sheep. I am the good shepherd. I know my own and my own know me, just as the Father knows me and I know the Father; and I lay down my life for the sheep. And I have other sheep that are not of this fold. I must bring them also, and they will listen to my voice. So there will be one flock, one shepherd. For this reason the Father loves me, because I lay down my life that I may take it up again. No one takes it from me, but I lay it down of my own accord. I have authority to lay it down, and I have authority to take it up again. This charge I have received from my Father.

As we contemplate Jesus' words, we can affirm that a more accurate picture of the Good Shepherd would portray Him as one who fights the wolves and protects the lambs. When the cowardly hired hands scurry away, our Lord Jesus Christ does the exact opposite. He lunges at the wolves and places Himself between His sheep and the hungry predators. Indeed, Jesus laid down His life for you and me. He put His body between the wolf of death and us. He allowed Himself to be gobbled by the jaws of sin and death at the cross. He was chewed up and put into death's belly, the tomb. This is what makes the Good Shepherd truly good. When all is said and done, the Good Shepherd does not remain as mere prey but erupts out of the belly of death—ripping the stomach and shattering the fangs of the wolf of death.

Considering this, how many pictures have we seen or can we find on the internet of the Good Shepherd caring for the sheep by defending them from the wolves? To be honest, it is very hard to find pictures that portray His masculinity like this. Rather, most pictures show the Good Shepherd metaphor with Jesus giving sweet, sentimental nurturing care to small lambs. With the exception of some older artwork portraying the Good Shepherd as one who fights against the wolves, the majority of modern artwork seems to support a feminized version of the Good Shepherd.

MASCULINE VS. FEMININE CHARACTERISTICS

Male and female is ascribed to sexes of people. Sex is based on the physiology of a person (i.e., sexual reproductive body parts). However, masculine and feminine characteristics are generally characterized by traits. Masculine traits include defending, forceful, competitive, confident, providing, sacrificial, etc. Feminine traits include nurturing, affectionate, sharing, tenderness, patience, yielding, etc. Generally speaking, masculine traits are ascribed to males and feminine traits are ascribed to females, though males and females can and do possess both traits to different degrees.

Egalitarianism, though, completely ruptures the masculine and feminine traits from male and female sexes, making the sexes indistinguishable.

Is this an entirely inaccurate image of the Good Shepherd though? No, it is not. There are plenty of verses and accounts of Jesus that demonstrate His compassion and nurturing care. What is inaccurate about Eva's view of Jesus is that this false christ is stripped completely of His traditional masculine characteristics.

I realized my conversation with Eva was far from over, so I suggested we move to a nearby table that allowed us to hear each other better. Once seated, I picked up our conversation. "Eva, it sounds like you are trying to ignore the masculinity of Jesus. But why is His masculinity such a threat?"

Nodding her head, she said, "Pastor, the masculinity of Jesus promotes an image of male superiority in the church, which, in today's culture, is simply unacceptable. I believe with all my heart that God is calling women out of spiritual imprisonment in the church. The glass steeple of the church is cracked and needs to be broken so women can finally be freed of the chains that limit and oppress them within the walls of their own churches. God has unlocked every prison gate for there is neither male nor female in the church; we women just have to be brave enough to stand up, get out, and leave the darkness behind!"

In Eva's previous comments we can identify an additional presupposition, one that is actually quite troubling. Her presupposition is that masculinity is seen as oppressive to women. While this may be true in many circumstances for Eva, is godly masculinity for the purpose of oppression? Absolutely not! Even though many masculine traits communicate forceful power, that power is not to be used to dominate people but to serve people.

What is especially troubling about this eleventh false christ is not only that all traditional forms of masculinity are stripped away but also that these traditional forms of masculinity are seen as oppressive in Christianity; therefore, they are seen as oppressive attributes in Jesus that need to be downplayed, minimized, or entirely removed.

But did Jesus have traditional forms of masculinity? Yes, He did. For example, Jesus was not afraid to confront, rebuke, and even offend people in the Bible. We cannot forget that He called the Pharisees vipers in Matthew 23:33 and called Peter "Satan" when Peter opposed Him in Matthew 16:23. We cannot forget that in Mark 4:39 Jesus rebuked the wind and waves of the Sea of Galilee and they quickly bowed to Jesus' authority as a submissive dog bows its head to its master. We cannot forget that in John 2:15 Jesus made a whip and cleared the temple—overthrowing tables and driving out animals. Considering this, was Jesus' masculinity responsible for oppressing? If we affirm Jesus' masculinity, are we automatically subscribing to and upholding oppression against women? The answer to both questions is a resounding no! Jesus' masculine aspects were never used to sinfully oppress His neighbors, but always used to serve God the Father and His neighbors.

A loud blast of noise came from the speakers. It was the DJ announcing the reception time was coming to a close, and they were calling the bridal party out onto the dance floor. Eva looked away briefly and then turned back to me saying, "Thank you for the short visit Pastor!" I thanked her as well, and we parted ways.

Responding to Eva

What is the main thing that drives and controls Eva's thoughts, logic, and decisions regarding Christianity and her views about Jesus? As we have learned, Eva is a third wave feminist, which results in her opposition to any and all male-influenced and male-dominated structures. The reason why she is so against such structures is that she sees all masculine characteristics as oppressive to women.

When we respond to Eva—and others like her—the most important thing to do is to immediately address the purpose and role of masculinity. Now, this may be quite tricky to communicate to her, but it is worth the try. The first thing we want to do is to help reveal why she is opposed to male-dominated systems in society. Most likely she will answer that these systems are bad because they oppress women. Now, here is the tricky part. We can ask Eva the following question, "How are male-dominated systems able to oppress women and keep women down?" The answer that Eva will most likely give us is that this ability is due to power. Generally speaking, we can affirm to Eva that men do have more power than women—that is, physical power that can be used to oppress. (We do not say this to be sexist by any means, but rather as a general observation.) Once we have established that Eva is fighting against a masculine power to oppress, we are then prepared to ask our next important question, "Can power be used in ways other than oppression?" This question allows us to confess that the real Jesus—who is all-powerful—did not use His power to suppress mankind, but to serve mankind.

By talking about power, we can certainly affirm with Eva that some men use power to oppress and abuse women, which is sin; however, we can also help Eva understand that the intended purpose of masculine power is to serve and defend one's neighbor. The Feminized false christ she has created does not do what Jesus did. The real Jesus did not shy away from death, the devil, and sin, but gave His life as a ransom for many. He did not do this to oppress us but rather to free us from the oppression of our own sin. He laid down his very life for the sake of taking it up again for humanity. He, being the first to rise from the dead, annihilated our true oppressor, the devil, and rescued us from the clutches of hell.

Masculine characteristics are not intended to oppress and abuse, but to serve and protect. Therefore, by making this distinction to Eva, we help her see that not only has sin perverted masculine characteristics into oppression and power but also that the real Jesus was indeed masculine and that His masculine characteristics of power, leadership, and dominance were at work for our salvation—leading Him to Mount Calvary.

Eva's creation of the Feminized and her adamant suspicion of any reference to masculinity actually exposes another struggle that may come out in conversations with her and others like her. Feminists commonly will do virtually anything to avoid appearing weak. Whenever they feel weak, they will condemn those who are making them feel that way. This is why they have created a more delicate false christ, for the Feminized false christ feels safer and gentler. In reality, though, they need to see that the Feminized false christ is neither safe nor gentle for he will leave her exposed and bare, clothed only in her own skin. He will abandon her at the first sign of danger. He will cower as the enemy throws daggers at her and as she is left for dead. He is the hired hand who flees at the first sign of trouble.

We can pray that our conversations with feminists will lead to a vulnerable place of confession where they share their story of why they struggle with men. When they do so, we can affirm that the men who wounded them were not just and that those wounds can be healed by the real Jesus who understands our every weakness. The real Jesus promises never to leave us and never to forsake us. The real Jesus fights for us, rescues us, and claims us as His bride and declares us perfect and spotless. He restores us. This is the message that I truly believe Eva longs to hear. In fact, it is the message we all long to hear.

Will the Real Jesus Please Stand Up?

To combat the Feminized, shall we simply offset the feminine characteristics with more masculine characteristics? No, we shall not, for if we try to offset the feminine qualities with masculine qualities, we risk the pendulum swinging the other way, resulting in a Jesus with large biceps, a deep voice, and a readiness to fight everyone who gets in His way! An overly masculine Jesus is also not consistent with how the Bible views Jesus—if we go this route we can create another false christ, maybe some kind of Rambo or Cage Fighting christ.

Jesus was absolutely compassionate, and He was also absolutely determined, truthful, and bold. His more traditional masculine characteristics, though, did not lead Him to oppressively rule over His subjects. Rather, Jesus' strength and what we perceive as masculine characteristics are displayed in His sacrifice for mankind. (See Matthew 26:53–54.) His leadership, power, and dominance were most clearly on display as He trudged the path to the bloody cross of Mt. Calvary, where He was made to be sin on our behalf. (See Isaiah 53:12.) As a man, He took the beating, the hardship, the ridicule, all for those He loved most—His bride the Church.

Unlike Eva, who sees traditional forms of masculinity as oppressive, the Bible speaks of these more masculine characteristics as acts of sacrifice. Indeed, Ephesians 5 is not about Jesus "lording" leadership, power, and authority over the Church, but rather, it is about Jesus sacrificing everything for the sake of loving His Bride—the Church.

In turn, what this means is that Ephesians 5 is not about the husband lording leadership, power, and authority over his wife, but rather, it is about the husband sacrificing everything—dying to self—for the sake of his wife, just as the real Jesus did for the Church. More specifically, what this means is that the wife is not to become a doormat to the husband, something he tramples to get his own way. Rather, a wife is called to trust her husband, knowing that he is to be a husband to her as Jesus is a husband to the Church. She is to trust that everything her husband does is ultimately for her good because he is called to give her everything he has and all that is needed, even laying down his very own life to save hers. He sets aside his own comfort to defend and protect his bride no matter the personal cost. To submit to a husband who is called to protect her with his very life truly means the wife gets to rest in the protection of his loving arms. And that is a great gift.

Let's discuss the *Feminized*

1. What are the main presuppositions of Eva that allow her to embrace the Feminized?

2. Read Galatians 3:27–28. Does this passage promote abolishing the gender-based roles that are established by God? According to these verses, does Baptism in Jesus eliminate gender distinctions?

3. Read Ephesians 5:21–33. Does this passage promote an oppressive male-dominance structure for marriage, the church, and our understanding of Jesus? Why?

4. Using the metaphor of the Good Shepherd and the sheep, how would we understand the Good Shepherd from a feminized perspective? Read John 10:10–18. How does the apostle John portray the Good Shepherd?

5. How do these questions and the verses shed light on the Feminized?

6. How can or do you discuss the real Jesus Christ with someone who sees Him as the Feminized?

Meet Gary and Amber Pederson,
the Glory Theologians

I clicked the refresh button on my email. A beep sounded, and a new email appeared on my screen. It was an email from Gary, one of my parishioners. Now I would never share confidential emails from parishioners, but here is the gist of what he said to me.

> Dear Pastor:
>
> I was wondering if you had time this week to visit with my wife and me about Sunday School? I am a bit concerned about some of the things being taught in Norah's third-grade class.
>
> I could certainly stop by anytime this week that you are free. Otherwise, we could meet for lunch. I'll buy, my treat!
>
> Thanks, Pastor.
>
> Gary

I hit the reply button and suggested we meet on Thursday morning.

Thursday came. Gary and his wife, Amber, had arrived a bit early for our meeting. They both came into my office and sat at my conference table. We exchanged several pleasantries regarding the weather and life in general.

"So, Gary and Amber, what can I do for you? What is on your mind?" I asked.

Gary's face went from a smile to a very concerned and troubled look. "Well, it's Norah's third-grade class, pastor. Her Sunday School teacher, Nate, is wonderful and caring; however, I think he is going too far in class."

Nate was a sophomore at our city's small four-year university. He was a faithful son of the church and had been seriously considering going to seminary to train to be a pastor someday. He was asked to teach Sunday School because he had a lot of passion for the Bible and teaching.

"What's going on with Nate?" I asked with a bit of unease and concern.

Gary leaned forward in his chair and with animated hands said, "He is going too far, simply too far, Pastor. He is going too far with the lessons. My little Norah is only nine years old and should not have to be subjected to gore and violence. And all those big words he uses, it's just too much."

"What gore and violence?" I said.

Shaking her head, Amber spoke up, "All the blood and gore of the cross, Pastor. That is all Nate talks about. He even wears a crucifix! My daughter is only nine; she does not need to hear about all of that, at least not yet. She came home last Sunday afraid of God and concerned about how cruel God was to Jesus by leaving Him to die on the cross."

I waited a couple of seconds to make sure Gary and Amber were finished. They clearly loved Norah a lot, which was why they had so much frustration in their voices.

Gary broke the silence, "Pastor, it seems like we focus too much on the cross and not nearly enough on the resurrection. The power of the Gospel is that Christ *rose* from the dead; it is our future hope that we will rise again. Shouldn't we focus more on the resurrected life rather than on the cross? Don't we limit the Christian faith and the message of Christianity when all we do is talk about the cross?" Gary paused, looked down, gathered his thoughts, and then continued, "Can't we lighten up our Sunday School lessons a bit? Why does everything have to be so heavy?"

Like the Jaegers in chapter 5, Gary and Amber Pederson have similar assumptions. Whereas Jim and Stacy Jaeger stressed that health, wealth, and success are the will of God for Christians, Gary and Amber struggle immensely with God's will being connected to suffering, sadness, loss, and pain. In other words, Jim and Stacy wanted good things from God such as health, wealth, and success, whereas, Gary and Amber wanted good things from God such as an absence of suffering, sadness, loss,

DIFFERENCES BETWEEN A THEOLOGY OF GLORY AND A THEOLOGY OF THE CROSS

A theology of glory and a theology of the cross are two completely different ways of understanding reality and life. They are different theological worldviews that cannot be mixed. In fact, it has been said that every major religion in the world can be categorized as a theology of glory, whereas Christianity stands alone underneath the banner of cross theology.

Briefly, a theology of glory leaves a person's will in control; therefore, glorious things (i.e., health, wealth, and prosperity) are easily accessible to people in this earthly life by applying their will to make glory happen. As a result, obtaining glory by some sort of human exertion is focused upon in life. A theology of the cross, though, understands everything through the suffering of the cross. In other words, a theologian of the cross knows that this life is impacted by sin and that God does allow His children to suffer, so that His children would cling to Him in faith. As a result, God's will is left in control and the story of Jesus' death for sinful mankind becomes the primary focus in life, as the Christian learns what it means to die with Jesus. As the Christian learns to die in Jesus (not only physically but spiritually), the Christian learns what it means to live with Jesus, too—being raised anew in faith in order to look forward to the resurrection at the Last Day where total glory awaits in the new heaven and earth.

and pain. Naturally, this all makes sense, since this is a very common human reaction; nobody likes bad things but everybody likes good things. What does this mean, though? It means that both the Jaegers and the Pedersons are representing two closely-related features of one idea: one family emphasized health, wealth, and success, whereas the other family is highlighting an absence of suffering. They indeed are two sides of the same coin—that coin is called a theology of glory.

A theology of glory teaches that the glory God promises through faith in His redemption in Jesus should be evidenced in our present life, typically through material blessings or good things. That means if there is suffering, a theologian of glory sees this suffering as a result of some particular sin or sins in a person's life. More specifically, theologians of glory—like the Jaegers and the Pedersons—consider suffering as evil. Because Christians are to abstain from evil, bad things should generally not be present in the lives of Christians. Therefore, anything related to suffering is branded as being evil, which results in a shying away from the depths of a messy, bloody, and painful cross. In fact, for a person who subscribes to a theology of glory, the idea that a Father-God would mandate the suffering of His Son on the cross is considered cosmic child abuse and simply too evil for a righteous and good God. Indeed, for a glory theologian, the idea that the cross is where God's wrath is poured out upon the Son of God who bore the sin of the world is opposed to Jesus' words of loving thy enemies and not repaying evil with evil. For a glory theologian, the cross of Jesus cannot be considered a sacrifice, for this is simply too sadistic, too cruel, and is too uncomfortable. As a result, glory theologians diminish, avoid, and try to move past the cross, rather than looking directly at the cross. They seek out more attractive, comfortable, and victorious things, such as the resurrection. That which appears good is exceedingly emphasized; therefore, creating a false christ called the Teddy Bear.

Meet our twelfth and final false christ: the Teddy Bear. This is a crossless christ with no blood, no wounds, and no suffering. This false christ has been sanitized from the messy blood and scary-looking cross. This false christ is rated G and is all about the resurrection, with intent to diminish Golgotha. Additionally, this false christ is anti-intellectual—he does not demand his followers to think much but only feel comfortable. The Teddy Bear is huggable and squishable—he is neither frightening nor demands reverence but instead is sanitized and spiritually safe—he is tame.

As with the other false christs, there are several presuppositions at work with Gary and Amber that lead them to create this false christ. Who the real Jesus is and what the real Jesus accomplished have been adjusted by Gary and Amber to match with their assumptions.

Understanding how a theology of glory works, we can now understand why Gary and Amber were so concerned about Nate's emphasis on the cross in Sunday School. Nate's stress on the cross to Norah was revealing a view of Jesus that was very different from the one her parents believed in (i.e., the Teddy Bear). Furthermore, through Nate's teaching he was beginning to make Norah into a theologian of the cross; however, that struggle of becoming a young theologian of the cross forces a person to begin to see all things in life through suffering and the cross—through the real Jesus, and Him crucified. That is to say, Norah was starting to see that in this life, God indeed allows His children to suffer so we would cling to Him in faith and bring glory to Him. While glory theology attempts to find glory in material blessings, the absences of suffering, and pleasantries, the theology of the cross attacks everything that mankind places trust in, to ascribe glory only to the crucified and resurrected Lord Jesus Christ. Nate's emphasis on the theology of the cross was creating an entirely different kind of theologian in little Norah, which would result in Norah being wholly different from her parents' glory theology. Therefore, Gary and Amber were attempting to protect Norah—and themselves—from the theology of the cross. They were endeavoring to protect the Teddy Bear.

"Why not focus more on the resurrection? That is a good question, Gary," I said. "Well, the reason is that the crucifixion of Jesus on the cross is the centerpiece of the Bible. All of Scripture funnels toward the crucifixion. In other words, the crucifixion is the 'high point' of the Scriptures where sin is atoned for, where the devil is defeated, where wrath is satisfied, and where death finds its end. In the Gospel of Mark, we especially see that Mark is so very concerned to pull us toward God's most dramatic display and accomplishment of love—the cross!"

"But Pastor, you are not defending Nate, are you?" Amber jumped in with amazement in her voice.

"Yes, I am, Amber. Think of what Paul says in his letter to the Corinthians, 'I desired to know nothing among you except Jesus Christ and Him crucified'," I responded.

Both Gary and Amber slowly sat back in their chairs. It seemed like they were a bit stunned.

After waiting a few seconds, I continued, "You know we are surely blessed to have Nate teaching our Sunday School lessons in our church. I'm not sure if you know this or not, but he spends several hours each week preparing to teach Norah and the rest of the children. He takes it seriously and prides himself in teaching the Christian faith. He wants the kids to know Christ-crucified for the forgiveness of their sins."

Looking a bit agitated, Gary seemed to shift the conversation by saying, "You know Pastor, you don't need a bunch of head knowledge to be able to serve the Lord—all you need is an experience. Our kids should not be expected to figure everything out, because if they do try to figure everything out, they will just be confused."

Nodding her head, Amber then said, "I want Norah to be spiritual, Pastor, not religious. I don't want her to be full of a bunch of head knowledge because that will cut away at the very heart of Christianity. Christianity is about the heart beating toward heaven, not a bunch of dead head-knowledge."

We are now introduced to Gary and Amber's second assumption, and that assumption is anti-intellectualism. This anti-intellectualism is not something Gary and Amber embrace in all aspects of their lives. They are very bright and curious people—Gary is a chiropractor and Amber is a stay-at-home mother who does some part-time financial consulting with area businesses. Both Gary and Amber are indeed very educated people; however, when it comes to the church and the Christian faith, their curiosity, learning, and intelligence all shut down. Theology as a discipline may as well not exist for Gary and Amber.

Some Christians—like the Pedersons—hold to an anti-intellectualism because they believe that internal subjective spiritual experiences take priority over rigorous biblical interpretation and sound doctrine.

But why an anti-intellectualism regarding the Christian faith; why the anti-intellectualism regarding understanding the work and person of Jesus? Some Christians—like the Pedersons—hold to an anti-intellectualism because they believe that internal subjective spiritual

WHAT ARE SPIRITUAL EXPERIENCES?

A spiritual experience is an encounter with God that leaves a person with an intense new awareness or understanding regarding God and truth. Typically, when referring to these religious experiences, they take place apart from God's Word and Sacraments.

As Christians, we can be tempted to interpret our lives, the Christian faith, and even the Bible through our experiences. On the other hand, we Christians can be quick to harshly reject experiences, coming across as insensitive jerks. Considering both of these options, how shall we understand experiences? We do not have to blindly accept or harshly deny Christian experiences, but we always reserve the right to assess and interpret these experiences in light of God's Word. In other words, God's Word—not a subjective experience—interprets our lives and our Christian faith.

experiences take priority over rigorous biblical interpretation and sound doctrine. These experiences might include the so-called powerful worship experiences when hearing a vibrant worship song or the potent adrenaline at work when responding to a moving altar call. For the Pedersons, it is more important for their daughter Norah to feel spiritually alive than to be presented with too much information about the details of Christianity.

I was a bit taken aback by Gary and Amber's wishes for their daughter. So I responded, "What I hear you say is that Nate is counterproductive by teaching too much about the cross? Is Nate too theological?"

Gary, nodding his head, said, "Kind of, Pastor. I just don't want Norah's faith journey weighed down with heavy doctrine so it loses relevance for her. I don't want the Christian faith to become like stale bread sitting in her brain. So, yeah, Nate is teaching too much suffering and blood and too many technical words, words like propitiation. These words are just too complicated for Norah."

"But Gary, aren't the kids learning in school about photosynthesis of plants?" I said.

Looking a bit puzzled, Gary said, "I am not following, Pastor."

I responded, "Aren't the kids learning about photosynthesis of plants in third grade? Yet you are suggesting that they are not able or should not learn about propitiation? They are learning about the structural unit of cells, but are you proposing they cannot and should not learn about Christians being simultaneously saint and sinner?"

Seeming a bit agitated with my question, Gary said, "That's different. That is school. It isn't the church."

I think Amber noticed Gary was a little hot under the collar because she put her hand on Gary's arm, smiled, and began to speak. "Pastor, what he means to say is that the emphasis of the blood and cross and all the big words are just too much, especially for Norah. If you are unwilling to talk to Nate, we feel that it would be best for us not to have Norah in Sunday School any longer."

This concerned me a great deal, "But how is she going to learn the Christian faith; how is she going to learn about Jesus?"

"Well, we have been talking about it, and we feel that we can just pass that down to her as we journey together in this Christian faith," Gary answered.

Gary and Amber are embracing two core beliefs. They obviously are impacted by glory theology, which leads them to want to limit the amount of suffering presented to Norah—including Jesus' suffering on the cross. Second, they are anti-intellectual regarding only the Christian faith because they hold to the priority of experience over sound doctrine.

At this point, we can clearly see the Pedersons' glory theology and anti-intellectualism. However, there is an angle of their perspective that has not yet been explored. That angle is that internal subjective experiences take priority over sound doctrine, which is why the Pedersons view the Christian faith as a religion of the heart. Indeed, the Pedersons are hesitant toward doctrine because objective doctrine exposes where their religious experiences may be in error. However, we have yet to answer the question of why they seem to be so resistant to theological concepts and doctrine when they do not appear to be anti-intellectual in the area of academic disciplines. Well, it's because they are trying to protect their false christ, the Teddy Bear. They are trying to protect the

WHAT IS A RELIGION OF THE HEART?

A religion of the heart looks internally to mankind's actions. It shifts the attention away from the real Jesus to the Christian. The focus is not so much on what Jesus did but on how the individual person is doing. Mankind's ongoing individual and personal performance, not Jesus' finished word, becomes the focus of sermons, books, and conferences. What I need to do and who I need to become becomes the end game. A religion of the heart looks inside, not outward to the Word and Sacraments.

false christ that they have constructed their whole worldview around. If their false christ were to be exposed, their worldview would come crashing down around them—something that would be too painful and too earthshaking for them to endure.

Responding to Gary and Amber

What is the main thing that drives and controls Gary and Amber's thoughts, logic, and decisions regarding Christianity and their views about Jesus? As we have learned, Gary and Amber want everything to be safe. As a result, they hold to a theology of glory and anti-intellectualism, as ways to keep suffering and challenging doctrine at a distance.

When we respond to Gary and Amber—and others like them—we must keep in mind that their false christ, the Teddy Bear, is the direct opposite of the real Jesus. As we will hear later on in this chapter, the real Jesus in the Gospels is not tame, and He is not predictable. He does not heed to mankind's timetable. He will not succumb to man-made agendas and plans. The Lion of Judah is not domesticated or harmless, but He is kind. The Pedersons, though, want a safe, comfortable, and predictable Christianity. They want pleasant and calm spiritual experiences. They want a huggable and squishable lovey figure. Therefore, they demand a tame and domesticated false christ—one that fits into their pleasant, calm, spiritual experiences. More specifically, they want a false christ who is predictable. They want a false christ who does not abruptly and gruffly intrude into their lives, but who is there to give hugs when comfort is needed.

This means the Pedersons will adamantly reject any teaching of doctrine and any teaching about the person and work of the real Jesus that undermines that which they hold most dear—their safety and comfort. Perhaps no other false christ is grasped as tightly as the Teddy Bear. Like a young child refusing to give up a comforting pacifier or a young teen not wanting to get rid of a childhood blanket, the Pedersons will resist letting go of this false christ. Fear is a powerful motive for clinging to the Teddy Bear.

As difficult as it may be, we can ask the Pedersons if the Teddy Bear they are clinging to desperately for comfort is in fact safe. Will the positive statements and sanitized stories actually protect them and their loved ones from harm and danger? One way to introduce this in a conversation is to ask them if they feel safe. We can ask them whether they feel their daughter will be safe as she grows up and goes off to college. A Teddy Bear false christ sounds so comforting, until an attack on one's faith comes.

The goal in our conversations with glory theologians is to try to help them understand that the enemy of our souls prowls like a roaring lion seeking to devour us. (See 1 Peter 5:8.) Our sins, doubts, and fears threaten to undo us. It may seem counterintuitive, but we can pray in our conversations with individuals such as the Pedersons that in discussing fears related to our salvation and Christian faith that they will realize that the Teddy Bear they have created really can do nothing at all. He is merely full of fluff. He is truly an impossible defender. We can pray that when faced with the gravity of our soul's true terror—sin and death—we can confess that all of Scripture proclaims the real Jesus, who does not flinch and proves Himself the victor over and over. The scariest reality would be to not hear all of Scripture. The real Jesus' blood-stained cross bears witness that He understands the gravity of our deplorable condition. The real Jesus' empty tomb declares Him untouchable. The Teddy Bear hangs limp in our hands, whereas the real Jesus is at the right hand of God the Father, from whence He will come to judge the living and the dead. Jesus indeed drank from the cup of suffering so that we do not have to. This Jesus has not left us defenseless nor does He soothe us with superficial and empty Christian clichés. Instead, He gives us His own spiritual armor and the sword of the Spirit, His very Word. (See Ephesians 6:10–18 for the description of the whole armor of God.)

We do not need to fear, for the real Jesus has promised to be with us and to be our rock and foundation. By God's grace, the Pedersons will see that this real Jesus is truly the safety of their daughter's life. Lord willing, they will see that the real Jesus is the place of rest—rest in the nail-scarred hands, rather than a fluffy embrace of the Teddy Bear.

Will the Real Jesus Please Stand Up?

The real Jesus is not so easily manipulated and managed by our attempts to box Him in. He will not be tied down or pushed into a box. As the Lion of Judah, He cannot be caged. (See Revelation 5:5, where Jesus is described as the Lion of Judah.) Indeed, the grace flowing from bloody Mount Calvary cannot be sewed up with pretty stitching. The Lion of Judah is not a pristine child's play toy sitting neatly on a shelf or bed. (See Matthew 21:12–13.)

Dear friends, take comfort, for the real Jesus is not a tame and inactive Teddy Bear full of fluffy stuffing. This Jesus does not need to be kept on a shelf or stuffed into a display case; rather, from the cross, He cried out, "It is finished!" (John 19:30). Instead of mint condition, collector-worthy qualities, this Jesus opens his bloody nail-scarred hands to us as He welcomes us into His Kingdom. (See Ephesians 1:7; Hebrews 9:12.) And rather than a perfectly-stuffed cuddly comfort, this Jesus' side is pierced, and His blood and water pour out in the blessed assurance that our souls can find true rest in Him. (See John 19:34.) For it turns out that indeed we are the ones who need to be held after all in the bloody embrace of the forgiveness of sins.

A Note on the Holy Spirit's Work

With all of the people we have met in this book thus far, we are powerless to affect any spiritual change in their lives, for we are not the Holy Spirit. What this means is that we are called to simply confess the real Jesus. Yes, sometimes by God's grace we work to clear away presuppositions by asking questions, challenging, and debating, but Christian apologetic work is one hundred percent about confessing the real Jesus. You see, in thinking about the people we have met in this book, we must guard ourselves against the temptation of wanting to rip the false christs out of their hands and force the real Jesus in the same exact spot. May God forgive us for thinking we can do the work of the Holy Spirit. That is to say, bringing about the death of a false christ and replacing it with faith in the real Jesus

> *The death of the idol and the emergence of faith in the real Jesus only happens by the Holy Spirit working through the Word.*

is not such a simple task for mere mortals. With these individuals, we cannot pry the false christs out of their hands and quickly replace them with the real Jesus. No, the death of the idol and the emergence of faith in the real Jesus only happens by the Holy Spirit working through the Word.

The individuals cannot drop their idols on their own for their fingers are dug in too deep. However, as we pray for them, we do have hope that the Holy Spirit will work by the Law to uncover their sin of idolatry, to drive them to the point of contrition when their fingers will release the false christ in horror of their idolatry. But the Holy Spirit will not stop there; through the Gospel, the Holy Spirit will call them unto the real Jesus, enlighten them with His gifts, declare them holy, and keep them in the true faith. All of this happens as the Holy Spirit works through the Word, the very word that we simply confess—words of God's true and perfect Law and words of God's true and perfect Gospel, words that we will gently share with them, when given an opportunity to confess.

Let's discuss the **Teddy Bear**

1. What are the central presuppositions of Gary and Amber that allow them to embrace and sponsor the Teddy Bear?

2. Imagine yourself in a tiny boat in the midst of a mighty storm. How would you react to the lightning, the large waves, and the blowing gusts of wind and rain? After thinking about this question, please read Mark 4:35–41. As you can see, Jesus and His disciples were caught in a great storm as well. Considering this, where is Jesus, what is Jesus doing, and why is this significant? (See verse 38.)

3. In verse 39, what happened when the disciples woke Jesus up?

4. Do Jesus' actions in verse 39 catch the disciples off guard? What do you think they were expecting Him to do? Do Jesus' actions catch you—the reader—off guard? Examine verses 40-41 for the disciples' reactions.

5. How do these questions and the verses shed light on the Teddy Bear?

6. How can or do we address someone who is presenting the theology of the idol the Teddy Bear?

Conclusion

We have been introduced in this book to a dozen christs who seem to fill the needs of our souls, but, in reality, attempt to push down the real Jesus. They attempt to steal the spotlight from the real Jesus. Indeed, we have met the following:

- the Mascot, an idol with pom-poms who encourages his followers in their pursuit of whatever makes them happy;

- the Option among Many, a champion of religious pluralism and pagan tolerance;

- the Good Teacher, who is not the incarnate Divine Lord and nothing more than a wise religious person;

- the Therapist, who reduces sadness, unfulfillment, stress, and averageness;

- the Giver of Bling, who grants health, wealth, and success to those whose faith in him reaches the level it should;

- the National Patriot, who is about life, liberty, and the pursuit of happiness—the American Dream;

- the Social Justice Warrior, who is all about liberating the oppressed from unjust economic, political, spiritual, and social conditions;

- the Moral Example, who emphasizes moralistic living at the expense of forgetting the cross;

- the New Moses, who is about giving new obscure laws that are used for a legalistic salvation and spiritual abuse;

- the Mystical Friend, who is a bodiless spiritualized being living in the heart that exalts signs, wonders, and emotions;

- the Feminized, who spends his time cuddling little lambs and coddling emotions because he has been stripped of his masculinity;

- and, finally, the Teddy Bear, who is a cuddly, safe, and tame crossless and anti-intellectual savior.

As this book concludes, it is important to understand that our intent is not to rudely judge the individuals we have met in this book; rather, through their stories, we raise awareness of the widespread idolatry problem within North America and recognize the idols we

HOW TO SPOT A FALSE CHRIST?

The quickest way to spot a false christ is to examine what verbs the christ is doing to and for his followers. In other words, if the verbs are something along the lines of cheering, modeling, befriending, and psychologizing, then there is most likely a false christ present. On the other hand, if it is the real Jesus who was crucified for sinners, His actions are suffering, bleeding, dying, and resurrecting. False christs will typically be doing something other than dying and rising for mankind's sin. False christs do absolutely nothing productive or helpful for their followers.

must not worship in our own lives. Idolatry is a problem because we do not have a right to define Jesus according to our own presuppositions, our own philosophies, and our own desires. It does not matter what we say about Jesus or what our neighbor says about Jesus. What matters is what Jesus says about Himself. How we comprehend and how we define Jesus is dependent not upon popular opinion polls, social pressures, prevailing beliefs, political hopes, or mindless conjectures, but upon the proclamation of God's Word—the Bible. As a matter of fact, who Jesus is and what Jesus has done and will do, are best summarized in what is known as the Apostles' Creed and the Nicene Creed—creeds that are a summary of the Bible's teaching about Jesus. (See Appendix for the Apostles' Creed and the Nicene Creed.)

Throughout the pages of this book, you have met Jillian, Tamar, Mr. Darby, Wendy, Jim and Stacy, Jack, Simon, Ruby, Walter, Zach and Mindy and Stephanie, Eva, and Gary and Amber. As you have gotten to know these individuals, you have heard their stories and interacted with their presuppositions. While these individuals and their stories are works of fiction based upon real experiences I've had over the past twenty years, I have one more person to introduce you to whose story is not a work of fiction. That person is me, and that story is my own.

WHY CREEDS ARE IMPORTANT

"Pastor, the creeds are not found in Scripture—we believe what the Bible says about Jesus." These words have most likely been echoed throughout history in resistance to creeds. However, the previous statement is actually empty. While it is good to believe the Bible, it is even better and necessary to ask the question, "What do I believe the Bible teaches and says about Jesus?" That is where creeds are important. They are clear in their content and function to unmistakably teach the faith. The earliest creeds (Apostles' Creed, Nicene Creed, and the Athanasian Creed) are not only based on the Holy Scriptures, but are also tested by time.

I felt like an utter failure. I felt lost as a pastor, running out of creative ministry ideas. I also felt like I was a complete disappointment as a husband, neglecting my wife as I worked some sixty to seventy hours a week. It was one of the darkest times in my life. It not only seemed dark, but the darkness clouded my mind; anxiety had inevitably led to depression. Though it is uncomfortable to admit, I remember one night curling up in the fetal position and weeping uncontrollably. The tears were not due to sadness, though; they were due to me coming to terms that I was not in control. The reality hit me that I had been entrapped in self-righteousness again. In effect, I had applied spiritual cosmetics to myself to cover my own sin. The tears were the outpouring of an anguish of my soul at the thought that I was just like the Pharisees of the New Testament times, white-washed caskets—clean and polished on the outside, but dead on the inside.

GREAT SINNERS; AN EVEN GREATER SAVIOR

When we assess the person, work, and nature of Jesus apart from the Bible, we typically commit to two identifiable and definable positions. Indeed, in all the false christs mentioned in this book, there are two common themes working within the created false christ idols. They are an underestimation of the depravity of mankind, which then diminishes the person and work of Jesus. For example, if we view ourselves as basically good, then a Jesus who is crucified and resurrected for poor miserable sinners is not needed; rather, a patriotic-mascot-mystical-friend-christ who gives bling and acts like a teddy bear could be handy to enhance our lives. Conversely, though, when we are assessed in light of the Bible, we come to see that our nature is always much darker than we usually believe it to be. A false christ who is a mere therapist or social justice warrior or good example or rabbi is not sufficient to deal with this biblical view of mankind. Rather, an all-powerful, all-knowing, sufficient Savior is needed to forgive and resurrect us from sin and death.

There is truly no bottom to the pit of our sinful nature, and as I was made aware again of the depths of my own depravity, I realized I needed an even greater Savior than I had previously understood.

As I came to terms with my own sinful self-righteousness, it was as if I was being ground to a fine powder in repentance. Repentance has a unique pain to it. There is a ripping—a tearing—a pulling sensation on a soul, which causes the soul to fall down and be smashed into a thousand pieces. Yet, that was not the only thing that was happening. The false christs I had drifted toward were also beginning to crumble, becoming as sand that sifts through open fingers. That is when I remember meeting the real Jesus.

To clarify, I did not meet the real Jesus, but rather, the real Jesus came to meet me. Also, it was not the first time that I met Him. Oh, no, I had met Him many, many times before, the first time being in my Baptism, when He washed me and placed His name upon my head and heart as I was marked by the sign of the cross. He continued to come to me

To clarify something, I did not meet the real Jesus, but rather, the real Jesus came to meet me.

throughout my childhood and high school, never leaving me and never forsaking me. In college when I questioned the Christian faith and almost abandoned it, the real Jesus did not shrink away but came for me yet again. And here in a moment of darkness, depression, shame, and guilt, the real Jesus did not despise my crushed, collapsed, and broken heart but came to me with forgiveness, life, and salvation. (See Psalm 51:17.)

The real Jesus originally met me in Baptism where I was buried with Him—united with Him in His death through water and the Word of God so that I might be united with Him in His resurrection. (See Romans 6:3–5, where we hear about being united to Jesus in Baptism.) From that time forward, Jesus continually came to me through His Word and Sacrament of the Altar, placing His saving Word in my ears and on my tongue. In college, I learned that I was crucified with Him and that I no longer lived, but I lived by faith in the Son of God who loved me and gave Himself up for me. (See Galatians 2:20.) But like a dog who returns to its own vomit, I continually drifted away from this real Jesus to my own self-righteousness and to the false christs that I had made up in my mind. (See Proverbs 26:11.) Indeed, as the hymn "Come, Thou Fount of Every Blessing" proclaims, I am prone to wander; I am prone to leave the God I love.

That night, with my soul in anguish, was simply another time when the real Jesus came to me in His Word. Reading through the blurriness of my tears and the fog of my depression, I read from Matthew's Gospel, the ninth chapter, "Those who are well have no need of a physician, but those who are sick. Go and learn what this means: 'I desire mercy, and not sacrifice.' For I came not to call the righteous, but sinners."

I can recall the relief—the pure joy—being gifted to me as I read those words. Such simple words; such a simple and powerful message: Jesus came for the sick, Jesus came for sinners! He came for sick sinners like me! Jesus is salvation and victory for sinners; He is release for sinners in captivity. He is the sinner's hope, the sinner's future, the sinner's eternity, and the sinner's forgiveness. He is the Christian's wisdom, righteousness, sanctification, and redemption as stated in 1 Corinthians 1:30. What good news! Hope and restoration filled my sin-wearied heart just as air fills lungs after a time under water.

As you have read this book, perhaps you have found yourself in a similar predicament as me, prone to wander and susceptible to these false christs in your own life. Others of you may have met several false christs here in this book for the very first time. You may have even questioned whether the false christ described in a chapter was in fact truly false, as you wrestled with the uncomfortable realization that the qualities described matched eerily close to the idolatrized christ on the throne of your own heart. Regardless of our circumstances, one thing is certain: we all need the

Regardless of our circumstances, one thing is certain: we all need the real Jesus.

real Jesus. We need Him daily and constantly, for all of these pseudo-christs are insufficient. They are indeed insufficient, for they are not able to forgive our sins—they have no power to recompense sin. Furthermore, none of these false christs can resurrect us from the dead—they have no power over the jaws of the grave. They crumble and fall at the slightest discomfort. They smash to the ground as we trip and fall into the traps of our own sin and despair. They stare back at us with vacant eyes as we plead for salvation.

The reason why these false christs cannot forgive sin and cannot resurrect dead people from the grave is simply that they are not real. Like a craftsman who cuts down a tree and carves the tree into an idol one day and then the next day decides to use it as firewood for his cooking stove, these false christs are essentially puppets of their creators. (See Isaiah 44:9–20 as a good description of idolatry.) In other words, since these false christs are created by individuals to match their own prevailing presuppositions, they are susceptible to changing presuppositions—an invented savior one moment and firewood the next. These false christs are frail and will never have more power than those who create them, which means that they cannot overcome sin, death, the devil, and the world. Because these false christs are created by individuals who would rather reinterpret Jesus than reject Him entirely, these false christs may possess qualities of the real Jesus, as described in Scripture, yet fail to capture the full essence of the Almighty One, the Savior of our body and souls.

These false christs are frail and will never have more power than those who create them.

Considering all of this, where shall we go from here?

We must stop right here and not move an inch. You see, when it comes to the real Jesus, we must understand that Jesus comes to us and for us. If we take off on a spiritual endeavor toward acquiring Jesus, we, unfortunately, will not end up with the real Jesus but with some false christ. That is to say, if we try to acquire Jesus through our own will, emotions, or intellect, we are inadvertently treating Jesus as if He is some motionless hidden prey that must be hunted and captured. This is completely backward! The real Jesus is not hidden. He is not off in the distance waiting for us to search for Him. He does not reside in some out-of-the-way region. He is not high above us or low below us. Instead, the real Jesus became one of us. In His humanity, He was born, lived, and died as fully human, yet fully God. And then He rose victoriously in His resurrection. And this crucified and resurrected Jesus *now* draws near to us in His Word and Sacraments. Jesus is the Word offering Himself and His righteousness to us! He is in, with, and under the bread and wine to give us His true body and true blood for the forgiveness of all of our sins. Therefore, the Christian faith is not one where we venture off to discover Jesus. The Christian faith is not us conjuring up faith that might somehow reach out and find Jesus. No! The Christian faith is you and me being pursued by the God of the universe whose Word stops us dead in our tracks, painfully exposes our deadness, and pours newness of life into our very souls. It is about stopping, listening, and receiving.

> *The Christian faith is you and me being pursued by the God of the universe.*

THE REAL JESUS DOES THE VERBS

An old professor used to say to his students training for ministry that it is important to make note of who is running the verbs. He would say something like, "If the 'Christian' runs the verbs in Christianity, it is a dead end. Only if 'Jesus' runs the verbs does it lead somewhere." Otherwise stated, in our modern Western civilization, we are a culture that likes to do things, which means we must guard against the temptation to take control of the verbs, which would result in the sheep serving the Shepherd, the clay forming the Potter, the branch producing fruit for the Vine, and the sinner saving the Savior. This inversion—as subtle as it is—results in undercutting everything about the real Jesus.

The Christian faith is receiving the real Jesus as the real Jesus reveals Himself and gives Himself to us in His Word and Sacraments. Christianity is about receiving the real Jesus by faith, as the real Jesus draws near to us.

Will the Real Jesus Please Stand Up?

In the introduction, I invited you to join me in asking, "Will the Real Jesus please stand up?" This has been not only a question that we have asked throughout the pages of this book but also our desperate plea of wanting the real Jesus to stand up in the midst of all the twelve false christs. It has been a question and a plea for the real Jesus *Here's the incredible news: Jesus is already standing.* to stand up so we can clearly see who He is and hear about what He has done. But here's the incredible news: Jesus is already standing. Yes, the real Jesus is already standing, whereas all the false christs we have encountered throughout the chapters of this book are truly not able to stand on their own. In fact, they are either propped up by our own strivings or dangled as puppets from the strings of our own presuppositions. The real Jesus, however, stood in our place as He became flesh and blood. He walked through the wilderness of depravity on our behalf. He conquered the temptations to which we so easily succumb. He truly stood in our place in every way, drinking the vile cup of our suffering and sin. He stumbled up a lonely hill and was displayed on a bloody cross. His body was pierced, and blood and water poured out for us—for each and every one of us who are desperately holding on to tattered, hollow, fake christs. I pray that these idols fall to the ground and smash open as we hear about the mighty earthquake and believe that the curtain that separated us from a holy and righteous God has been torn in two.

The real Jesus declared from His cross, high above the false idols of our own creations, that "It is finished!" All our sins have been atoned for. Then, after having done what He came to do, dying in our place, He rises up, takes His seat at the right hand of the Father in glory, and makes Himself known through His Word and Sacraments. Indeed, through the Word and Sacraments, we not only hear who Jesus is and what Jesus did, but we receive Him and His benefits of forgiveness, life, and salvation. And even though our culture and our own lives are like a bunch of reeds blowing in the winds of change, the Word of God does not change. It remains forever. (See Isaiah 40:7–8 about the unchanging Word of God.) What this means is that we can meet the real Jesus right here and right now. Through God's Word, we hear that the real Jesus is God of God (John 1:1), Light of Light (1 John 1:5), very God of very God (1 John 5:20), begotten, not made, being of one substance with the Father (John 10:30), by whom all things were made (Colossians 1:15–17); who for us men and for our salvation came down from heaven (John 6:38) and was incarnate by the Holy Spirit of the virgin Mary and was made man (Matthew 1:18); and was crucified also for us under Pontius Pilate (Mark 15:15). He suffered and was buried. (Matthew 16:21). And the third day He rose again according to the Scriptures (1 Corinthians 15:3-4) and ascended into heaven and sits at the right hand of the Father (John 20:17). And He will come again with glory to judge both the living and the dead (Acts 1:10-11), whose kingdom will have no end (Luke 1:33).

This is the real Jesus, the real Jesus you and I do not deserve, but certainly need. This is the real Jesus who is for you. This is the real Jesus who has drawn near to you in His Word to reveal Himself to you, so you might receive Him by faith and be His own. This is the real Jesus: Christ crucified and resurrected, the only one who forgives sin and grants everlasting life.

Amen. Come Lord Jesus, Come.

+ Solus Christus +

Let's discuss Will the Real Jesus Please Stand Up?

1. In your own words, what is a creed and why is it important?

2. Read the Apostles' Creed and the Nicene Creed in the Appendix. How are they similar and how are they different?

3. When we ask, "Will the Real Jesus Please Stand Up?," what are we actually asking?

4. From your reading of this final chapter and the book in its entirety, how would you define the real Jesus Christ? Who is Jesus and what has He done for you?

5. Look back at what you wrote down for question 6 in the Introduction Study Guide. Can you match what you wrote down to any of the 12 false christs presented in the book? Were there any idols that weren't addressed in the book that you wrote down?

6. What is your biggest takeaway from the book? What has been the most edifying part of this study in your learning?

Appendix 1

Leader Guide

Introduction

Read Matthew 16:13–28. The following questions are going to force you to consider the topic of Jesus' identity and what happens when people set their minds on the things of man.

1. During the time of Jesus, what were people saying about His identity? Did everybody agree? (See Matthew 16:13–14.) Who do people say Jesus is today?

During Jesus' ministry, not everybody agreed on His identity. Some thought He was John the Baptist; others said He was Elijah; still others said He was Jeremiah or one of the prophets who had reappeared in their midst.

It is no different today, as people have all sorts of different opinions on who Jesus is. (For this question, consider listing all the definitions of who Jesus is on a dry-erase board or a notepad—definitions according to the talking points of culture.)

2. As we look at Matthew 16:15–19, what was Peter's confession about Jesus' identity? According to Jesus, how was this confession revealed to Peter? What does this revelation mean regarding the Church and the gates of hell?

Peter's confession is excellent: You are the Christ, the Son of the living God! Jesus' response to Peter is profound as well. Jesus states that Peter's confession did not come from Peter's superior understanding, but by revelation (i.e., revealed truth). In other words, it is important to note that the identity of Jesus cannot come forth from mere opinions of mankind, but must come forth by the Bible's revelation of who Jesus is. Furthermore, Peter's confession was rocklike. It was reliable and accurate. Therefore, Jesus states that the confession of Peter is that solid foundation that the Church would

WILL THE REAL JESUS PLEASE STAND UP?

be built upon, as well as the fact that the gates of hell will not overcome the confessional truth of Jesus. In summary, the Church is not built upon mankind's reason, opinions, or upon a denominational polity, but upon the solid confession of Peter, the revealed confession that Jesus Christ is the Son of the living God.

3. In verse 21, how did Jesus further expound on Peter's confession? In verse 22 how did Peter respond to Jesus' further explanation of His identity? Did he accept it or reject it? Why do you think Peter responded the way that he did?

When Jesus told the disciples about His upcoming suffering and death and resurrection, Peter literally freaked out. He took Jesus aside and rebuked Him. Peter could not handle the idea of a suffering and dying Messiah because He obviously loved Jesus and wanted no harm done to Him. Peter, though, also struggled with the idea of Jesus suffering and dying because it conflicted with his presuppositions and worldview of who Jesus was. In other words, this is an example of Peter's cognitive dissonance.

4. What was Jesus' response to Peter in Matthew 16:23? Why did Jesus respond the way that He did? Does Jesus' response surprise you? Why or why not?

Jesus spoke to Peter as if he was Satan's representative. "Get behind me Satan!" Jesus' response was stern but good. It was needed because Peter was attempting to be a stumbling block to Jesus. Peter was setting His mind on the things of mankind. He was not allowing Jesus to define Himself but was attempting to explain Jesus the way that he wanted Jesus to be (i.e., idolatry). Peter was trying to create a false christ.

5. What happens when we set our mind on things of man and not the things of God when attempting to define Jesus? What happens when our minds are set on the things of God (i.e., the Scriptures) when trying to identify Jesus?

This question is intended to connect Matthew 16 to the topic of this book. Stated in another way, when we set our minds on things of man and not the things of God, we not only create false christs, but we also become a stumbling block to the confession of Jesus. If we talk about the real Jesus, we must do so by the Bible's confession of who Jesus is and what He has done—mere opinions and conjectures and hypothesis about Jesus' identity will not do.

6. Before you read the rest of the book, write down some of the examples of false christs you have experienced in your life. What context did you experience these idols in? After you finish the book, look back at your list and see if you can match any of them to a specific chapter.

In discussing these questions, it is important to ask questions to identify the mission of the false christs, as well as the relationship of the false christs to their followers. In other words, what are these false christs about (i.e., what is the false christ's mission or purpose), what do these false christs expect from their followers, and what do these false christs do for their followers. By describing the purpose of the false christ as well as the dynamics of the relationship of this false christ to its followers, we will then be able to clearly distinguish the false christ from the real Jesus of the Scriptures.

Chapter 1:
The Mascot

1. What are the three main characteristics of the Mascot?

The three key characteristics of this false christ are (1) an avoidance of the Law, (2) the denial of hell, and (3) an acceptance of ethical hedonism. This false christ avoids the Law and denies the doctrine of hell because they undercut this false christ's ethical hedonism. Indeed, this false christ is nothing more than a hedonistic idol with pom-poms. With his pom-poms, this idol stands on the sidelines of life encouraging people in their pursuit of happiness. He always cheers and always supports. Since this false christ goes the way of hedonism, he will never bring about any pain for the individual. In other words, the Mascot will never confront the sinful nature with God's Ten Commandments unto repentance; he will never talk about hell and damnation. Indeed, he will never condemn, correct, or criticize, which means that he waters down the Word of God by avoiding the Law and abusing the Gospel to dodge unnecessary conflicts. He is an all-around nice guy who encourages his followers in their pursuits of pleasure and happiness.

The following questions should cause you to contemplate ethical hedonism, lawlessness, and the doctrine of hell. As you discuss these ideologies, contemplate how they are embedded in the Mascot; consider how they are diametrically opposed to Biblical Christianity and the Real Jesus.

2. What does the Bible say about ethical hedonism?

a. Read Ecclesiastes 2:1–11. Solomon said, "And whatever my eyes desired I did not keep from them. I kept my heart from no pleasure" (2:10). In other words, Solomon tested the pleasures of the world and his reaction to them. After this hedonistic experiment of Solomon, what was Solomon's conclusion about pleasure? What can you expect if you were to center your life on the pursuit of pleasure?

The pleasures of this world are empty. The person who goes the way of pleasure—the ethical hedonist—is going down a path of enhancing selfishness and that is about it. In the grand scheme of everything, nothing is obtained or advanced by hedonistic pleasure. Pleasures are just pleasures; here for a moment and gone the next. Seeking pleasure as the goal of humanity is like chasing the wind. It is futile at best.

b. Read Philippians 3:12–20. The apostle Paul describes certain people who live by the god of their belly. How does Paul describe these people? Who are these people in relation to Jesus? What is their end? On what do they base their mind-set?

Paul warns the Philippians about fake Christians who lived by their appetites. These false Christians made their cravings and yearning their god. To make matters worse, they boasted about their shame—they made their ungodly desires good. Tragically, they are enemies of the cross of Jesus, and their end is destruction, for their minds are set on earthly things.

3. What does the Bible say about lawlessness?

a. Examine Romans 3:20 and Romans 7:7. What is the primary function of the Law? What happens when we reject the Law?

In Romans 3:20, Paul shows us that the main function of the Law is to bring about the knowledge of sin. Furthermore, in Romans 7:7, Paul teaches us that we cannot know sin if we don't have the Law. While it is true that the Law is inscribed on our hearts (see Romans 2:15), the Law has been dulled because of mankind's fall into sin. In other words, the Law is intended to bring out what was originally painted on mankind's heart but has faded due to our sinful nature. When a person rejects the Law and dismisses it, mankind is choosing to walk in blindness and is essentially fighting against repentance. Without the Law revealing sin, there is no godly sorrow for sin. If there is no godly sorrow, there is no need of a Savior.

b. Why can the Christian not keep on sinning that grace may abound? See Romans 6:1–11.

Paul's answer to this question is a big "no!" Why? The Christian is baptized. Indeed, through Baptism, we Christians partake of Jesus and the fruits of His death, which means that we do not have a license to sin, even though we regrettably do sin.

4. Consider what the Bible says about the doctrine of hell, its implications, and the final judgment of mankind. Read Matthew 25:31–46. What does Jesus say about the great judgment? Does Jesus say there is or is not a judgment? Does Jesus say there is or is not hell?

If there is no hell, then our thoughts, words, and deeds really do not matter in this life. Why should anything matter if we live in a morally inconsequential world? That is to say, if there is no Law and no Judge and no consequence for our actions, then nothing matters and anarchy rules. Moral chaos! However, there is a great judgment. As we see in Matthew 25, the sheep are taken unto salvation and the goats are left for damnation. The Lord only remembers the good works of believers and does not remember their sin, for they are covered in the forgiveness of sins. As a result, the sheep—by grace—inherit eternal life and the goats—by their rejecting unbelief—are accursed unto eternal damnation.

5. In your own words, why does the Mascot avoid the doctrines of hell and the Law so much?

The simple answer to this is because the doctrine of hell and biblical Law destroy and undercut ethical hedonism. With that said, this question is to allow the group to be able to articulate this answer and to ensure that they have understood this chapter.

6. Why is the real Jesus not compatible with ethical hedonism, lawlessness, and the denial of hell?

As question 2 points out, individuals who live by the god of their belly are enemies of the cross. Why? If one denies sin, there is no need for Jesus dying on the cross to forgive sins. The real Jesus and ethical hedonism are not compatible. Furthermore, Jesus does not support lawlessness. The reason why? We learned in question 3 that Jesus is not the author of sin. Indeed, we who are baptized into Jesus are not granted a license to sin, for in Baptism we have been joined to Jesus and the fruits of His death. Jesus' death on the cross is not an instrument that promotes sin but is the very place that sin was atoned for. The real Jesus and lawlessness are not compatible. Finally, regarding hell? From question #4 it's obvious, we live in a morally consequential world where the ultimate end is heaven or hell. Indeed, we read in Matthew 25 that Jesus will be the great judge, taking the sheep unto himself and judging the goats. While this can be frightening for humanity, we must hear the Gospel continually that in Jesus there is no condemnation (see Romans 8:1). The real Jesus and a denial of hell are not compatible.

7. With all of these texts in mind and what you read at the end of chapter 1, how can or do you interact with someone who has the Mascot as their idol?

By the time that each chapter is read and the study guide is completed, we will have learned about a false christ, a person who subscribes to the false christ, and how the Scripture responds to the false christ. For example, from this chapter we have learned about the characteristics of the Mascot, we have also learned about Jillian, and in the study questions we have learned more about the real Jesus from the Bible. While each of these three segments can be thought of independently, this final question is attempting to pull all three together.

As a way of answering this question in your own personal study or with a group, con-sider writing out on the left side of a horizontal sheet of paper the things that you have learned from the chapter 1 Study Guide as well as any portions of the Apostles' Creed or the Nicene Creed that might apply to chapter 1. (See Appendix for the Apostles' Creed and the Nicene Creed.) Then on the right side of the sheet of paper, write out the characteristics of the Mascot in the top right and the presumptions of Jillian in the bottom right.

Once completed, take what you have learned from this Study Guide and the Creeds (on the left side of the paper) and simply draw lines to the Mascot and to Jillian. Then ask the question, "On the basis of the biblical confession, what characteristics of the Mascot and what presuppositions of Jillian can be affirmed as correct?" (Keep in mind that many of these false christs do contain aspects of the real Jesus, which should be affirmed.) The second question to ask is, "On the basis of the biblical confession, what characteristics of the Mascot need to be considered heretical and what presupposi-tions of Jillian need to be repented of?" The final question to ask is, "On the basis of the

Biblical confession, what characteristics of the real Jesus is Jillian missing? What verses of the Bible speak to the characteristics of the real Jesus that Jillian is overlooking?"

From these three questions, we now have a very concrete outline for a conversation with someone who has the Mascot as their idol. We understand what they have right (i.e., what we can affirm and have common ground on), what they have wrong (i.e., where repentance is needed), and what they are missing (i.e., where we can confess about the real Jesus).

Note: This exercise can be done with the other chapters as well if so desired.

Chapter 2:
The Option among Many

1. What are the three key characteristics of the Option among Many?

This false christ is not the way, truth, and life, but a way, truth, and life—he is non-exclusive and like all the other religious leaders. Furthermore, this false christ comes from a pagan and modern view of tolerance and most definitely will not speak the truth for the sake of maintaining peace at all costs. Finally, this false christ will reject binary oppositions.

Using the provided verses below and the Leader's Guide in the Appendix, contemplate the following ways in which the real Jesus Christ qualifies as the exclusive Lord and Savior, not just the Option among Many:

2. Read Isaiah 7:14, Matthew 1:18, and Luke 1:26–38. How was Jesus exclusive in His conception and birth? How are His conception and birth different from other religious leaders?

There are many pagan myths of gods being born of virgins; however, when a person takes a closer look at these myths, it becomes apparent that none of the myths are the same as Jesus' conception and birth. In other words, many of these myths feature a special person born by way of sexual intercourse or born miraculously by a woman who already had children. Many of these accounts involve Greek mythological figures and not real historical persons.

Considering this, only Jesus was conceived without sexual intercourse, born of a woman who had never had children before, and was a real historical figure. Jesus' conception and birth are exclusive—unlike any other.

3. Read John 1:14. How was Jesus exclusive in His incarnation? How is His incarnation different from other world religions? *Note: For a definition of "incarnation," see chapter 3.*

Only Hinduism has anything remotely close to the Christian view of the incarnation. Hinduism teaches about something called "the Avatar." Unlike the Christian incarna-

tion, though, the Avatar only appears to put on flesh—the flesh is like a garment. Furthermore, the Avatar is not fully God and fully man at the same time, and the Avatar returns to its former way. This is not true of Jesus. Jesus is fully God and fully man—and continues to be. As God, Jesus can atone for the sins of the world; as a man, Jesus can take the place of mortal man by dying a death on the cross. Jesus' identity is exclusive—unlike any other.

4. Read Romans 5:19 and Galatians 4:4–5. How was Jesus exclusive in His life? How is His life different from other world religions?

Among some devout Muslims, Muhammad is considered sinless. Among other Muslims, Muhammad was only deemed to have small errors or seeming weaknesses. However, examining the Qur'an a bit more carefully, it is clear that Muhammad was commanded to ask Allah for forgiveness (Sura 47). Jesus, however, is commended by the Scriptures as perfect. Jesus was born under the holy Law of God so that He could live a sinless life. This was so that through His perfect obedience to the Law, many would be declared righteous. Jesus' life was exclusive—unlike any other.

5. Read Isaiah 53:6 and 2 Corinthians 5:21. How was Jesus exclusive in His death? How is His death different from other world religions?

Look in Isaiah 53:6, 2 Corinthians 5:21, and other passages that your group may bring to the discussion. Consider for a moment the ancient pagan god Molech. The ancient Canaanites worshiped the god Molech and at the time the Israelites did as well. Molech was worshiped when his subjects sacrificed their own children to him. Children were placed into the hands of a Molech statue and then rolled into a fire pit below as a sacrifice. This is a common theme among most pagan religions—mankind must give some sort of sacrifice to a deity to get some favor in return.

On the other hand, Jesus did not offer up a sacrifice for sin, but rather, He offered up one sufficient sacrifice for the sins of the world—Himself. As God in the flesh, He died a substitutionary death; He who knew no sin was made to be sin on our behalf so that we might become the righteousness of God. Jesus' death was exclusive—unlike any other.

6. Read Romans 6:9 and 1 Corinthians 15:3–7, 17. How was Jesus exclusive in His resurrection? Why is the resurrection of Jesus so incredibly important to the Christian faith and how is it exclusive?

> *The apostle Paul makes a profound claim in 1 Corinthians 15:17, "And if Christ has not been raised, your faith is futile, and you are still in your sin." In other words, if Jesus stayed in the tomb, victory over sin would be incomplete. Indeed, the resurrection from the dead shows that Jesus was triumphant over sin, death, the devil, and the world. No one has been raised from the dead victorious over sin, death, the devil, and the world. Jesus' resurrection was exclusive—unlike any other.*

7. As we consider our friends who are "spiritual, not religious", how can we most effectively communicate the truths we just studied—the ones proclaimed in the Apostles' Creed and the Nicene Creed?

> *Typically, those who say they are spiritual and not religious mean that they take issue with organized religion. This means that they are people who tend to reject old religious explanations but still want to be spiritual. This means that they may take issue with the creeds and various Bible passages, which may sound very formal and stuffy to them.*

> *A possible inroad to this mind-set would be to state the fact that these creeds and the Bible are literally confessed and read by millions of people each year, not only in church, but also as acts of piety. In fact, they are confessed and read at bedsides, on deathbeds, at baptisms, during persecution, etc. Furthermore, they are confessed and read by millions of people from many different denominations, on all the continents of the world, and throughout the last approximate 2000 years. That said, the creeds and the Bible do not belong to a bunch of religious elites but to the Church. Indeed, spiritual people are those who are grounded in the creeds and the Word. The Bible and the creeds that stem from the Bible offer a very practical and important anchor point that provides the church—and humanity—its purpose, destiny, and identity. This may help individuals realize that to be spiritual, their spirituality must be anchored in something secure, something time-tested, and something rooted in real historical events—the testimony of the Bible and the confession of the creeds.*

Chapter 3:
The Good Teacher

1. What are Mr. Darby's main presuppositions that created the Good Teacher?

Mr. Darby has atheistic tendencies that cause him to reject the Creator, which therefore leads him to dismiss the divinity of Jesus. Mr. Darby also uses a magisterial use of reason, which places his reason above Jesus and Jesus' Word.

The questions below at first may seem disjointed and unrelated. However, as they are studied, it will be clear that these questions, with their verses, are showing that Jesus is not just a mere man (i.e., the Good Teacher), but God in the flesh who came into the midst of mankind.

2. Read Genesis 3:1–10. After Adam and Eve had sinned, it says that the Lord came to them in the midst of the garden. What is the significance of the Lord drawing near to Adam and Eve right after they sinned?

It is important to note that in Genesis 3, right after Adam and Eve sinned, the Lord God drew near His creation. Indeed, Adam and Eve sinned and felt shame and fear. The Lord God, though, despite their sin, came toward them. Even when they hid from Him, the Lord God still called out to them.

This is the way it is with the Lord. He draws near His creation. We see this throughout the Scriptures as the Lord never forsakes humanity. We especially see this in the incarnation of the Son of God—God is with us.

3. Read Exodus 25:8, 21–22 and 40:34–38. What was the purpose of the Old Testament tabernacle? Who would draw near the people of Israel in the tabernacle? What is the significance of this?

In the Book of Exodus, we read about the commands of God to build a tabernacle (i.e., a moveable sanctuary). The purpose of the tabernacle was so God would dwell among His people. Even though God is omnipresent (present everywhere), He promised the Hebrew people that He would locate Himself in their midst. Just as the Lord came to

Adam and Eve in the garden, He would tabernacle among the Hebrew people in the wilderness. What a profound gift of God coming to the Israelites!

4. Read John 1:1–16. In these verses, we read about the Word and the True Light. Who is the Word and the True Light that is coming into (drawing near) the world?

As we examine John 1:1, we see that the Word is God. We also hear later on in verse 9 that the True Light was coming into the world. But who is the Word and the True Light specifically? As we read verses 14–16 it is clear that the Word and the True Light are referring to Jesus. Certainly, the Word and True Light—Jesus—is God. Indeed, God is coming into the world, just as He came to Adam and Eve, as well as the Hebrews.

5. According to John 1:14, how exactly did Jesus—the Word and True Light—draw near and live among the world?

Jesus did not come to the world in a tent, but rather He put on flesh—He became flesh. This is what the Christian Church calls the incarnation. Jesus—true God—becomes true man in the incarnation.

6. Take a special note of the word *dwelt* in John 1:14. This word in the Bible's original language is technically *tabernacled*. It is a word that means to pitch a tent, tabernacle, dwell. What is the significance of this word *dwelt* regarding the person of Jesus? What is the significance of this word in regard to the Exodus passages in question 2?

The word dwelt (i.e., tabernacled) most assuredly brings forth to the readers of the Gospel of John how the Lord dwelt among the Hebrews in the Book of Exodus. As the glory of the Lord dwelt in the Old Testament tabernacle, the glory of the Lord was made known in Jesus. The Lord comes to mankind in the flesh—in the incarnation— just as He came in the Old Testament.

7. Considering the verses from Genesis, Exodus, and the Gospel of John, what do we learn about Jesus? Is He just a mere man or more than a man? Who does Jesus draw near to?

Clearly, Jesus is no mere ordinary man. He is God with us. Jesus is the God-man. The first chapter of the Gospel of John clearly teaches this, and He does so by appealing to the narrative of Exodus. Truly, the Lord God draws close to mankind with grace upon grace. He comes to go to the cross of Calvary, to atone for the sins of the world.

8. What are ways that you can or have spoken the truth about Jesus to people who hold that He was only a Good Teacher? How can you utilize what we have just learned to help you in those conversations?

It cannot be stressed enough. The key to chapter 3 is to understand the incarnation. Jesus—the Son of God—put on flesh and dwelt among us. Jesus is no ordinary man. He is so much more.

Besides the incarnation, multiple miracles of Jesus are recorded in the Gospels of Matthew, Mark, Luke, and John that testify to His divinity (i.e., calming the sea, walking on water, raising the dead, rising from the grave, etc.). These miracles are visible signs that are done in order to testify to the truth of Jesus and Jesus' message. In other words, many of these signs and miracles of Jesus were done not as a means to their own end, but they were done so that people might believe that Jesus was the Messiah (John 20:31). The signs and miracles are like a catapult that grab ahold of people and launch them to the person of Jesus Himself and His faithful/true words. They show us that Jesus is no ordinary man but the God-man who came for humanity. In other words, the testimony of the Gospels—which function like a biography for Jesus—tell not of an ordinary teacher but a person who has supernatural abilities, capacities and attributes that are only ascribed to and done by God.

Chapter 4:
The Therapist

1. What are Wendy's main presuppositions that created christ, the Therapist?

A two-tiered Christianity and a false christ who functions as a means to another end are the two key features of Wendy's theology and the heartbeat of Wendy's Growing More sessions.

The New Testament Church of Colossae was full of heresy (false teaching). One of the false ideas that had been spread throughout the Colossian Church was that the Gospel they had come to believe in was inadequate and lacking. False teachers were saying that the simple Christian message the Colossians embraced was not enough. The Colossians needed a higher understanding and great wisdom, which the false teachers were ready to give out.

Consider the following questions regarding the Colossian heresy and regarding ideologies presented by the Therapist in chapter 4. Read Colossians 2:6–15.

2. Consider Colossians 2:6. Since the Colossians already received Jesus, who are they to walk in (i.e., keep in line with)?

It is important to note that the apostle Paul (the author of Colossians) does not call the Colossians to move on to other things since they have already received Jesus. No, Paul directs the Christians in Colossae to walk in Jesus—to keep in step with Jesus. Paul is advocating that they do not stray from the one that they have already received. Jesus is not a stepping stone toward something else.

3. In what two ways are the Colossians to walk in the Lord continually? In what two ways are we Christians to walk in Jesus?

Two verbs are important to note in verse 7: "rooted" and "built up." These two verbs are in the perfect passive. In other words, we Christians are to presently walk in Jesus (v. 6), while continuously being rooted and built up in Him. The perfect tense of the verbs "rooted" and "built up" inform us that the rooting and building are ongoing and continuous. The passive voice of the verbs "rooted" and "built up" show us that this is to be done to us. This cannot be stressed enough at this point! We Christians are to presently walk in line with Jesus, as we are continually being rooted and built up into Jesus. More specifically, though, where do we walk with Jesus? We walk with Jesus where He has promised to meet us with forgiveness, life, and salvation—His Word and Sacraments.

Verse 6 shows us that Jesus is not a stepping stone, and verse 7 shows us that we Christians are being rooted into Jesus (like a plant being rooted to the ground) and that we are being built up in Jesus (like something being built by a construction worker). This "rooting" and "building up" are not one-time events, but are ongoing; they are not something we do, but something that happens to us as we walk in Jesus by faith receiving Jesus' gifts.

4. Where and of whom are the Colossians and the Christian complete? What does it mean to be complete?

With bold words, the apostle Paul points to Jesus as the whole fullness of deity. Paul then goes on to say to the Colossians—and us—that we have been filled (i.e., completed) in Jesus. Yes, we Christians have everything we need in Jesus. We are not lacking. We do not need some new doctrine or some second tier. We do not need some new leader to show us how to get to another level.

5. How do these verses speak to Keswick theology and the idea that Jesus is some means to another end—some Therapist?

These verses show us that the Christian's focus is Jesus, for the whole fullness of the deity dwells in Him. Jesus is not some lame therapist, but God in the flesh. Because Jesus is God, we Christians, and Colossians, are not directed away from Jesus but are directed back to Jesus. Considering the heresies in Colossians to direct people away from Jesus to perverted and extreme forms of piety, it is most reassuring to hear about the simplistic message of the completeness of Jesus for Christians.

6. In keeping with the Eighth Commandment of not giving a false testimony against our neighbors, can you describe a situation (generically) that you have experienced the Therapist?

In thinking about this question, try to identify the theology that was being presented. While it may be easy to think of the group or the group leader holding to the Therapist false christ, it is more important to think about the theology that they were presenting. How did they talk about the false christ? What did they emphasize? What did they not emphasize?

7. Hypothetically, if you ended up in a situation where a group was presenting Jesus as the Therapist, how would you respond? What actions would you take?

While there are all sorts of different ways to respond, the key thing to keep in mind with this question is that those holding to the Therapist are all about trying to make their followers respond and move to a second tier. What this means is that if you meet the Therapist, you will be challenged to move to a second tier. You will not need to challenge to the Therapist, but rather, you will need to be ready to give a sure defense when the Therapist challenges you. Put another way, the faithful confession against this false theology is for you to stay put—to remain in the grace that you have been given in Jesus. Yes, you will not need to challenge this false christ, but this false christ will come to you and demand that you move to some second tier, in which you can be ready to confess that you already have every spiritual blessing in the real Jesus.

WILL THE REAL JESUS PLEASE STAND UP?

Chapter 5:
The Giver of Bling

1. What are the main presuppositions of the Jaegers that make up the Giver of Bling?

The Giver of Bling is a false christ that dispenses health, wealth, and success to those whose faith reaches the level it should. Furthermore, this false christ is a result of an over-realized eschatology. Finally, this false christ does not mess with suffering.

It should also be noted that the Jaegers view this false christ in an "if-then" relationship. The Giver of Bling functions like a generous slot machine—put money in, pull the lever, and he will pay out twofold!

In the Old Testament Book of Job, we read about the afflictions of a man named Job. Job was pronounced as blameless three times in the first two chapters of the book; however, as we read through this book we hear about the decline in Job's health, the loss of his property, and the loss of his children. In the story, we hear about Job's three friends and their attempts to make sense of Job's disasters. The following questions will show us that there is nothing new under the sun, regarding the false ideology that makes up the Giver of Bling.

2. Read Job 11:13–20. Take note of the "if-then" construct. What things does Zophar say that Job should do in verses 13–14?

Job is told to stretch out his hands as a way of showing that he is ready to worship God. Furthermore, he is being called to put sin out of his life. Zophar incorrectly assumes that Job is unrepentant (which is not the case) and that Job is able to dismiss his sin (which mankind cannot do).

3. If Job does the things mentioned in verses 13–14, what does Zophar say will happen to him? See verses 15–19.

According to Zophar, if Job prepares his heart to worship God (gets his heart right with God) and puts away his sins, then his suffering will fall away and his life will shine

brighter than the noonday. Again, take note of the "if-then" construct. If Job stretches
out to God and removes his sin, then Job will feel secure, have rest, and have favor.

4. Consider verse 20 for a moment. Zophar assumes that the wicked will fall and that they will have no hope. Is this always the case? Do bad things happen to bad people only and good things happen to good people only? Why or why not?

Zophar is tragically mistaken in his thinking. While it is true that bad things happen
to us when we sin, this is not always the case. In many circumstances, wicked people
prosper in this life, while faithful people suffer and are persecuted.

What we can take away from Zophar's terrible theology is that mankind wants to have
control over suffering. We want to believe that we can turn suffering on and off, like a
light switch, by regulating our sin and righteousness. However, the fact of the matter
is this suffering sometimes happens to us, and we do not know why.

Even though suffering happens to us and we do not know why, we always have the
hope of the Gospel. Indeed, in the midst of the suffering, the Gospel is clear that our
Lord will never leave us nor forsake us (He will be with us to the end of the age) and
that the suffering in this life will only be a little while.

5. Is Zophar saying that Job can change his suffering and condition if he changes his behavior and puts away his sin? How is this problematic?

Yes. As with the last question, we want to believe the idea that we have control over
our suffering. We like to believe, like the Word-Faith Movement, that we can easily al-
leviate our struggles by simply doing XYZ. The reality, though, is that we do not always
understand suffering, nor do we need to. Rather than trying to determine the source
of our suffering, the better stance is to ask the question, "Where do I go in the midst
of my suffering?" As we heard in chapter 4, our focus and destination are always Jesus.
We do not go to Jesus as a means to get us out of suffering, but we go to Jesus because
His grace is sufficient for us in our weaknesses, trials, and tribulations. The real Jesus
will not forsake us when we are crushed, crippled, and broken by our suffering, but He
will be with us in His Word and Sacraments until the end of the age.

6. How do these questions and the verses shed light on the Giver of Bling?

The Giver of Bling supposedly grants health, wealth, and success to those whose faith in him reaches some undefined but satisfactory level it should. He is clearly not the one and only God-man Savior of the world who died for sin and was raised from the dead for our justification. The Giver of Bling is obviously not the same as the Jesus of the Bible and historic creeds. (See the Apostles' Creed and Nicene Creed in the Appendix for further study)

7. Maybe more than any other false christ today do we experience the Giver of Bling in our day-to-day interactions. How can or do you share the truth of Christ-crucified for your sins with people who hold to this idol?

Much like the Therapist, this false christ is about trying to get you somewhere—not to the second tier but to health, wealth, and prosperity—bling! More specifically, though, this theology is all about actualizing a person's faith through positive faith confessions. Therefore, nothing destroys this false christ more than the trustworthy saying of the apostle Paul, "Christ Jesus came into the world to save sinners, of whom I am the worst" (1 Timothy 1:15). Indeed, confessing that we are great sinners in thought, word, and deed, will irritate those holding to the Giver of Bling. But do not let their irritation bother you, for when we confess that we are great sinners, we then get to confess that we have an even greater Savior, Jesus Christ crucified and resurrected!

Chapter 6:
The National Patriot

1. What is the main presupposition of Jack that makes up the National Patriot?

Jack is unable to distinguish between the two kingdoms of the right and the left. As a result, he has absorbed characteristics of the left-hand kingdom into the realm of the church and the person/work of Jesus.

Perhaps no better passage of Scripture shows the confusion of the two kingdoms than Matthew 20:20–28. Read these verses and consider the following questions.

2. What was the request by the mother of the sons of Zebedee? (See vv. 20–21.) Why did she ask what she did?

The disciples witnessed Jesus' miracles; they saw Him transfigured like the sun; they knew His authority, and they dreamed of how He was going to make things happen; put things into action, if you will. They anticipated, like many others, that Jesus would arrive in Jerusalem, fireworks would go off, the fight would be on, and Jesus would overthrow the Roman Empire and usher in an independent Jerusalem with a powerful reign like King David's.

To sit at the right- and left-hand of Jesus—the King—would be to sit in the highest places of honor in this new kingdom. The mother was asking that her boys be placed in the highest rank of Jesus' kingdom.

3. Did the mother and her two sons truly understand what they were asking by sitting at the right- and left-hand of Jesus? (See vv. 22–23.) What were they thinking when they asked?

They had an entirely different understanding of what it meant for Jesus to obtain glory than Jesus did. They were ignorant of what their request involved. They didn't understand the real kingdom that Jesus was building. They wanted glory but didn't understand the pain that Jesus was about to go through. This is why Jesus asked them if they were able to drink the cup (cup of suffering) that He was going to consume.

4. How does Jesus contrast His kingdom of grace with the kingdom of power? (See vv. 24–28.)

Jesus points out to the disciples that the way to glory and greatness is not through overthrowing the Roman Empire and being victorious. Rather, the way to glory is through the cross, through suffering, and through humiliation. The kingdom of God is not like the ways of this world. In other words, they were severely mistaken about Jesus' kingdom. While they were hoping for joy, glory, and power, Jesus' kingdom was about sacrifice, suffering, and death. Indeed, the kingdom that they wanted was one of glory in the world; whereas, Jesus' kingdom is the kingdom of the cross—suffering to accomplish the forgiveness of sins.

5. As a way to summarize, how do these questions and the verses shed light on the National Patriot?

The National Patriot is about life, liberty, and the pursuit of happiness—the American Dream. He is clearly not the one and only God-man Savior of the world who died for sin and was raised from the dead for our justification. The National Patriot is obviously not the same as the Jesus of the Bible and historic creeds. (See the Apostles' Creed and Nicene Creed in the Appendix for further study.)

6. In the United States it can be challenging to address the false christ, the Patriot. We have such national pride ingrained into our DNA. How can we lovingly teach about the true Jesus and challenge the false one?

Though it might sound simplistic, the key to this question is to learn the distinction between the two kingdoms. Indeed, the biggest mistake in talking about our nation is either to not distinguish the two kingdoms of the church (right-hand) and state (left-hand) or to overlook one of the kingdoms at the expense of the other. Only when both of the kingdoms (the right- and left-hand kingdom) are established and understood, are we able to start teaching about the true Jesus and challenge the false one.

Some important scripture passages on the Doctrine of the Two Kingdoms are:

Kingdom of the Right (Church): Matthew 28:16–20; Colossians 1:13–18; Philippians 3:20; Matthew 16:16–18; John 18:33–27; Luke 12:13–14.

Kingdom of the Left (State): Romans 13:1–7; 1 Peter 2:13–15; John 19:10–11; Romans 2:14–16.

Chapter 7:
The Social Justice Warrior

1. What are the main presuppositions of Simon that make up the Social Justice Warrior?

> Simon creates an oppressor-oppressed construct with people in society. As a result, he makes Jesus into a warrior who fights for the oppressed and fights against the oppressors.

Jesus Christ did not go to cross to die for victims; He went to the cross to die for sinners who sinned against God in thought, word, and deed. Furthermore, even though He could have called down twelve legions of angels—countless angels—to stop the actions of the ruthless Romans and sly religious leaders, He chose the cross instead. Read Isaiah 52:13–53:12 and Matthew 26:47–54, and then consider the following questions.

2. Applying the oppressed-oppressor construct to the verses in Isaiah, who is the oppressor and who is the oppressed? What are the implications of Isaiah 53 upon the Social Justice Warrior false christ?

> Isaiah 53 talks about Jesus' passive obedience—it talks about how Jesus suffered because of mankind's sin and suffered because it was a part of God's plan to crush Him. In other words, Jesus was a true victim—He was truly oppressed with the sin of the world and the crushing will of God. However, He was innocent and sinless; He did not open His mouth. He was oppressed and suffered the judgment of sin and considered it well worthwhile.

> Mankind is truly the oppressor in the case of Jesus. It is because of our sin that He was smitten and made to be an offering for guilt.

3. In considering the verses in Matthew's Gospel, a great crowd with swords and clubs approached Jesus. This said, who were the oppressors and who was the oppressed? Who had the upper hand? Why did Jesus do what He did?

Clearly, the mob was coming to take Jesus by force toward the crucifixion. They had swords and clubs, a lot of force. Jesus, though, had the upper hand. He could have called down twelve legions of angels and settled everything but did not. The reason why? He was not about toppling the chief priests, Pharisees, Sadducees, or even the Roman Empire. Rather, He was about fulfilling God's will in being the suffering servant who would die for sins. Jesus was all about drinking the cup of wrath for the sins of the world.

4. Did Jesus have any other choice but to be the suffering servant (i.e., the ultimate oppressed one suffering for the sins of the world)? Did Jesus have the ability to usurp the powerful systems that brought about His crucifixion and death on a cross? How would someone like Simon respond to the real Jesus Christ?

Jesus was not forced into the crucifixion. He could have avoided it. Furthermore, He could've stopped the crucifixion any time that He wanted. He could've overthrown the abusive and oppressive religious system. However, He did none of this. He chose the cross and chose passive obedience for the sake of salvation.

5. Consider John 10:17–18 and Mark 10:45. What was the mission of Jesus Christ? How was His mission different from a mission to topple oppressive political, economic, and religious systems?

Jesus' mission was to be a ransom for many. He did this on His own accord, for He had authority to give His life and authority to take it up again. While he could have toppled the political, economic, and religious systems by a forceful upheaval, He chose a different way—the cross. He chose the cross to be the victor not over politics, economics, and man-made religious systems but over sin, death, the devil, and the world—He was the victor over that which is visible and that which is invisible.

6. Is there a time and place to work for change against abusive and oppressive systems? If so, consider what we learned about the left-hand kingdom in chapter 6.

Much of this can occur within the realm of the left-hand kingdom. It can happen through voting, petitioning, and running for political office. To learn more about the differences between the right- and left-hand kingdoms, see chapter 6.

Regarding abuses within the church, parishioners have several options here as well. They can leave an abusive and spiritually oppressive church or they can work through existing ecclesiastical authority to make amends.

Note: It is interesting to take notice at this point that the National Patriot and the Social Justice Warrior have a lot in common. They both fail to distinguish the left and right-hand kingdoms to certain extents.

7. As we consider the Social Justice Warrior, how do we take what we have just learned and challenge the worldview of that false christ?

I have heard it said before that if Christianity were to be viewed through an old Western story, everyone would be wearing black cowboy hats and there would only be one person wearing the white cowboy hat—Jesus Christ. This is exactly what the apostle Paul does in the beginning portions of Romans. He levels the playing field by putting pagans and the Jewish people under God's Law and wrath, so that no one is righteous, not even one. Then Paul exalts righteousness—Jesus—for all of humankind. In John 8:1–11, Jesus does something very similar by showing us that there are really only two categories of people—not the oppressed and the oppressor, but those who confess sin and those who do not confess sin. What this means is that the main goal of Christianity is not to gain victory for the oppressed over and against the oppressors, but rather, that the oppressed and oppressors would realize their sin and that everyone would be brought to repentance and forgiveness of sins in Jesus. And when this happens, those who oppress may then not only confess their sins before God, but also confess their sins to those whom they have hurt and make gracious amends for their wrongful actions. Christianity and the real Jesus Christ are about all parties being delivered repentance and faith, for only through the Word of God can there be true healing and true change to injustices.

Chapter 8:
The Moral Example

1. What are the main presuppositions of Ruby that allow her to embrace and sponsor the Moral Example?

> *Ruby has five presuppositions. First, she fails to understand the continued implications of original sin for Christians, which causes her to think about original sin and justification in the past tense. Second, she sees sin as a series of separate naughty events; avoidable with some effort (in doing so, she overinflates mankind's abilities). Third, she has a very low view of God's Law. Fourth, she attributes lawlessness to a Gospel that is too free or too unconditional. Finally, she sees the Christian as having the freedom to choose to sin or not to sin.*

Perhaps no better portion of Scripture captures the life of a Christian than Romans 7, where we read about the struggle between the new man created at Baptism and the old Adam that remains. They are at constant war.

Consider the following questions on Romans 7 and how the apostle Paul speaks about himself and the person of Jesus.

2. Read Romans 7:14–23. Is the apostle Paul speaking about himself in the past tense or present tense? What is the significance of knowing this difference?

> *It is important to note that in verses 14–23 Paul changes from the past tense to the present tense. In other words, the struggle against the sinful nature is a present reality—Paul is speaking about the Christian experience in these verses.*

3. According to these verses, does the struggle against sin continue after conversion and Baptism?

> *The reason why Paul is struggling with the flesh (old Adam) is that the new man was created at Baptism. In other words, the struggle against the flesh is evidence that the Holy Spirit is at work in Paul—warring against sin.*

4. Does the apostle Paul see his sin as avoidable? Does he have power to overcome sin by his strength?

Paul clearly acknowledges that there is a difference between how he should act and how he acts. He furthermore recognizes that he is completely powerless to act the way he should. In fact, he says that he does the exact opposite. He knows the goal, but simply cannot achieve it—what a wretched man that he is. Who will rescue him from this awful predicament? Not Paul, not his efforts, and not his abilities, but Jesus Christ.

5. Through the Law (7:7), Paul's sin is revealed to him. Furthermore, Paul acknowledges that the good that he wants to do, he does not do. And the evil that he despises, he keeps on doing. All of this said, he cries out, "Wretched man that I am! Who will deliver me from this body of death?" What kind of action does Paul cry out for? What doesn't he cry out for? Why is this significant regarding this chapter's false christ?

It is important to note that Paul desires "deliverance" not an "example." He desires to be delivered from his predicament. He wants to be rescued and snatched out of the part of himself that is addicted to sin. He knows that he can't maneuver out of or away from his sin. He needs to be delivered from it.

6. Read Romans 7:25–8:1. Who rescues Paul and what is done for him?

It is the real Jesus that rescues Paul; this is why he gives thanks to God. Furthermore, we read in Romans 8:1 that in Jesus there is "no condemnation." In other words, Romans 8:1 does not say that there is now no sin in Paul, but rather, it states that there is now no condemnation for his sin, for he is justified in Christ Jesus.

7. As a way to summarize, how do these questions and the verses in Romans help us better understand the Moral Example?

The Moral Example emphasizes moralistic living at the expense of forgetting the cross. He is clearly not the one and only God-man Savior of the world who died for sin and was raised from the dead for our justification. The Moral Example is obviously not the same as the Jesus of the Bible and historic creeds. (See the Apostles' Creed and Nicene Creed in the Appendix for further study)

8. When you cross paths with this false christ, how can or do you respond?

As it is true with many of these false christs, there is always a small element of truth in their identity and teaching. In regard to the Moral Example, it is true that mankind does have the freedom and power to imitate and externally follow the Moral Example; however, this does not mean that mankind can truly fear, love, and trust the Lord. Indeed, Christians and even unbelievers can externally fulfill what is commonly called civil righteousness; however, no one without the operation of the Holy Spirit through the Word and Sacraments can fear, love, and trust God, which is called spiritual righteousness.

The point to this is that believers and unbelievers can—to a certain extent—mimic and follow the Moral Example; however, when it comes to the real Jesus, we must confess that our human hearts lack the fear of God and trust in God—that we can do nothing, unless the Holy Spirit gives us holy impulses. A person holding to the false christ must be steered away from civil righteousness to spiritual righteousness to see the futility of their ways.

Chapter 9:
The New Moses

1. What are the main presuppositions of Walter that allow him to embrace and sponsor the New Moses?

> *Walter elevated his traditions to the level of Scripture and then clung to these traditions as a basis for his justification. The New Moses was then embraced to validate Walter's traditions and thus affirm Walter's self-justification.*

The real Jesus and His followers did not follow the traditions of the Pharisees. Mark 7:1–13 records the confrontation that resulted from their conflict. Read Mark 7:1–13 and consider the following questions.

2. In verse 7, Jesus quotes Isaiah the prophet. According to verse 7, what are the Pharisees doing with the commandments of men?

> *As with Walter, the Pharisees were raising the commandments of men up to, and often times above, God's divine commandments.*

3. Consider verses 8–13. Once the Pharisees raised the commandments of man up to the level of God's divine commandments, what resulted?

> *Once the commandments of mankind were raised up to and above God's divine commandments, God's commands were not only left but also rejected. Jesus gives a specific example in verses 9–13, where he shows that the Pharisees have neglected the Fourth Commandment by thinking that it was more vital to give a contribution than to sustain aging parents.*

4. What happens if a person goes the way of the Pharisees and elevates the traditions of mankind, rejects God's divine commands, and then validates all of this in the name of Jesus Christ?

> *Elevating the traditions of mankind, rejecting God's divine commands, and then validating all of this in the name of Jesus Christ is how the New Moses is created. Not*

only is the New Moses a false christ, but this false christ also does not speak about the
Gospel whatsoever.

In chapter 8 we met the Moral Example and here we met the New Moses, false christs who both go the way of works-righteousness. They also tend to see sin as something external and goodness as something inherently internal. In light of this, consider the following question regarding Mark 7:20–23.

5. Both Ruby (chapter 8) and Walter not only keep up good external appearances but also tend to see sin as something outside of themselves. However, where does the real Jesus locate the problem of sin? What are the implications of where Jesus locates the problem of sin?

See Mark 7:20–23. Jesus clarifies that sin comes out of a person's heart. In other words,
a person can clean himself up—they can quit their habitual drinking, stop their foul-
mouth cursing, end extramarital affairs—and still end up in hell. While it is good for all
of us to discipline our lives, we must understand that merely polishing the outside is not
sufficient. Indeed, not only are our words and deeds stained with sin, but our thoughts
are stained as well. Our condition is such that we are fallen people with defiled hearts.
Merely cleaning up the external outside—which is possible to a certain extent by per-
sonal effort and discipline—does nothing to crucify the sinful heart. Only the real Jesus
Christ can deal with the depravity of mankind's sinful condition, and for mankind's sin-
ful condition mere rules, traditions, and examples are not sufficient. The real problem is
not the stuff on the outside of the whitewashed tomb, but the dead bones on the inside.
Only the real Jesus Christ can deal with the deadness and sin within.

6. To summarize, how do these questions and Mark 7 shed light on the New Moses?

The New Moses is about giving new obscure laws that are used for legalistic salvation
and spiritual abuse. He is clearly not the one and only God-man Savior of the world
who died for sin and was raised from the dead for our justification. The New Moses is
obviously not the same as the Jesus of the Bible and historic creeds. (See the Apostles'
Creed and Nicene Creed in the Appendix for further study.)

7. How can we help address the Law/Gospel confusion people have when they follow the New Moses?

The Small Catechism is a great place to start, especially the Ten Commandments and the Apostle's Creed. The reason why this is so is that the Ten Commandments are God's Law, His Law that curbs our sinful nature, reveals our sin, and shows us God's good will. The Ten Commandments capture our relationship towards God (Commandments 1–3) and our relationship to our neighbors (Commandments 4–10). The Ten Commandments are God's Word of Law, His divine No. On the other hand, the Apostles' Creed is Gospel. The Apostles' Creed talks about our Triune God who creates us, redeems us, and sanctifies us. It is all about what the Lord does for us. The Apostle's Creed is God's Word of Gospel, His divine Yes.

In going to the Ten Commandments and the Apostles' Creed, confusion may be able to be avoided, as Law and Gospel are rightly distinguished from each other.

Keep in mind that the goal is never to get the right balance or mixture of Law and Gospel (50 percent Law and 50 percent Gospel), but rather, it is to distinguish Law and Gospel. They are not one word, but two different doctrines, with two different effects with the same aim of salvation: Law unto repentance; Gospel unto faith.

Chapter 10:
The Mystical Friend

1. What are the central presuppositions of Zach, Mindy, and Stephanie that allow them to embrace and sponsor the Mystical Friend?

> *Jesus was separated from the Word and Sacraments. He was also stripped of His humanity and reduced to a bodiless fairy-like mystical being that was then relocated within their hearts. From their hearts, this false christ would speak to them by impressions, signs, and wonders.*

As a way of review, consider these comments about Gnosticism in regard to the following questions:

In the Early Church, there was a heresy called Gnosticism. Gnosticism didn't like the material world but favored the spiritual world. This became especially troubling when Gnostics began to teach that Jesus did not have a body. They believed that it only seemed that Jesus had a body. This becomes problematic, for if Jesus was not fully man, then salvation is not possible.

2. Read 1 John 1:1. What three human senses does John talk about? What do these senses have to do with Jesus?

> *John mentions three senses: sight, touch, and hearing. It is by these three senses that the disciples can affirm that Jesus was fully man. They heard Jesus with their own ears; they saw Jesus with their own eyes; they touched Jesus with their own hands. Jesus was fully man.*

> *Why is it important for Jesus to be fully man? If He is not a man, He can't be nailed to the cross. If He was not nailed to the cross, God could not condemn sin in the flesh of Jesus, and God could not justify mankind by His blood.*

3. Read Acts 1:6–11. What do these verses teach us about where Jesus is now?

> *These verses tell us that Jesus ascended upward—rising—until a cloud received Him. And then Jesus passed from human sight. Other verses, such as 1 Peter 3:22, tell us*

that Jesus has gone to heaven and is at the right hand of God. All this said, it is important to note that Jesus rose bodily. He reigns at the right hand of the Father until He will come back at His second coming to judge the living and the dead.

4. If Jesus is at the right hand of the Father—bodily—is He somehow confined or restricted to a particular place in heaven so that in His body He can't be present with mankind? Examine Jesus' Words of Institution in Matthew 26:26–28. What does Jesus promise in the Lord's Supper?

Jesus promises that He is present with us in the Supper. In, with, and under the bread and wine, Jesus is truly present to give Himself to the Church for the forgiveness of sins. That is to say, the true body and blood are present and distributed and received in Communion. The bread and wine do not symbolize an absent body and blood, but they truly are Jesus' body and blood.

5. Read the following verses in the order they follow: Romans 10:17; 1 Corinthians 1:21; 1 Peter 1:23; Hebrews 4:12; and 2 Timothy 3:16. What do these verses teach us about the Word of God?

It is through the proclaimed Word of God that faith happens, and we are saved, or we could say, "born anew." Furthermore, it is through the Word of God that the thoughts and intentions of our hearts are judged. The Word of God interrogates us and shapes and forms us. Indeed, it is useful for reproof, correction, and training. The Word stands above and over mankind. The Word of God is the final influential authority for faith and conduct.

6. How do these questions and the verses shed light on the Mystical Friend?

The Mystical Friend is a bodiless spiritualized being living in the heart that exalts signs, wonders, and emotions. He is clearly not the one and only God-man Savior of the world who died for sin and was raised from the dead for our justification. The Mystical Friend is obviously not the same as the Jesus of the Bible and historic creeds. (See the Apostles' Creed and Nicene Creed in the Appendix for further study.)

7. If one of your friends said to you: "I don't need to go to church anymore because I am getting everything I spiritually need in the joy I experience in my small group," how would you respond?

> While there are indeed blessings in meeting in small groups and opportunity to con-
> nect with others easily, nothing can replace gathering with a faithful congregation
> to receive the gifts of Jesus in Word and Sacrament. More specifically, the blessing of
> receiving the body and blood of Jesus in Communion only happens when you gather
> with other Christians in a congregation, something that typically does not occur in a
> small group.

> If Communion is being conducted in a small group along with a Bible study, this does
> not remedy the concern stated above but makes it worse. That is to say, if the Word
> and Sacrament are given in a small group apart from a local church and pastor, and
> people are disconnected from the local church, whether the small group knows it or
> not, they have essentially become a separate church. If this is the case, the severity of
> the situation increases, for now it must be asked, who is the pastor of the small group?
> In fact, who in the small group is trained for professional pastoral care? Who will
> conduct weddings, pastoral care, funerals, baptisms, etc.? Furthermore, is the church a
> non-profit entity? How is money handled? Who is the governing council of the group? Is
> there ecclesiastical oversight of the group to help prevent scandal? If the small group is
> functioning as a church, are they violating city code by meeting in a house?

> More to the point, the real Jesus is not fragmented into our lives and groups. We do
> not divide up Jesus and fit him into our personal identities. Rather, we are unified into
> Jesus. When we look at the Church, we do not see groups such as farmers, ranchers,
> businessmen, housewives, students, bankers, secretaries, grandmas, grandpas, etc.
> No, we see a bunch of different people who have been called together into the real
> Jesus. We see various people finding their rest and identity—their oneness—in Jesus.
> As members of the church, we join as common sinners with the same Savior—Jesus.

Chapter 11:
The Feminized

1. What are the main presuppositions of Eva that allow her to embrace the Feminized?

   Eva was triggered by the word submit. She was concerned about any male-dominated structure that oppresses women. As a result, she wants to separate male and female, to prevent the female from either depending upon the male or being dominated by a male and to free the female from gender-oppressive roles. Once separated, she then desires to downplay and diminish any traditional masculine attributes that can contribute to oppressiveness. Generally speaking, Eva sees masculine characteristics as oppressive toward females.

   Regarding Jesus, the same is true. Jesus as a groom and the Church as the bride is a construct that needs to be diminished, for it can lead to a male-dominated oppressive structure. A masculine-looking Jesus is detrimental to Eva's feminized agenda, for a masculine-looking Christ summons and supports ideas of male dominance.

2. Read Galatians 3:27–28. Does this passage promote abolishing the gender-based roles that are established by God? According to these verses, does Baptism in Jesus eliminate gender distinctions?

   Galatians 3:27–28 is often used in liberal denominations as a basis to negate gender specific roles. It is argued that since we have been clothed in Jesus, there are no longer male-female role distinctions. That is to say, it is argued that these verses replace the old creation order of Genesis 1–3. However, when we read this passage in context of Galatians 3, we can see that it is not speaking about equal rights, the qualifications for pastoral ministry, the elimination of gender, or about civil rights; but rather, these verses are all about the fact that status, sex, and ability do nothing or contribute nothing to our justification. These verses in Galatians 3:27–28 are not Law that should be used to tear down supposed oppressive structures, but rather, these verses are Gospel, showing that justification is not based on a person's race, gender, age, or national origin, but upon the real Jesus' death, burial, and resurrection.

3. Read Ephesians 5:21–33. Does this passage promote an oppressive male-dominance structure for marriage, the church, and our understanding of Jesus? Why?

Ephesians 5 is not about Jesus lording leadership, power, and authority over the Church; but rather, it is about Jesus sacrificing everything for the sake of loving His Bride—the Church. What this means for our human relationships is that Ephesians 5 is not about the husband lording leadership, power, and authority over his wife, but rather, it is about the husband sacrificing everything—giving up his life if needed—for the sake of his wife, just as Jesus did for the Church. More specifically, what this means is that the wife is not to become a doormat to the husband, so that she can get walked on, but rather, she is called to trust her husband, knowing that her husband is to be a husband to her as the real Jesus is a husband to the Church. She is to trust that everything the husband does is ultimately for her good because he only has good things in store for her. Ephesians 5 is the Biblical view of marriage—the way a healthy and godly marriage can and should be.

4. Using the metaphor of the Good Shepherd and the sheep, how would we understand the Good Shepherd from a feminized perspective? Read John 10:10–18. How does the apostle John portray the Good Shepherd?

We often see pictures of the Good Shepherd cuddling little lambs. This picture is a feminine and maternal depiction of the Good Shepherd. While it is true that there is comfort in the Shepherd's care, a more accurate picture is portraying the Good Shepherd as the one who fights the wolves to protect lambs. In other words, the strength, fearlessness, and dominion of the Shepherd are not for the sake of oppressing the sheep, but for protecting, loving, and sacrificing for the sheep. The point being, the masculine aspects of the Shepherd are not for oppression but rather for protection. The power and might are for sacrifice, not for tyranny.

5. How do these questions and the verses shed light on the Feminized?

The Feminized spends his time cuddling little lambs and accentuating emotions because he has been stripped of his masculinity. He is clearly not the one and only God-man Savior of the world who died for sin and was raised from the dead for our jus-

tification. The Feminized is obviously not the same as the Jesus of the Bible and historic creeds. (See the Apostles' Creed and Nicene Creed in the Appendix for further study.)

6. How can or do you discuss the real Jesus Christ with someone who sees Him as the Feminized?

We often base our view of Jesus upon art that is displayed in the halls of the church, included in childhood curriculum, or from movies about Jesus. Considering this, a good place to start a conversation with someone embracing the Feminized is identifying what artistic expressions of Jesus they have been exposed to (i.e., pictures in the church, pictures in Sunday School curriculum, movies, etc.). Then identify if these artistic expressions are masculine, feminine, or both. If they are feminine, another question that could be asked is this: what would artwork look like if it was produced to capture the more masculine aspects of the real Jesus? What would be different? What would be the same?

Keep in mind that this chapter on the Feminized is not saying that Jesus did not have feminine characteristics (i.e., caring, loving, nurturing), but rather, it is addressing the fact that the masculine characteristics of Jesus are many times eliminated, which lead to a false christ named the Feminized.

Chapter 12:
The Teddy Bear

1. What are the central presuppositions of Gary and Amber that allow them to embrace and sponsor the Teddy Bear?

Gary and Amber have a theology of glory. This theology of glory is unable to deal with the reality of suffering, which results in seeing suffering as evil and wrong. This then causes Gary and Amber to avoid the aspects of the cross, as well as Jesus' suffering.

Furthermore, Gary and Amber are anti-intellectual when it comes to their faith. They are governed by their experiences and tend to resist any teaching about Christianity that will unsettle their non-challenging false christ.

With this stated, we can conclude that both their glory theology and anti-intellectualism exist for the purpose of keeping their false christ—the Teddy Bear—as tame, safe, and unchallenging as possible.

2. Imagine yourself in a tiny boat in the midst of a mighty storm. How would you react to the lightning, the large waves, and the blowing gusts of wind and rain? After thinking about this question, please read Mark 4:34–41. As you can see, Jesus and His disciples were caught in a great storm as well. Considering this, where is Jesus, what is Jesus doing, and why is this significant? (See verse 38.)

Jesus was not majestically walking on water. He was not rowing an oar with confidence or scooping water up with determination. None of these were the case. He was quietly asleep in the boat, in the stern.

3. In verse 39, what happened when the disciples woke Jesus up?

When the disciples woke Jesus up, He looked at the situation, and then with four simple and direct words made everything right, "Be still; be silenced!" Like basically turning off the faucet, the rain stopped. Like simply flipping the switch on a fan, the wind ceased. A great calm settled.

4. Do Jesus' actions in verse 39 catch the disciples off guard? What do you think they were expecting Him to do? Do Jesus' actions catch you—the reader—off guard? Examine verses 40–41 for the disciples' reactions.

The disciples were most likely not expecting Jesus to calm the storm but to probably scoop water out of the boat or help row an oar. However, when Jesus exercised His authority over creation itself, they were afraid. They were filled with great awe.

The reason for the fear and awe was that this calming of the sea was more than they bargained for. They simply wanted another person to row, maybe another person to scoop water, or maybe their teacher to at least pray. But to turn off the raging sea, like switching a light to the off position? They had not asked for this, nor were they prepared to process it.

This incredible miracle shows us that Jesus is no tame, powerless, squishy teddy bear. But rather, Jesus is the one who exercises authority over nature. He is the one who has authority over a legion of demons. (See Mark 5:1–20.) He is the one who has power over sickness and even death itself. (See Mark 5:21–43.) The point being, Jesus is not tame but can tame things like nature itself.

5. How do these questions and the verses shed light on the Teddy Bear?

The Teddy Bear is cuddly, safe, tame, crossless, and anti-intellectual. He is clearly not the one and only God-man Savior of the world who died for sin and was raised from the dead for our justification. The Teddy Bear is obviously not the same as the Jesus of the Bible and historic creeds. (See the Apostles' Creed and Nicene Creed in the Appendix for further study.)

6. How can or do we address someone who is presenting the theology of the idol the Teddy Bear?

As we have learned in chapter 12, there is an enormous amount of fear involved in the Teddy Bear. He is seen as safe and comfortable. But, as said in chapter 12, the key with someone holding onto the Teddy Bear is to help them see that, when an attack comes on one's faith, this false christ will not endure. In other words, this false christ is clung to for the supposed comfort that it gives; however, the catch-22 is this, even though this false christ seems comforting and secure to its followers, it cannot stand against the ideological assaults of our culture and it cannot endure the fire arrows of the evil one. So, while it may seem a bit aggressive, this false christ needs to be brought in front of the ideological assaults of the world's ideology and it needs to be brought before the battering of the devil, in order to show that this false christ cannot and will not endure—to show that this false christ is not as safe and secure as one might think.

Conclusion:
Will the Real Jesus Please Stand Up?

1. In your own words, what is a creed and why is it important?

   The word creed comes from the Latin word credo which means, "I believe." Therefore, a creed is a succinct profession of what an individual or church believes. Two of the most important creeds—the Apostles' Creed and the Nicene Creed—seek to answer the question of "Who is Jesus?" They answer this question by defining who Jesus is in relationship to God and in relationship to humankind. They do this on the basis of Holy Scripture—the Apostolic Teachings.

2. Read the Apostles' Creed and the Nicene Creed in the Appendix. How are they similar and how are they different?

   The creeds share a lot of similarities; however, the most substantial difference is that the Apostles' Creed highlights Jesus' humanity (e.g., born, crucified, dead, buried), whereas the Nicene Creed highlights Jesus' divinity (e.g., God of God, Light of Light, very God of Very God). Together, both of these creeds show forth Jesus' humanity and divinity.

3. When we ask, "Will the Real Jesus Please Stand Up?" what are we actually asking?

   By Scripture, we are asking that Jesus be defined according to Christianity—the Bible and creeds—and not according to what every Tom, Dick, and Harry might personally believe Him to be according to their experiences and presuppositions.

4. From your reading of this final chapter and the book in its entirety, how would you define the real Jesus Christ? Who is Jesus and what has He done for you?

   The best way to answer this question is with the Explanation of the Second Article of the Apostles' Creed according to Martin Luther's Small Catechism. It states, "I believe that Jesus Christ, true God, begotten of the Father from eternity, and also true man, born of the Virgin Mary, is my Lord. He has redeemed me, a lost and condemned creature, purchased and won me from all sins, from death, and from the power of the devil. He did this not with gold or silver, but with His holy, precious blood and with His innocent suffering and death, so that I may be His own, live under Him in His kingdom, and serve Him in everlasting righteousness, innocence, and blessedness, just as He is risen from the dead, lives and reigns to all eternity. This is most certainly true."

5. Look back at what you wrote down for question 6 in the Introduction Study Guide. Can you match what you wrote down to any of the 12 false christs presented in the book? Were there any idols that weren't addressed in the book that you wrote down?

If talking about this question in a Sunday School class or a group of people, consider making a list of the false christs that you identified in the introduction and then seeing how many of those fit with the false christs identified in this book.

For the false christs that have not been identified in this book, consider taking some time to determine the characteristics of these false christs and then identify what pre-suppositions a person might need to have to subscribe to each particular false christ.

6. What is your biggest takeaway from the book? What has been the most edifying part of this study in your learning?

What false christ has stuck out to you the most and why? Did this false christ stick out to you because you may have subscribed to this false christ yourself? Or, did this false christ stick out to you because you see this false christ at work in your family, friends, or church?

Also, what character stuck out to you the most and why? What was it about their pre-suppositions that you found intriguing? Are these presuppositions that you have held to before or presuppositions that you see at work in your family, friends, or church?

Finally, consider contrasting all the false christs with the real Jesus. If you were to summarize the differences between the false christs and the real Jesus in one to two sentences, what would you say?

Appendix 2

The creeds are special statements of faith that have been used by Christians for hundreds of years as the basis of what we Christians believe and why. The Apostles' Creed was not formulated by a specific council or by a group of theologians but developed over time in the church as a tool to summarize the Christian faith. On the other hand, the Nicene Creed was drafted in the context of great confession in the church and serves to grant clarity on the essence, person, and work of God. Both of these creeds set out to answer the question, "Who is Jesus?" They also define mankind's relationship to God and God's relationship to mankind.

Since these statements are rooted in the Scripture, they summarize the message of the Bible. This means the creeds are helpful in protecting the Church from errors that attempt to ensnare and destroy, as well being helpful tools that help teach the faith to Christians young and old.

We live in a day and age where a deeper study of what we believe and why we believe what we believe is often needed. That is why I placed references to the creeds throughout this book and included them here in this Appendix. Please keep in mind, though, that these creeds are not intended to intimidate, but to help you reflect upon what you have learned in this book and upon Jesus' identity and His work.

The Apostles' Creed

I believe in God, the Father Almighty, maker of heaven and earth. And in Jesus Christ, His only Son, our Lord, who was conceived by the Holy Spirit, born of the virgin Mary, suffered under Pontius Pilate, was crucified, died and was buried. He descended into hell. The third day He rose again from the dead. He ascended into heaven and sits at the right hand of God the Father Almighty. From thence He will come to judge the living and the dead. I believe in the Holy Spirit, the holy Christian Church, the communion of saints, the forgiveness of sins, the resurrection of the body, and the life everlasting. Amen.

The Nicene Creed

I believe in one God, the Father Almighty, maker of heaven and earth and of all things visible and invisible. And in one Lord Jesus Christ, the only-begotten Son of God, begotten of His Father before all worlds, God of God, Light of Light, very God of very God, begotten, not made, being of one substance with the Father, by whom all things were made; who for us men and for our salvation came down from heaven and was incarnate by the Holy Spirit of the virgin Mary and was made man; and was crucified also for us under Pontius Pilate. He suffered and was buried. And the third day He rose again according to the Scriptures and ascended into heaven and sits at the right hand of the Father. And He will come again with glory to judge both the living and the dead, whose kingdom will have no end. And I believe in the Holy Spirit, the Lord and Giver of Life, who proceeds from the Father and the Son, who with the Father and the Son together is worshiped and glorified, who spoke by the prophets. And I believe in one holy Christian and apostolic Church, I acknowledge one Baptism for the remission of sins, and I look for the resurrection of the dead and the life of the world to come. Amen.

About the Author

Rev. Dr. Matthew Richard has been the pastor of Zion Lutheran Church of Gwinner, North Dakota, since 2013. He was previously a Senior Pastor in Sidney, Montana; an Associate Pastor in Williston, North Dakota; and an Associate Pastor in Rancho Cucamonga, California.

He received his undergraduate degree in Finance and Economics from Minot State University in North Dakota. After a short career working as an Investment Representative, he moved to Minnesota to obtain his Master of Divinity from Lutheran Brethren Seminary, Minnesota. In 2005, a year after graduating from seminary, he was ordained into the ministry by the Church of the Lutheran Brethren of America. About eight years later (2013), he transitioned to the Lutheran Church—Missouri Synod and was certified for ministry. Furthermore, in 2013, he obtained a Doctor of Ministry Degree from Concordia Seminary, St. Louis, Missouri. His doctoral thesis explored the journey of American Evangelicals into Confessional Lutheran thought.

Pastor Richard is married to Serenity, and they have three children. He enjoys fishing, pheasant hunting, watching movies, writing, golfing, spending time with his family, and a good book with a warm latte!